Transforming Church Conflict

Transforming Church Conflict

Compassionate Leadership in Action

Deborah van Deusen Hunsinger
Theresa F. Latini

WESTMINSTER
JOHN KNOX PRESS
LOUISVILLE · KENTUCKY

First edition
Published by Westminster John Knox Press
Louisville, Kentucky

13 14 15 16 17 18 19 20 21 22—10 9 8 7 6 5 4 3 2 1

Book design by Sharon Adams
Cover design by Night & Day Design

Library of Congress Cataloging-in-Publication Data
Hunsinger, Deborah van Deusen.
 Transforming church conflict : compassionate leadership in action / by Deborah van Deusen Hunsinger and Theresa F. Latini. — First edition
  pages cm
 Includes bibliographical references and index.
 ISBN 978-0-664-23848-3 (alk. paper)
 1. Church controversies. 2. Interpersonal conflict—Religious aspects—Christianity. 3. Interpersonal communication—Religious aspects—Christianity. I. Latini, Theresa F. II. Title.
 BV652.9.H86 2013
 253—dc23

2012033260

Most Westminster John Knox Press books are available at special quantity discounts
when purchased in bulk by corporations, organizations, and special-interest groups.
For more information, please e-mail SpecialSales@wjkbooks.com.

For our families, our students, and dear friends in the NVC community.

Contents

Appendixes

Acknowledgments

While I first became acquainted with Marshall Rosenberg's work in 1987 in the context of my study of psychology and pastoral care, it was not until 2004 that I glimpsed its transformative promise. In my first nine-day international intensive training, the teaching and skill of Robert Gonzales helped me find hope in the wake of my despair about the United States' decision to wage war against Iraq. During the next six years, I received countless gifts from the Nonviolent Communication (NVC) community—gifts of insight, compassion, love, and companionship—as I undertook intensive NVC study, training, and practice. I am indebted especially to NVC trainers, Inbal and Miki Kashtan, Susan Skye, Robert Gonzales, Dominic Barter, and countless others who have enriched my life and given me a renewed appreciation for the healing and energizing power of community. The students at Princeton Theological Seminary, with their hunger for learning and growth, have kept alive my love for this work. Finally, the love, faithfulness, challenge, and support of my family undergirds and upholds me every day of my life. I thank God for you daily.

Deborah van Deusen Hunsinger

I first discovered Nonviolent Communication at a time in my life when, unbeknownst to me, I desperately needed it. Ruptures in close relationships, animosity in my denomination, and the challenge of living well as I completed a doctoral degree and worked as a pastor called for new capacities in staying connected to God, myself, and others. Though initially tentative—given my intellectual questions about NVC—I eventually threw myself headlong into the NVC community. I am particularly grateful to Robert Gonzales, Susan Skye, and Myra Walden, from whom I not only have learned the skills of compassionate communication but also have received an abundance of empathy and care. With the 2008 LIFE (Learning & Integration, Full Embodiment) program cohort, I experienced the delight of fellowship in the Spirit, which comes both as a gift and from a common commitment to seeing and hearing one another, bearing one another's burdens, and participating in one another's healing and growth. My students, two NVC practice groups, and the leaders of Lake Nokomis Presbyterian Church have inspired me by persisting in authentic relationships in the midst of anxiety and ambiguity. Most of all, I am deeply grateful to friends and family whose single-minded and openhearted love nourishes my soul daily.

Theresa F. Latini

Illustrations and Tables

Illustrations

Tables

Introduction

Living Peaceably with All

"If it is possible, so far as it depends on you, live peaceably with all."
Romans 12:18

The apostle Paul's exhortation to the church at Rome stands as a powerful challenge to the church in America today. Congregations floundering in intractable conflict may read such words with incredulity; how, they may wonder, is it possible to live peaceably with those determined to get their way at any cost? Congregations recovering from clergy misconduct may be seething with so much anger that any vision of peace is completely untenable unless yoked to an understanding of a justice that includes real repentance. Congregations in mainline Protestant denominations rent apart by polarizing discourse may be so disheartened that they are tempted to withdraw altogether. The complexity of church life today in myriad subcultures, both religious and cultural, makes any kind of true and lasting peace sometimes seem completely out of reach. How are pastors and church leaders to tackle such complexity with any clarity of purpose or vision of a happy outcome?

Pastors burn out at an alarming rate, and lay leaders grow weary of keeping all the church's programs afloat. Both pastors and lay leaders falter under the weight of their own and others' expectations to do it all—to develop programming in adult education, youth groups, and Sunday school; to provide pastoral care for the sick and dying; to work with church committees and governing boards; to preach every Sunday; and, perhaps most difficult, to maintain harmonious relationships with people who won't talk to them directly about their concerns but complain instead to their friends and neighbors. These are not the only challenges church leaders face.

What about the pastoral care situation in which siblings come together over the imminent death of a brother after being estranged for decades? Each blames the others for the hurt, anger, loneliness, and emptiness that they feel inside, but no one wishes to take responsibility for contributing to the impasse. How can a pastor guide such a family in untangling the chaotic threads of a lifetime of mutual resentment?

Scripture exhorts us to live in harmony with others, taking "thought for what is noble in the sight of all" (Rom. 12:17) no matter what our circumstances. It encourages us to practice hospitality toward strangers as well as compassionate care toward those we consider our enemies. We are not to repay evil for evil but to overcome evil with good. Such a vision could be exhilarating, serving as a beacon of hope, but for those mired in conflict, it might be more disheartening than inspiring. When we consider the interpersonal impasses, entrenched power struggles, and ongoing frustration at many levels of the church's common life, we might admit to seasons of hopelessness. The violence that we deplore in the world exists, if we are honest, in our own hearts as well. Though we may not have murdered our brother or sister, there are times when we might admit to harboring feelings of murderous rage. When we find ourselves caught up in a polarized struggle, we may rightly wonder how we can serve as ambassadors of reconciliation.

How is it possible to retain an authentic connection to the New Testament's enduring vision of reconciliation in today's church? Can conflict in the church be transformed so that it revitalizes the church rather than enervates it? We are writing this book because we believe that with skilled and compassionate leadership, conflict can be honestly confronted and transformed at every level of church life. Moreover, when we dedicate ourselves to learning certain skills, not only is the conflict transformed, but so are we. Though the skills we will describe obviously cannot usher in the promised kingdom of God—for no human undertaking can bring about the redemption we long for—they can keep churches connected to a common vision and working together toward life-giving purposes. For the past nine years we have both been immersed in intensive study of *nonviolent* or *compassionate communication* as developed by Marshall Rosenberg. In our personal experiences, and in the lives of the students, pastors, and lay leaders that we have taught, we have witnessed inspiring parables of grace in which paralyzing conflict has been transformed into caring connection. Compassionate communication has taught us how to:

1. transform criticism into opportunities for mutual understanding;
2. stay in dialogue in the midst of difference and disagreement;

3. heal pain from unresolved conflict, guilt, and shame;
4. express ourselves so that we are heard more fully;
5. develop compassion for ourselves and others;
6. transform anger so that others will take our urgent needs to heart;
7. mediate between two or more others, helping them to speak the truth in love; and
8. build authentic community based on honesty and empathy.

We have become convinced that *nonviolent or compassionate communication* is the best single resource available for learning the complex interpersonal and pastoral leadership skills needed by today's church. This is the motivation for writing this book: to describe the knowledge and skills that offer such promise and to place them into theological context so that they can function as a practical guide for revitalizing the church.

Nonviolent Communication (NVC) emerged in an era of ferment and change. In the turbulent 1960s, Marshall Rosenberg, a clinical psychologist, became increasingly disturbed by the dissension, antagonism, and violence he witnessed. Having moved to Detroit as a child in the 1940s, he had already lived through a race riot that left more than forty people dead. "Why," he wondered, "were some people able to respond compassionately to others under the most terrible conditions, while others became exploitative and violent?"[1] He longed to find a way to facilitate mutual respect among people, particularly those who were violently at odds with each other. Rosenberg believed that the entire culture desperately needed the invaluable skills of empathy and honesty that formed the core of his training as a psychologist. He thus sought to develop an educational model that would teach these skills to anyone who wished to practice them in everyday interactions. He has spent virtually his entire career developing this model. With a special charism for this work, he has mediated between warring tribes in Rwanda, between Palestinians and Jews in the Middle East, and between gang members and police in the inner cities of the United States.

During the past twenty years, NVC has grown into an international training and peacemaking organization[2] with certified trainers and teams in more than thirty countries. It is taught in prisons and schools, community centers, and universities. Preschool teachers even use it with toddlers and teach it to their parents. Practice groups have sprung up around the world. Online courses, leadership training programs, and intensive residential workshops are offered every year by a wide variety of instructors.[3]

College, university, and seminary professors have developed courses contextualized for particular subject areas.[4]

We are writing this book for church leaders because we believe that these skills can contribute significantly to the flourishing of Christian ministry. In a foreword to Peter Steinke's book, *Congregational Leadership in Anxious Times*, Bishop Rick Foss writes: "Whether conflicting approaches to mission and ministry lead to creativity and growth or to polarized stand-offs is largely a matter of how the key leaders are able to respond to the situation."[5] When a church is in conflict, most pastors and leaders are as well. The conflict, in other words, does not reside *outside* the pastor or only among the church's most vocal members. It resides within every person in the church. We internalize our context and are an integral part of the emotional system in which we reside. This is why the anxiety that runs through the church also runs right through the heart of every pastor or church leader. Non-anxious presence—that interpersonal ability to stay focused and calm in the midst of emotional chaos—does *not* mean that the skilled pastor or leader is in fact *not feeling* anxious. On the contrary: in the midst of an emotional maelstrom, pastors, being human, are inevitably affected by the anxiety of the systems in which they work. As Edwin Friedman argues in his classic work *Generation to Generation: Family Systems in Church and Synagogue*, the anxiety of the work system can significantly raise the level of anxiety in the home and vice versa. Any model that intends to transform conflict on a systems level needs to begin with the person of the leader. For this reason, we shift our focus throughout each of the chapters, moving from the leader's core needs to those of the community, to various interpersonal conflicts that affect the emotional system, whether in a family or church committee. In every case, *how leaders position themselves vis-à-vis the conflict is the key to transformation.*

Conflict need not be destructive. In fact, conflict faced honestly is far healthier for any individual or community than suppressed or denied conflict. There is a great deal of difference between conflict and violence. Violence is always destructive. It inflicts anguish, and often enduring trauma, on persons, communities, and nations. Conflict, when openly acknowledged and courageously embraced, can be constructive. When undertaken with an attitude of hope and expectation, and with certain skills in hand, open conflict can actually be life-giving. In her groundbreaking book, *Toward a New Psychology of Women*, Jean Baker Miller writes:

Conflict, seen in its fullest sense, is not necessarily threatening or destructive. Quite the contrary. . . . We all grow via conflict. . . . Growth requires engagement with difference and with people embodying that difference. If differences were more openly acknowledged, we could allow for, and even encourage, an increasingly strong expression by each party of his or her experience. This would lead to greater clarity for self, greater ability to fulfill one's own needs, and more facility to respond to others. There would be a chance at individual and mutual satisfaction, growth, and even joy.[6]

When the church is bogged down in what seems to be an intractable conflict, and when the leaders of the church have little skill or confidence in engaging that conflict openly, it is little wonder that so few imagine conflict as an opportunity to find mutual satisfaction, growth, or joy.

By teaching three skills sets—self-empathy, empathy, and honest expression—and by grounding these skills in the gospel's overarching aims, we hope to contribute to the living out of this vision of mutual joy. The more deeply we are each rooted and grounded in the love of God, the further we can reach out to others with the compassion that we ourselves have received. Leaders who work from a place of mutuality and joy have a wellspring of compassion toward others, even those with whom they disagree.

At the beginning of the third millennium we live in an increasingly complex world marked by rapid change in every sphere of life: political, economic, communal, religious, and domestic. Such widespread and ongoing change gives rise to pervasive feelings of uncertainty and anxiety, sometimes even fear. The church lives in the midst of this maelstrom of change. It is called to be responsive to the world, to serve it gladly, and to witness to God's compassionate care in the midst of its anxious foreboding. Theological educators are particularly concerned about training ministers who have the capacity to provide compassionate leadership in these challenging times. We want ministers not only to serve the members of their congregations faithfully but also to provide vision and leadership as each congregation seeks to serve the world.

The church also needs leaders who negotiate the complexities of the Christian world and cooperate with persons of widely different backgrounds and belief systems. These leaders will need to be so firmly rooted in their Christian identity that they are capable of reaching across profound religious and philosophical differences. They will need to build bridges of understanding with those who do not begin with the same premises or have the same worldview. They will need to treat those who have a different national identity with honor and respect. They will need to have the personal resources to enter what is unfamiliar and complex with confidence and competence.[7]

The skills of compassionate communication help us to reach across national, religious, cultural, and class boundaries to affirm our common humanity. We live in a world where diverse religious beliefs and practices coexist in the same place, and compassionate communication offers us ways to connect with people who have widely different customs and different understandings of the world, of God, and of the purposes of human life. At the same time, NVC is indispensable in more intimate situations of interpersonal conflict that are crucial to understand for the sake of effective pastoral care. It helps foster mutual understanding between teenagers and their parents, between husbands and wives on the verge of divorce, among family members who envision their lives unfolding in widely divergent ways. Perhaps most important of all, compassionate communication helps us maintain our inner clarity and sense of direction in the midst of challenging situations in which we have significant personal investment. It gives us tools to make healthy and faithful choices when we ourselves are in danger of reacting out of anger rather than responding with compassion. We believe that competence in these skills can mean the difference between success and failure in building bridges with those who are different, whether they are in the pew next to us, the mosque down the street, or in communities across the city or the globe. Equipped with compassionate communication, pastors and church leaders will not only have finely honed their skills in pastoral care and self-care, but they will also have the tools needed to exercise public leadership.

NVC eschews official alignment with any particular religion in order to connect with each person's common humanity. Since religion often divides people, Rosenberg and other practitioners often steer clear from placing NVC into any specific religious context. Instead they emphasize its irreducible spiritual nature. Many will explicitly call it a spiritual practice but are loath to call it a religious one. Indeed, NVC itself does not recommend any specifically religious practices. Nevertheless NVC is practiced by people the world over who are rooted in *particular* religious communities. Over the years we have worked alongside Hindus, Buddhists, atheists, agnostics, New Age seekers, Jews, and Christians across the denominational spectrum who see NVC as an indispensable tool for resolving differences effectively in their respective communities.

We are committed to placing NVC into a specifically Christian context so that it will support the ministry of the church. Our overriding aim in this book is to bring the skills and consciousness of compassionate communication into the worldwide church so that the church can more faithfully live out the gospel of Jesus Christ. We intend to fulfill this aim in three ways:

1. First, we will set forth our understanding of compassionate communication in concrete, practical, and accessible terms, describing the specific skill sets needed for effective pastoral and lay leadership.

2. Second, we will delineate some of the theoretical richness that feeds compassionate communication by entering into conversation with closely related psychological theories that both illuminate and deepen our understanding of the need for these skills in resolving difficult situations of conflict.

3. Finally, we will put compassionate communication into theological perspective, engaging its implicit (or explicit) theological assumptions about the nature of humanity in relation to Christian teachings. While acknowledging the conceptual tensions between compassionate communication and Christian theology, we seek to place the core tenets of compassionate communication into a Christian theological framework so that Christian leaders can use it with integrity.

The book begins with a basic overview of compassionate communication, interpreting it theologically in relation to church conflict. Chapters 2–4 teach the basic skills of making clear observations, sharing one's feelings and needs without judgment or defensiveness, and making requests. As these basic skills are internalized, they provide the foundation for the fundamental skill sets of empathy, self-empathy, and honest expression (chapters 5–7). These skill sets in turn provide the necessary foundation for more advanced capacities: healing hurt through mourning, staying in dialogue when it is difficult, and transforming conflict in community-wide crises (chapters 8–10).[8]

We are persuaded that these skills can help Christian pastors and leaders, as well as people in the pews, to face conflict honestly, to hear one another with mutual understanding, and to live out their vocation with more zest and joy. We trust that they will help the church to live peaceably with all and thus become a more faithful witness to the Prince of Peace.

Part 1

Basic Skills
in Compassionate Communication

Chapter 1

By the Renewal of Your Mind

Transforming Church Conflict

> Do not be conformed to this world, but be transformed by the
> renewing of your minds, so that you may discern what is the will
> of God—what is good and acceptable and perfect.
>
> Romans 12:2

The key to transforming conflict in the church is developing skilled leaders who are not afraid to engage conflict. These leaders will trust the Spirit of God to renew their minds as they learn how to speak (and listen to) the truth in love. No longer conformed to the ways of the world, such leaders will understand the difference between conflict (which can be constructive) and violence (which is always destructive). Conflict allows for many points of view to be shared openly, for people to learn from one another's perspectives and to hear what matters most to them. Violence arises in situations where differences are denied and voices for change are silenced. Those who long for change, as well as those who are determined to preserve the status quo, become frustrated and begin to operate by the familiar cultural norms of a win/lose strategy. Seeking to win at all costs, each side sets about to defeat the other who, even in the church, may come to be seen as the enemy.

We are conformed to the world whenever we perceive conflict as a determined battle that we must win at all costs. When we hold enemy images of those with whom we disagree, we fuel polarization of persons and groups in our congregation. Widespread judgmentalism immerses the entire community in pain. As Franciscan priest Richard Rohr states, "pain that is not transformed is transferred."[1] It may be transferred to those around us through mutual blaming, or it may be internalized and passed along to other persons in the system through our attitudes and unresolved grief. For pain to be transformed it must be acknowledged, brought into the light of day, and healed through the caring of the community.

This book is designed to nurture caring communities by teaching compassionate (or nonviolent) communication. Those who internalize the practical skills and the modes of awareness presented here will know how to lead their congregations toward constructive conflict, a dynamic process of creative change that promises to renew the church. When leaders engage conflict openly and skillfully, they give the community an opportunity to talk about, clarify, and live out their most deeply held values.[2] Those who long for change will learn ways to bring it about without alienating those who desire to preserve the status quo. And those who are happy with the way things are will genuinely open themselves to hearing from those members of the body with whom they disagree. Mutual respect and basic trust will be core values for all members as they remember that God wills communities of peace. In this way, church conflict will not be resolved as much as it will be transformed.[3]

What Is Nonviolent or Compassionate Communication?

In this first chapter we provide an overview of the essential conceptual framework of *nonviolent or compassionate communication* (NVC) that needs to be understood by church leaders aiming to lead their congregations *through* constructive conflict, transforming pain and alienation into joyful connection. Compassionate communication nurtures a kind of consciousness and teaches a set of skills that train people in a unique kind of practical wisdom. As a communication model, it helps us speak with clarity and passion as we learn to stay connected to what matters most to us. At the same time, it assists us in listening for what is in another's heart, especially when we find the other's words difficult or painful to hear. In the midst of conflict, it provides a reliable process of discernment that enables us to decide where to direct our energy as we make particular choices about how to engage those with whom we (perhaps strongly) disagree.

Compassionate communication teaches a way of being with ourselves and others that builds trust because it enables us to share what is in our hearts, without defensiveness, no matter how challenging. We are given the courage to speak honestly without fearing that we will alienate the other. We speak our truth with care as we try to imagine how our words may affect our hearers. When compassionate communication is practiced faithfully over time, the congregation grows in trust that conflict can provide rich opportunities for deepening mutual understanding. Faithful practice of NVC also enables us to face our feelings of regret and guilt when we have not lived according to our own values. It offers concrete steps by which we can mourn choices that we regret and it sheds light on the process of making amends to those we have hurt. When we dare to act on our feelings of remorse, we gain inner strength because we are in alignment with our core value of integrity. Especially when relationships are bogged down with mutual recrimination and historical pain, compassionate communication offers a clear set of guidelines about how to work toward reconciliation. Whenever a single relationship improves, hope flares up with a sense of possibility for other relationships as well.

The overall purpose of compassionate communication is interpersonal connection. NVC assumes that a trustworthy connection between people is the precondition for finding *any* satisfactory way to transform conflict because it is the basis for any kind of cooperative human activity or fulfilling emotional relationship. In order to achieve mutual understanding and connection, NVC aims for three things: authentic connection with oneself; empathic reception of the other; and honest expression toward the other.

We aim first to connect authentically with ourselves so that we can speak honestly about our experience. Though we cannot control another person's reaction to our words, we aim to express ourselves in ways that minimize defensiveness and encourage receptivity. We also aim to hear the other with such a depth of understanding that she actually understands herself better after we have listened to her. In Hermann Hesse's novel *Siddhartha*, the ferryman Vasudeva embodies the kind of listening we aspire to.

> Of the ferryman's virtues, this was one of his greatest. He knew how to listen as few people do. Though Vasudeva spoke not a word himself, the speaker felt him receiving his words into himself, quietly, openly, unhurriedly, missing nothing, not jumping ahead through impatience, attributing neither praise nor blame—just listening. Siddhartha felt what happiness can come from opening to such a listener, having one's own life—one's seeking, one's suffering—enter this other's heart.[4]

As Vasudeva quietly steers his ferry through the water, his passengers find themselves opening their hearts to his receptive presence. His qualities of patience and quiet attentiveness provide the spaciousness that is needed for the unburdening of their hearts. Because he attributes neither praise nor blame, his passengers do not fear judgment and so can speak freely.

Whenever we listen without praising or blaming, simply receiving what the other longs to say, we create the conditions for an emotional connection to be forged. Similarly, whenever we speak without judging the other, we increase the likelihood for a sturdier connection to grow between us. When we honestly communicate what we are observing, feeling, and needing in our particular circumstances, as well as make any requests we might have of the other (or ourselves), we typically find more freedom and ease in our interpersonal relationships.

The OFNR Template of Compassionate Communication

The four basic skills of the NVC template are: observation (O), feeling (F), need (N), and request (R).[5] While they can be cognitively grasped relatively easily, the more challenging task of truly internalizing them requires a commitment to ongoing practice. The third skill, identifying needs, is the conceptual linchpin of the whole. Learning how to connect with our own and others' needs is the key to transforming animosity or indifference into constructive, life-giving relationships. The OFNR template for learning compassionate communication is a useful tool for guiding our conversations, but it is not a formula for a particular way of speaking. It helps us to understand ourselves and others in the midst of difference and disagreement. In other words, there is no right or wrong way to speak in NVC. NVC helps us to speak authentically in our own idiom what is truly in our hearts.[6] We have found the template extremely useful, however, for learning each of the discrete skills. Once we internalize the template, we can communicate in compassionate and colloquial ways. Here we will briefly describe each of the four steps involved in a complete, compassionate communication, which will then be elaborated in subsequent chapters. Though these steps are by no means linear, they are presented in a step-by-step fashion for the sake of clarity.

Observations

Whenever we seek to communicate clearly with others it is helpful to let them know which of their words or actions are affecting us. Whenever we can describe what we are observing without at the same time evaluating it, connection is facilitated. Especially if we have a negative reaction to another's words or behavior, it helps simply to describe it while remaining as free from any evaluative comment as possible. Negative judgments tend to evoke defensiveness. When we criticize or label others, we are therefore likely to contribute to disconnection.

Observations describe what is available to our senses: what we can see, hear, touch, taste, or smell. They are specific to time and context. If your colleague arrives for an appointment thirty minutes later than you expected, you might say, for example: "I'm puzzled because I expected you a half hour ago. I had written 2 p.m. in my calendar." Even to say, "You are late," is to make a kind of evaluation, rather than a simple observation because you don't actually *know* that she is late; all you know is that your calendar says that she was due to arrive at two. She may have a completely different understanding about the time you were to meet. The intention in making an observation is to share helpful information about what in particular you are reacting to, not to criticize or lay blame at the other's door. Separating an observation from any possible evaluation facilitates connection because it gives no offense.

In making an observation, the aim is to describe what you have seen or heard as if a video camera were recording the incident. If you say, for example, "Ellen procrastinates," you would be using a verb that has evaluative connotations. If you were to say instead, "Ellen told me that she had to leave for the airport in twenty minutes and that she hadn't yet started packing," you would be offering a precise observation devoid of evaluation. Generalizations are similarly avoided because they don't give a concrete description of a particular event. Thus we seek to avoid comments that use such words as *always, never, everyone,* or *nobody,* as in, "You are always late." We seek, as much as possible, to speak concretely about specific events and to see others without preconceptions.

Feelings

The second step in the NVC template is stating what we are feeling. We continually assess what is happening around us through our emotional capacities. In his book, *Emotional Intelligence,* Daniel Goleman argues that we are capable of appraising situations with lightning speed. Laboratories can now measure the interval between a stimulus and our emotional response to it in the thousandths of a second.[7] Such speed, says Goleman, helped guarantee human survival when even a millisecond might make the difference between life and death. If a snarling dog lunges toward me, my intense fear will send hormones to my brain that will activate a fight or flight response before I have time consciously to assess the dog's relative danger.

Besides acting as a kind of radar for danger, our emotions are also closely tied to our thoughts. Anyone who practices cognitive behavioral therapy or mindfulness meditation will know how intimately interwoven our emotional state is with our beliefs, judgments, and thoughts. Here it becomes apparent that many of our emotions are not triggered directly by a change in the environment, but rather by our rational assessment of that change. If you conclude that your congregation's accountant is embezzling church funds, you would likely feel angry. However, if you suddenly realize that you have misread his report, your feelings would likely change. No longer believing that he is stealing from your church, you would likely feel relieved. The emotions you have, in other words, depend on the cognitive assessment you make. Learning to take note of your intervening thoughts and connect them with your feelings is also a key skill in compassionate communication.

Needs

NVC not only acknowledges the integral connection between feelings and thoughts, it seeks deeper understanding by connecting feelings with needs. Assessing what we need is the third step in the NVC template. It is a basic presupposition of compassionate communication that we are trying to get our needs met in every moment. We are motivated to act, speak, keep silent, and move toward or away from someone on the basis of our needs. Virtually everything we do (or choose not to do) is an attempt to meet a need. Thus, our needs are the source of our underlying motivation. What are we fundamentally desiring, wanting, working toward, hoping for, or valuing at any particular moment in time? If our basic needs are met, we might feel contented, excited, relaxed, delighted, joyful, moved, or happy. If our basic needs are not being met, we might feel frustrated, angry, sad, discontented, bored, disappointed, or anxious. In the examples given above, the pertinent need in relation to the church accountant would likely be for trust. In order to work effectively with the accountant you need to trust him. Your initial feelings of anger as well as the subsequent relief are likely connected to the essential need for trust. The need I have regarding the snarling dog would be for safety. It is clearly my need to be safe that would spur me into action. The need regarding the appointment with your colleague might be for clarity or for consideration, depending on how you interpret the other's actions. If you tell yourself that she is being inconsiderate of your time, it becomes clear that you need consideration. If, on the other hand, you are puzzled by the miscommunication, your main need probably would be for clarity.

In compassionate communication, needs by definition contribute to the flourishing of human life. Though they are often met in different ways in different cultures, human needs are universally shared. All people, no matter what their culture, have a need for food, water, clothing, warmth, and shelter. All human beings need rest. All persons have basic needs for safety, connection, community, support, respect, and understanding as well. People everywhere need love, hope, and meaning.

Knowledge of our own needs also enables us to understand what others might be experiencing when we seek empathically to grasp the essence of their experience. Knowing that others' feelings point to their underlying needs, the key skill lies in learning how to connect those feelings with needs. This can be challenging given that many people in our culture are not familiar with expressing either their feelings or their needs directly, sometimes having only a vague sense of discomfort or a strong judgment about how others are doing the "wrong" thing. Offering empathic understanding to others requires us to connect with what their need might possibly be. For example, if a member of your church describes her life in a way that evokes a feeling of loneliness, you might guess that her underlying need is for connection, intimacy, companionship, or community. You would get clues as to which need is most alive for her by noticing her concrete circumstances (in the observation). Feelings of loneliness that surface the day after her dog has died would be different from the loneliness she might feel living in a foreign country where nothing is familiar and her loved ones are a continent away. The quality of a new widow's loneliness would be different from the loneliness of someone in an unhappy marriage, though both of them may long for intimacy. So, even though the feeling of loneliness would be present in each circumstance, the underlying need is always context-dependent. Needs, in other words, are interpreted within a specific context. Observations that are context-specific therefore help us to connect the feelings we hear with the possible underlying needs. Thus, each component of the OFNR template is deeply interrelated to every other part.

In situations where we cannot find words that adequately describe what we are feeling and needing, we would do well to seek out friends or colleagues that have skill in empathy. We can request that they simply hear us, to listen to us with caring as they seek to understand our experience. We might ask them to guess at our feelings or needs by paying attention to our words, tone of voice, body language, or overall context. Or we might request them simply to be present to us, listening in silence to all we have to say. What we need when we ask for empathy is not someone to solve our problems or even to make us feel differently, but rather to give us the opportunity to be heard by someone who cares about us.

Compassionate communication practice groups typically give us training not only in listening with empathy but also learning how to listen to ourselves empathically (self-empathy) as well as speaking honestly. These skill sets all build on an ability to identify and accurately name our feelings and needs. NVC books and workshops provide lists of feelings arranged in family clusters to encourage finely differentiated feelings such as irked, miffed, irritated, annoyed, angry, furious, irate, and livid (see Appendix 1: Feelings Inventory). They also provide lists of needs clustered in family groupings: needs having to do with personal autonomy or choice; an array of interdependent needs; needs for physical nurture and well-being; and basic needs for integrity, play, celebration, and spiritual communion[8] (see Appendix 2: Needs Inventory). In addition, a wide variety of methods have been devised in recent years to help people gain fluency in identifying both feelings and needs, including card games, NVC dance floors, an empathy labyrinth, creative journaling assignments, and interactive group activities.[9]

Requests

The process of finding a strategy to address the need is the fourth step in the OFNR template. Once we have clarity about what we need, we can make a request that we believe will contribute to its being met. Effective requests are time-specific and doable, what Rosenberg calls positive action language. It is important to ask specifically for what you want, *not* for what you don't want. Thus, you might say, "I'd like you to call me once a week" *not* "I don't want you to call me so often." The request also needs to be specific and doable: "Would you be willing to give me a hug right now?" *not* "I'd like you to be more affectionate."

Rosenberg comments that we should never agree to fulfill another's request unless we can do so "with the joy of a small child feeding a hungry duck."[10] In other words, requests are understood as gifts, not as demands. They give us an opportunity to contribute to another's life, itself a fundamental human need. If we say no to someone's request, it is likely because we are saying yes to some (perhaps unstated) need of our own and we cannot figure out a way to meet both needs at the same time.

Conversations around requests are thus opportunities to become more deeply aware of our own needs as well as those of the other as we try to find a strategy that will meet both sets of needs.

Compassionate communication jealously guards the freedom of each person's choices, valuing the autonomy of every human being (even while emphasizing our interdependence). Requests are quite different from demands. If the other responds to our no by blaming, coercing, ridiculing, or pleading with us, the request may have been a demand in actuality. Demands contribute to disconnection because the need for choice is universal. Anytime we agree to do something out of fear, shame, or coercion and not freely and gladly, we build up resentment. We may submit now, only to rebel later. There is little chance for joyful fellowship with someone who uses power to force us into doing something that we do not wish to do. Thus a commitment to eschew using demands to get one's own way is particularly important in situations of conflict, and especially in those situations where there is an uneven power differential (for example, between pastor and parishioner). If one is able to stay on a committed path of equally valuing all persons' needs, trust will be engendered.

Honesty and empathy are the cornerstones of connection: honesty about what is going on in ourselves, and empathy for others. If we are unable to identify others' underlying needs, we cannot hear them with empathy. If we stand in judgment of them, or diagnose or label them in some way, we will fail to make an empathic connection. Other obstacles to empathic connection include: language that denies choice, such as "you have to," "you must not," or "you should"; language that expresses demands such as "If you don't do this, I'll do that"; or language that seeks to induce guilt such as "If you don't do such and such, I'll feel so disappointed in you." Any time we make demands, we fail to acknowledge basic respect for the other person's power to make choices.

Using OFNR to Translate Hard-to-Hear Messages

When we value the needs of others as well as our own, we can use the four basic skills of compassionate communication (OFNR) to gain mutual understanding and to fulfill as many core needs as possible within our human limits. When we use these skills to listen empathically, we can translate criticism or judgment into feelings and needs. We hear critical messages in one of the following four ways:

1. First, we might hear the other as attacking or blaming us. If so, we might think we are justified in attacking them back. With this response, negative energy escalates. We may become intent on proving ourselves right and the other wrong. Or we might see others as deserving punishment for whatever we judge problematic about their behavior or attitude. This choice typically intensifies anger and perpetuates self-righteousness and moralistic thinking. It is also the baseline for situations that can devolve into violence.

2. The second option for hearing criticism is basically to agree with it and magnify our own faults, judging ourselves. With this choice, we proceed to criticize, blame, or otherwise shame ourselves for whatever it is that we have done (or chosen not to do). Our self-talk might sound like this: "I should have known better." "What an idiot I am; I can't believe I said that." "I'll never learn." With this kind of response to criticism, we set ourselves up for chronic stress, guilt, and shame. If it becomes a deeply entrenched pattern, it can lead to depression.

3. A third option is to translate the criticism that others are making into the feelings and needs they might be having. We do this by making empathic guesses, imaginatively placing ourselves in their shoes. "Are you upset because you'd like your needs to matter, too?" "Are you annoyed because you value consideration and respect?" "Are you frustrated because you are longing for more fun in your life?" This option seeks understanding of the other's critical message, not in terms of what you might have done wrong or failed to do, but in terms of what the other person might be feeling and needing.

4. The fourth way to hear a critical comment is by engaging in an inner process of self-empathy. Instead of saying to yourself, "I can't believe what an idiot I am!" you would have compassion for yourself. "When I hear that she was hurt by my comment, I feel really upset because I wanted to contribute to her understanding. I'd like some acknowledgment of my intention."

As we develop our ability to translate painful messages into feelings and needs, it is helpful to notice the kinds of messages that are particularly hard to hear. We then can practice translating those difficult messages into the underlying feelings and needs, whether our own or others'. For example your colleague, the senior pastor, might say to you, "You really ought to try to preach on more culturally relevant topics." This may be painful to hear because you already feel discouraged about your preaching style. You might judge your colleague as rude or even tell yourself that he is intentionally trying to demean you. Alternatively, you might berate yourself, calling yourself a lousy, boring preacher (as if his comment were a confirmation of your worst opinions about yourself).

If you were to use your newfound NVC skills and guess at his feelings and needs in this situation, a different perspective would arise. In this case, you would try to imagine the feelings and needs that might prompt such a comment. Perhaps he is worried about your ability to connect with young adults in the congregation and is convinced that preaching about the latest trends in popular culture would be a good strategy for doing so. Perhaps you hear his words as an insult when he means them as an encouragement or even an expression of support. Of course, you don't actually know why he made the comment until you ask him. The best way to do so nondefensively would be either to make an empathic guess or to engage in honest expression. "John, are you worried about my connection to young adults in our church and want me to preach on topics that you think would be meaningful for them?" would be one possible empathic guess. Or instead of empathy you might offer honest expression (focusing on your feelings and needs rather than his): "You know, John, when you tell me that I ought to preach on more culturally relevant topics, I feel completely discouraged because I've been working so hard on improving my preaching. I guess I could use some acknowledgment for the efforts I have made."

If John's comment triggers your inner judgments, you may become even more disconnected from your true needs. For example, you might begin to tell yourself that he is right, that you should be a more engaging preacher. What feelings and needs might be hidden under that single word: *should*? Here you may need to spend some time in self-empathy, asking yourself: "Am I frustrated because I want more competence in my ability to preach? Am I upset because I'd like more self-acceptance with where I am? Am I discouraged because I'd like to contribute to the spiritual growth of our young adults?" In giving yourself empathy, you would grow to understand *from the inside* your own desire to connect meaningfully with your congregants in your preaching. You would not be submitting to or rebelling against either the senior pastor's judgment or your own. Your desire to change your preaching style would just be one strategy for competence, self-acceptance, or contribution, which you could choose to meet in other ways as well. If you are truly aware of this cluster of needs, it becomes much easier to find strategies to support the changes that would help you to carry out your vocation in a more life-giving way. (Chapter 6 on self-empathy will explain this process of self-connection, while avoiding self-judgment, in more detail.)

Working through these four steps of compassionate communication may seem mechanical or awkward, especially at first. Yet, even at their most mechanistic, they have the potential to make us aware of our habitual dynamics. Using the OFNR template for developing our skills is similar to practicing scales at the piano. If we want to make music, we need daily practice. We have found that using these steps as a mental guide facilitates clarity and contributes to ease in learning. Even a little OFNR can go a long way. Just as a simple Italian phrasebook can find us a place to sleep, enable us to buy groceries, or navigate our way through an unfamiliar Italian city, so knowing these NVC basics has contributed to our lives in fundamental ways. This is so because NVC helps us become aware of our habitual ways of communicating and provides ready tools for change. By consciously working through each of the steps, we may become aware, for example, of how frequently we label or judge others, or how in certain situations we feel helpless and believe that we truly have no choice. Or we may see how often we express our feelings without any real awareness of what underlying needs they are connected to. Or we may realize that certain feeling words are not in our vocabulary because they are somehow linked with feelings of shame. For example, we don't allow ourselves to feel sad because we have been taught that it is shameful to express sadness. Long-standing, habitual patterns of interaction with ourselves and others become readily apparent.

Compassionate Communication as a Christian Spiritual Practice

Marshall Rosenberg describes NVC as a spiritual practice.[11] Jewish by heritage, he speaks of God as "Beloved Divine Energy" that is the basis for every human being's connection to life. NVC arose out of Rosenberg's expressed desire to manifest love by connecting with the "divine energy" in himself and others. He writes:

> If we get in touch with each other's Divine Energy, it's inevitable that we will enjoy giving and we'll give back to life. I've been through such ugly stuff with people that I don't get worried about

it anymore, it's inevitable. If we get that quality of connection, we'll like where it gets us.

It amazes me how effective it is. I could tell you similar examples between the extremist Israelis, both politically and religiously, and the same on the Palestinian side, and between the Hutus and the Tutsis. . . . With all of them it amazes me how easy it is to bring about this reconciliation and healing. Once again, all we have to do is get both sides connected to the other person's needs. To me the needs are the quickest, closest way to getting in connection with that Divine Energy. Everyone has the same needs. The needs come because we're alive.[12]

The central purpose of NVC, according to Rosenberg, is to connect with oneself, other human beings, and the divine. NVC provides tools to increase awareness of one's own and others' needs as well as skill in speaking about them. Its purpose, in other words, is not to get one's needs met but rather compassionate connection with oneself and others. Once we connect with others' needs in an open-hearted way, our common humanity becomes the fundamental point of connection. Even if we don't agree with their point of view, we can understand and acknowledge their heart's longing.

When we put NVC into an explicitly Christian context, we understand the joyful mutual giving and receiving that Rosenberg describes as central to NVC as descriptive not only of our being created in the image of God but also of our being redeemed for life together. God created us to live in rich fellowship with each other, and this richness of harmony and love will be made manifest in the kingdom of God. Karl Barth, a Swiss theologian of the twentieth century, asks "What does it mean to be human?"[13] He argues that we cannot fully understand what it means to be human simply by looking at ourselves and our own experience. The only one who perfectly reveals the nature of true humanity is Jesus Christ because he is the only one without sin. In other words, Jesus Christ not only reveals true God to us but also true humanity. He shows us what our created existence was meant to be: a human being for and with others[14] because self-giving love marks his entire life. In the cross of Jesus Christ, God is *for us* as savior and *with us* as fellow sufferer. Although our suffering cannot redeem others in the way that Christ's suffering can (for we are not one another's saviors), we can be fully with one another in compassion and tenderness. We can share the other's pain and help bear the other's burdens: "Rejoice with those who rejoice, weep with those who weep" (Rom. 12:15); "Bear one another's burdens, and in this way you will fulfill the law of Christ" (Gal. 6:2). By sharing in one another's lives in this way, we live out the human interconnectedness for which we were created.

The basic form of humanity is what Barth calls *Mitmenschlichkeit*, translated into English as "being-in-encounter." This means that we are only fully human in relation to others. Only as we live in community do we reflect the image of God who in God's Trinitarian identity is a union and communion of love and freedom. The biblical witness shows that human beings are created to live in fellowship with one another. "It is not good that the man should be alone" (Gen. 2:18). As Ray Anderson puts it, "The picture of the solitary Adam in Genesis 2 is one of self-alienation rather than self-fulfillment. . . . The divine image is not a religious quality of the individual person, but a spiritual reality expressed through the interchange of persons in relation."[15] To be made in the image of God is to be made for glad fellowship with God and other human beings. Adam is not fully human until he has found his counterpart in Eve. Only then does he exclaim joyfully: "This at last is bone of my bone and flesh of my flesh" (Gen. 2:23). Though our capacity to be in perfect communion with God, each other, and the rest of creation has been marred by sin, the image of God in us has not been completely eradicated.[16]

Our human interdependence (or "being in encounter") with one another, according to Barth, consists in mutual seeing, hearing, speaking, and assisting one another with gladness. The four basic skills of the NVC template—observing without evaluating, stating feelings vulnerably and openly, connecting feelings to underlying needs, and making clear requests—provide concrete guidance for us as we seek to live in this kind of encounter. Barth's four marks of our basic humanity can fruitfully be correlated with observations, feelings, needs, and requests:

1. Mutual Seeing: The first mark of our humanity, according to Barth, is that of mutual seeing. When we look another person in the eye, we also consent to being seen by the other. Others cannot know us unless we consent to making ourselves known. They may be able to surmise something about us, but if we want to be fully human, we need to reveal ourselves to them. Barth writes, "This two-sided openness is the first element of humanity. Where it lacks, and to the extent that it lacks, humanity does not occur. To the extent that we withhold and conceal ourselves, and therefore do not move to know others and to let ourselves be known by them, our existence is inhuman." In so far as we seek to know and be known by another, we create a bridge, a way of connecting with him or her. "I should not take him seriously as a human being if I did not seriously try to find the way from me to him."[17] To see the other truly, we need to set aside our own preoccupations, biases, and prejudices. ***Observations:*** This mark of our humanity corresponds to NVC's first skill. Here we aim simply to see the other without any judgments that would obscure their God-given humanity.

2. *Mutual Speaking and Hearing:* In order to be known by others, we must risk revealing who we are by speaking to them. In addition, we must listen with care to their own self-revelation. They interpret who they are by addressing us in our particularity. As Barth says, "Each fellow human being is a whole world, and the request which he makes of me is not merely that I should know this or that about him, but the person himself, and therefore this whole world." Barth comments trenchantly that "two monologues do not constitute a dialogue,"[18] thereby reminding us how "barbaric and inhuman" our speech can become when we are not truly seeking to connect with the other but are concerned only with ourselves.

Feelings and Needs: NVC provides clear guidelines about how to let others know us by identifying as best we can what we are feeling and needing. It also helps us to listen to the heart of the other's message. In the midst of all that others say, we listen intently for the crucial information about how they are feeling as they connect with their underlying needs and values. When we listen in this way, it shows our willingness not only to be known in our vulnerability but also to hear others with respect and care for their vulnerability.

3. *Mutual Assistance:* This mark of our humanity recognizes our fundamental need of one another. "The eye cannot say to the hand, 'I have no need of you,' nor again the head to the feet, 'I have no need of you'" (1 Cor. 12:21). No human being is self-sufficient. All human beings need the assistance of others from cradle to grave. Though only God can offer saving help, we can offer penultimate help by sharing our burdens with one another, by offering each other comfort, encouragement, companionship, and support. We can pray for one another and uphold each other in love. Barth underlines the centrality of mutual need as a basic mark of our humanity: "My humanity depends upon the fact that I am always aware, and my action is determined by the awareness, that I need the assistance of others as a fish needs water." He also reverses it, saying, "My humanity depends upon the fact that I am always aware, and my action is determined by the awareness, that I need to give my assistance to others as a fish needs water."[19] Thus mutuality and reciprocity in both offering and receiving help is an essential mark of what it means to be human. *Requests:* The four basic skills in compassionate communication provide a concrete means for offering and receiving mutual assistance. It involves expressing honestly what our needs are and crafting requests to others on the basis of those needs. We also listen to others with requests in mind. Making requests potentially unleashes our creativity. At the same time, it is a step where people frequently experience conflict. A strategy that meets my need for intimacy might not meet your need for autonomy, for example. Though those needs do not inherently conflict, it calls for creativity to find a strategy that will meet both sets of needs. When we cannot find a way to meet both sets of needs, we have to acknowledge our failure of imagination and actively mourn our limitations.

4. *With gladness:* The fourth mark of our humanity, according to Barth, is that we see and are seen gladly, we speak and hear one another gladly, and we offer mutual assistance to one another with gladness.

> What we indicate in this way is really the *secret* of humanity. . . . in doing so we presuppose as the living center of the whole the decisive point that they meet gladly and in freedom. . . . there is a discovery, the mutual recognition that each is essential to the other. . . . [There is] an active willing of this fellowship, a willing which derives quite simply from the fact that each has received a gift which he necessarily desires to reciprocate to the best of his ability. And if it is asked in what this gift consists, the answer must be that the one has quite simply been given the other, and that what he for his part has to give is again himself.[20]

Our encounter with one another is thus a matter of mutual joy in which we receive one another as a gift. According to Barth, only in gratitude and freedom can our encounter with each other truly be human. Only in relationship with others do we discover our own "uniqueness and irreplaceability."[21]

Barth's "gladly" and "in freedom" resonate with Rosenberg's admonition to meet requests only when one can do so in pure gladness of heart. To be human for Rosenberg is to live in life-giving connection to one another and our own selves; to delight in contributing to the well-being of others; to recognize the essential "gift" of our interactions with others.

> To give a gift of one's self is a manifestation of love. It is when you reveal yourself nakedly and honestly, at any given moment, for no

other purpose than as a gift of what's alive in you. Not to blame, criticize, or punish. Just "Here I am, and here is what I would like." This is my vulnerability at this moment. To me, that is a way of manifesting love.

And the other way we give of ourselves is through how we receive another person's message. To receive it empathically, connecting with what's alive in them, making no judgment. Just to hear what is alive in the other person and what they would like. So Nonviolent Communication is just a manifestation of what I understand love to be.[22]

Both Christian theology and NVC recognize the importance of honoring the freedom of each person's choices and understanding the gift character of our life together. When we respond to others out of a sense of obligation or try to motivate ourselves or others by guilt or demands, we are disconnected from the life-giving values that truly motivate us.

Conclusion

"The fear of the Lord is the beginning of wisdom, and the knowledge of the Holy One is insight" (Prov. 9:10). Any wisdom that we find is therefore subsequent to the fear of God. Here fear means awe and reverence for God and respect and honor for all that God has made. Fearing God means that we seek to live our lives in accordance with God's life-giving will. As we lead congregations we seek that will through prayer, discernment, and constant attention to the Spirit of God as it moves in our lives, both individual and corporate. It means we study Scripture to hear what God may be saying to us through the Bible. NVC gives us tools for discernment and listening to God as well as to our own hearts and the hearts of those with whom we live.

Compassionate leadership, which has the potential to transform conflict, respects the creatureliness of human beings. Compassionate leaders see others in their full humanity: as made for life in community. Whenever we address one another with openness and respect in the church, we honor our humanity. Whenever we acknowledge our mutual need of one another, we honor our humanity. Whenever we listen to others with compassion and love, we honor our humanity. Whenever we support the freedom of each individual to take responsibility for his or her thoughts, feelings, and actions, we honor our humanity. NVC supports compassionate leadership by helping us to honor human beings as God's beloved children, creatures made to live in loving fellowship with God and each other. As we will see in the next chapter, connecting with others' needs is precisely what enables us to see their humanity. Once we recognize others' longings as the same longings of our own hearts, we can encounter them with mutual respect, openness, care, and freedom—the very qualities of life we seek in the kingdom of God.

Chapter 2

Rooted and Grounded in Love

The Beauty of Human Needs

For this reason I bow my knees before the Father, from whom every family in heaven and on earth takes its name. I pray that, according to the riches of his glory, he may grant that you may be strengthened in your inner being with power through his Spirit, and that Christ may dwell in your hearts through faith, as you are being rooted and grounded in love. I pray that you may have the power to comprehend, with all the saints, what is the breadth and length and height and depth, and to know the love of Christ that surpasses knowledge, so that you may be filled with all the fullness of God.

Ephesians 3:14–19

Compassionate communication understands human needs as universal qualities that are life-giving by definition. We thrive whenever our basic needs are met, whether they are physical, emotional, or spiritual in nature. In this sense, every human need is a fundamental value that serves life. This means that whenever we identify our needs accurately, we contribute in a basic way to enhancing our life. Even if a need remains unmet, once we recognize it, name it, and truly connect with its value, we will experience a greater sense of peace. We will also have clarity about what is causing our discontent, which puts us in a better position to make a request that might eventually fulfill our need. Moreover, because of our fundamental interdependence with others, we paradoxically contribute to the well-being of others when we have clarity about our own needs.

Let us first review some key points about needs from an NVC perspective:

- By definition, needs contribute to life.
- All human beings have basic physical, emotional, and spiritual needs.
- Needs are the underlying motivation for all our choices, whether we are conscious of them or not.
- We are trying to get our needs met in every moment.
- Needs themselves are universal although they may be expressed differently in different cultures. Needs transcend any cultural, religious, racial, ethnic, or gender differences.
- We are able to relate authentically with people we perceive to be different from us by connecting with their needs.
- Everyone's needs are equally valued. Therefore, in a conflictual situation we will seek resolution by finding strategies that attempt to take everyone's needs into consideration.
- Human needs are rich, multivalent, and full of meaning. When we are fully connected to their beauty,[1] we have no shame about asking for what we need.
- To express our needs vulnerably to another human being is, paradoxically, a sign of human strength. To make a request of another to meet our need is a gift.
- All persons have a need to contribute to the well-being of others.
- Needs themselves never conflict; only strategies to meet needs can truly conflict.
- When our needs are met, we typically feel happy or satisfied. When our needs are unmet, we feel unhappy or dissatisfied.
- When our chronically unmet needs are triggered, we may experience emotional pain and need empathy.
- Empathy means a caring attunement to another's feelings and needs. Self-empathy means a caring attunement to our own feelings and needs.

For all these reasons, the capacity to identify and connect with the needs of others and our own is the heart of compassionate leadership. By communicating their own needs and empathizing with the needs of others, compassionate leaders build bridges that connect formerly divided and isolated persons and groups. When we see and hear each other at the level of our common need, we can move toward each other in authentic encounter. Our judgments fade, our "enemy images"[2] are transformed, and we are moved by compassion for ourselves and others when we realize that we all long for the coming of God's kingdom in all its peace, well-being, beauty, and love.

Throughout this chapter we will explore in depth the centrality of needs in compassionate communication by placing them in the context of contemporary understandings of human psychology. We will then turn to a discussion of NVC's conception of human needs in relation to our understanding of the kingdom of God and Christian spirituality.

Needs as Life-Serving

During the twentieth century, a range of psychologists endeavored to base their understanding of human psychology on fundamental human needs. Some tried to reduce human needs to a single drive or core striving. For example, Sigmund Freud conceived of a basic life instinct, called *eros* or libido, which he believed grew out of our sexual impulses from the earliest years of life. Though he eventually countered it with an equal and opposite death instinct (*thanatos*), he considered *eros* to be the fundamental drive that motivated all life-serving human action, whether conscious or unconscious. By contrast, Alfred Adler spoke of the will to power (meaning the personal empowerment to reach one's life goals) as the basic need that motivates human behavior. Viktor Frankl spoke eloquently of the central need to find meaning in life, particularly in relation to one's suffering. Erik Erikson's understanding of the normal psychosocial crises in human development is yet another way of conceiving of our core human needs. In this sense, trust, autonomy, initiative, industry, identity, intimacy, generativity, and integrity can all be seen as fundamental needs that are necessary for human thriving.

Perhaps the most comprehensive account of basic human needs was developed by American psychologist Abraham Maslow in the mid-twentieth century.[3] Human beings, according to Maslow, are motivated by a number of essential needs that are species-wide and unchanging, though they typically express themselves differently in different cultural contexts. Maslow believed that needs have a biological basis in human instincts, and are therefore intrinsic to human nature. They cannot be eradicated, though they can be weakened, repressed, or distorted. Maslow arranged needs hierarchically, postulating that the "lower" needs must be met or fulfilled before one can move toward fulfilling the so-called higher needs. In ascending order, Maslow's hierarchy is as follows:

Physiological needs: food, drink, sleep, shelter, sex, oxygen
Safety needs: security, order, stability, freedom from danger, fairness, consistency
Belonging and love needs: love, affection, belonging to a group
Esteem: confidence, competence, mastery, self-worth, recognition, acceptance, appreciation
Self-actualization: Full development and expression of innate talents, capacities, gifts

The self-actualizing needs (level 5) are considered to be growth needs, as opposed to levels 1 through 4, which are described as deficiency needs. Growth needs include core values such as truth, goodness, beauty, justice, simplicity, playfulness, and meaning. Ultimately, Maslow conceives of these "Being values" as meta-needs that do not function in the same hierarchical way as levels 1 through 4.

Maslow teaches that once a need is gratified, it has little effect on motivation. As the lower needs are fulfilled, the higher needs emerge. Generally speaking, Maslow believes that adults who were not deprived of their basic needs when they were children grow up to be emotionally healthy. The main path to health for Maslow is through the gratification of needs, not through their frustration. This claim stands in contrast to Freud, who implies that one's impulses (the "id") are basically antithetical to cultural aims and must be fought or transformed in order to be acceptable.

Rosenberg also identifies a multiplicity of human needs, though he does not arrange them hierarchically. Rather, he sees the fulfillment of all human needs as enriching life; they are the fundamental motivation, the life energy, for all human action. Our need for play or meaning is neither more nor less basic than our need for bread and water. A child at play may completely forget about dinner, so absorbed is she in meeting this basic human need. Similarly, a baby at her mother's breast meets multiple needs simultaneously: her need for basic sustenance (nutrition) as well as needs for love, belonging, touch, and communion. Which is more basic? A child who is fed without being held will not thrive; love and belonging are just as basic as daily nutrition.

Below is a typical NVC list of needs (though not comprehensive or definitive):[4]

Table 2.1. Universal Human Needs

Connection	*Physical Well-Being*	*Peace*
acceptance		beauty
affection	air	ease
appreciation	food	inspiration
belonging	movement/exercise	order
cooperation	rest/sleep	
companionship	sexual expression	*Meaning*
consideration	safety	celebration of life
consistency	shelter	clarity
empathy	touch	competence
inclusion	water	contribution
intimacy		creativity
love	*Honesty*	effectiveness
mutuality	authenticity	growth
respect/self-respect	integrity	hope
security	presence	learning
support		mourning
to know and be	*Play*	purpose
known	joy	understanding
to see and be seen	humor	
to understand and		*Autonomy*
be understood		choice
trust		freedom
		spontaneity

When we look at this chart delineating core human needs, we see that they fall into several categories: needs for connection, physical well-being, honesty, play, peace, and autonomy. Various NVC teachers and groups organize them differently, but each one tries to capture the essential qualities of being and relationship that make life worth living. What are often called virtues in the Christian life are here identified simply as universal human needs. All persons need love, integrity, hope, and purpose. Christians may define each of these words in a specifically Christian way, and they can use these words as pointers toward universal qualities of being that enable them to connect meaningfully with the humanity of others.

Other psychologists have written about those things that are essential to human thriving. Remarkably similar to Rosenberg's list, they use different words but point to the same underlying human needs. An alternative list, for example, can be found in Gershen Kaufman's seminal book, *Shame: The Power of Caring.*[5] In his study of human development, Kaufman identifies feelings, drives, and needs as three major sources of motivation. He makes explicit the conceptual link between feelings of shame and parental failure to meet the child's most basic developmental needs. Any of the child's needs can become bound with shame when a parent disparages a child for having certain needs or in some way ignores the need or refuses to meet it. For example, when their son is sad over a loss, his parents might say, "Don't be sad; big boys don't cry. Cheer up. That's a good boy." A boy in this situation would likely suppress awareness of his need to mourn. This need might become so tied up with painful feelings of shame that whenever he began to feel sad, he would be immersed in shame. Instead of feeling sad, in other words, the child—and then adult—would feel ashamed, and perhaps not even be aware of his sadness. Over time, he may become chronically disconnected from any unmet needs that he feels sad about. They will feel dangerous because they have become attached to feelings of shame, evoked in the original parental relationship.[6]

Let us compare Kaufman's and Rosenberg's understanding of our interdependent needs. The six fundamental developmental needs that Kaufman identifies are:

1. Need for relationship: "Forming, having, and maintaining a mutually satisfying relationship with a significant other is perhaps the most fundamental interpersonal need of all."[7]
2. Need for touching/holding: "The purely physiological component of the need for touching does not communicate what I shall contend to be its more significant, developmental *meaning.* . . . It is the kind and quality of holding which form the earliest sense of self and lay the groundwork for a later secure, self-affirming identity."[8]
3. Need for identification: "Knowing how another human being lives and functions on the inside—how he or she handles the vicissitudes of life, copes with its joys and its frustrations, faces critical choices, meets failure and defeat as well as challenge and success—is what especially enables us to feel prepared for life. . . . Identification is one of those vital sources from which identity springs forth."[9] Here we "derive that precious sense of belonging *somewhere.*"[10]

4. Need for differentiation: "If identification confers that special feeling of belonging, then differentiation embraces no less a striving for separateness and for mastery. . . . Strivings for autonomy and independence emerge from this fundamental need that begins to manifest itself with the dawn of the locomotive capacity."[11]
5. Need to nurture: "We come now to that kind of interpersonal interchange in which the child is not so much in need of receiving something emotionally as giving it to another. . . After having been given to, the child will eventually *want* to give something back."[12]
6. Need for affirmation: "Each of us needs to feel that who we are, the person inside, is worthwhile and valued. It is through having someone significant provide that affirmation of self for us that we can gradually, and over time, learn how to give it to ourselves."[13]

By comparing this list with Rosenberg's, we can see that both lists represent overlapping ways of conceptualizing essentially the same interdependent needs. For example, Kaufman's understanding of the need for differentiation is represented by Rosenberg as a basic need for autonomy—that is, to make one's own choices in life. Needs for competence and empowerment in Rosenberg are closely related to Kaufman's description of the need for mastery. Similarly, Rosenberg's identified needs for love and belonging, trust and support are represented in an overlapping though not identical way on Kaufman's list by the first three needs: relationship, touching/holding, and identification. Both Kaufman and Rosenberg recognize the universality of the need to contribute to the well-being of others, Kaufman calling it the "need to nurture," with Rosenberg naming it simply "contribution."

Rosenberg's unique contribution to our understanding of human motivation lies in his explicit conceptual linking of feelings and needs. Many psychologists focus on the importance of feelings but neglect to mention needs at all, while others, like Kaufman, recognize both feelings and needs as motivating factors but do not explicitly link them conceptually. For Rosenberg, every so-called negative feeling we have means that there is an unmet need (or perhaps many) underlying it. Every so-called positive feeling means that one (or more) needs has already been met. Feelings, while important, are thus only the tip of the iceberg. If the real motivating factor comes from our underlying needs, then we are able to make choices that align with our needs only when we are consciously aware of them. It is the needs themselves that have the power to move us. Hence knowledge of what we are feeling is necessary, but not sufficient to bring about change. People can be capable of differentiating nuanced feelings, but if they are unable to identify the corresponding needs, then they can get stuck repeating the same feelings over and over without being able to work through them to some kind of action. Rosenberg provides tools for transforming our feelings by identifying the corresponding needs and developing strategies for meeting them. His detailed conceptual map—which links observations, thoughts, feelings, needs, and requests—combined with the concrete tools he offers for deep connection with oneself and others comprise what we see as his most valuable contribution.

It is important to establish that needs are by definition life-enhancing. This idea is particularly uncommon in a North American context where "being needy" can be considered a sign of human weakness. As stated in chapter 1, compassionate communication considers needs to be a source of strength, not of weakness. Yet to affirm this is to set one's foot on a distinctively countercultural path. Typical responses to the question— "What are your thoughts and feelings about the fact that human beings are 'needy' creatures?"—include the following:

- Having needs is a sign of weakness.
- I am a failure if I have needs.
- I feel angry about being dependent on anyone.
- I feel guilty when I ask anyone to meet any of my needs.
- Needy people are annoying and clingy.
- To be needy is to be "high maintenance."
- If you acknowledge your need, you are not a "real man."
- Women are supposed to focus on meeting the needs of others, never their own.
- Other people's needs are more important than mine.
- I hate needing people; I'd rather be completely self-sufficient.
- There is never enough to go around; not everyone's needs can be met.
- Needs are something you have to fulfill or you won't be happy.
- Needs are something you have to get rid of or you won't be happy.

It makes a great difference whether we think about our needs in terms of something that we lack or something that is evidence of our basic humanity. If needs are the latter, they represent life-serving values. If the former, they are experienced as painful deficits. If we see our needs as a sign of our basic humanity, we can move *toward* them as qualities that have intrinsic value rather than as something to be gotten rid of. We can acknowledge them as qualities that intrinsically contribute to our sense of well-being.

Needs can become stumbling blocks if we think about them as deficits. Consider this example. If I think about my needs for physical well-being and exercise and remember that I've failed to do this for most of my life in ministry (a negative judgment), I could regard this need as an albatross around my neck. I could tell myself a story about how hard it is to practice self-care, or about how I never have time to exercise. I might try to motivate myself to exercise by saying, "You are so out of shape; you've got to take better care of yourself." Or, I might say, "You hypocrite. You teach about self-care as part of honoring our call to ministry but fail to do it yourself." However, such self-talk would likely only mire me in inertia. It would deepen my sense of discouragement and may even induce feelings of shame. Compassionate communication stresses the importance of holding judgments at bay, even judgments of ourselves. In order to connect with myself compassionately, I would shift my focus, seeing my needs for physical well-being and integrity as life-serving gifts rather than as sources of pain and frustration. The shift from one (needs as deficits) to the other (needs as life-serving values) involves transferring my focus from what I *don't* want (the pattern of not exercising) toward what I *do* want (physical vitality).

To bring about such a shift, I might imagine taking a bike ride after work each day and experiencing the joy of having more strength and energy. I might become aware of the *beauty* of physical zest. I might notice my inner calm as I visualize myself taking time to exercise. The relaxation would become palpable when I hear myself sigh: "Ahhh, this is the kind of balanced and healthy life that honors my body as God's gift to me." As I move from the pain of unmet need ("You are so out of shape") to the beauty of the need ("Ahh, I enjoy the strength and energy and integrity that comes from exercising"), I move from a sense of deficiency to a sense of longing to live out these values. Even imagining my daily bike ride, I can experience peace in the midst of unmet need. Even though I am still as "out of shape" as ever, having *connected inwardly with my needs*, I am now motivated to act. Though I might still feel disappointed by my lack of physical energy, I am also aware of wanting to exercise in order to have a more balanced, healthy life. I move with a sense of anticipation toward the pleasurable feeling of exercising rather than with an angry "should" driving me like a stern taskmaster.

In this process of shifting from the pain of unmet need to recognizing our needs as something life-affirming, it is important to notice what happens in the body. Whenever we think about our needs as something to be discarded, we will notice a corresponding tension in our bodies. We might note shallow breathing, for example, or tightness in the abdomen or chest, a clenched jaw, tension in the shoulders, or locked knees. There is a noticeable shift that occurs when we relax into the place of recognizing the beauty of human needs, whether they are currently met or not. Whenever tension arises, we can find our center by focusing on our core need. Once connected to our need we are empowered to take the next step: making a doable request of ourselves or others. Such a process is very different from driving ourselves with "shoulds" or "musts" or calling ourselves names. When we see how our needs serve life, we can move toward them as something valuable. Attuning ourselves to our bodily responses when our needs are met helps us to recognize their intrinsic, life-affirming goodness.

Our bodies know what serves life when they taste, touch, smell, hear, or see it. To discover our true needs is not a mere intellectual enterprise. Instead, we connect inwardly with the quality or living energy that is indicated by what the word points to. We not only notice certain positive emotions but also sense an inner expansiveness and relaxation in our bodies.

What happens in your body when you recall a sense of satisfying collaboration with a colleague, or quiet companionship with a loved one, inspiration from a magnificent night sky, or a sense of community with a highly valued group of friends? In each case, a sense of fullness or expansive relaxation might be detected. Similarly, when you are confident that you have contributed to someone else's life, you might notice feelings of elation along with a sense of physical well-being. The life-giving value of contribution becomes noticeable when you experience the joy of giving to others what they need.

Developing a needs vocabulary helps us to increase our fluency in the use of compassionate communication. But it entails more than simply identifying which word corresponds most to what we are longing for. In order to integrate NVC into our everyday functioning, we need to connect with the need's life-giving qualities beyond the word or concept. This entails connecting with the difference that we notice both in our body and feelings when the need is truly identified. It has an "aha" quality to it, giving us a sense of recognition, of having landed on the exact need we are searching for.

Distinguishing Needs from Strategies

Intractable conflict occurs when two or more people are wedded to differing strategies and unaware of their common needs. Forms of conflict resolution or mediation that seek compromise typically bypass needs; they begin and end with strategies. Thus persons may debate the merits of their competing strategies without ever identifying the values from which they emerge. Or they may adopt a strategy that appears to keep the peace but actually undermines stability and trust. In contrast, Nonviolent Communication aims to transform conflict by focusing on needs, rather than strategies. Needs connect us at the level of our common humanity. When we understand the needs of others and ourselves, we are more likely to have compassion on all those embroiled in whatever conflict we find ourselves in. We also are more likely eventually to find creative strategies that contribute to all these needs.

People often confuse the simplicity of their need with a strategy for meeting the need. Because we are daily surrounded with advertising that intentionally mixes together strategies with needs, it can be challenging to differentiate them. Advertising's efficacy depends on its ability to evoke the deep needs that motivate our actions. By associating the fulfillment of those needs with a particular product, advertisers enhance their ability to sell the product. For example, beer or soft drink commercials will often picture young people glowing with good health. Attractive young men and women are seen relaxing in a beautiful environment (on the beach, in the mountains, by a gorgeous lake). The picture seems to suggest that if you buy this product, your needs for fun, relaxation, beauty, good health, companionship, play, and community will all be met. Successful advertisers want you to confuse the needs with the particular strategy that they have to sell.[14]

Compassionate communication stresses the importance of differentiating between our needs and strategies to meet those needs. A need, as stated earlier, is a shared universal value that is life-giving. It is fundamentally independent of any specific person, location, action, time, or object. By contrast, a strategy for meeting the need is concrete and context-specific. When formulating a request to meet any particular need (or brainstorming a strategy that we believe will be mutually beneficial for all parties), all of these variables—**P**erson, **L**ocation, **A**ction, **T**ime, and **O**bject **(PLATO)**—need to be included in one way or another. In the following sentence, for example, the need is not differentiated from the strategy: "I need you to clean the fellowship wing today." Even though the word "need" appears in the sentence, the speaker (the pastor) does not actually identify her need. Contrast this with a clear communication that differentiates feelings, needs, and requests: "I am *feeling* overwhelmed with all the tasks to be done before we host the regional conference meeting at our church, and I *need* some support. Would you be willing to dust and vacuum the rooms in the fellowship wing before our guests arrive?" Here the speaker clearly differentiates between her need for support and the specific request that she believes will meet that need: that the other person dust and vacuum rooms in the fellowship wing of the church. The request includes the crucial context-specific data of the **p**erson (you), the **l**ocation and **a**ction (dust and vacuum the fellowship wing), the **t**ime (before the guests arrive), and the **o**bject (implicitly understood as the floors and furniture in the rooms).

When we clearly differentiate between needs and strategies, we see that there are many ways to meet our needs. Knowing this enables us to let go of having to have things done in a particular way. It takes away the sense of desperation (or the shift from request to demand) that can creep into our requests when we believe that our needs can be met by only one particular strategy. In the example above, there may be various reasons why the sexton cannot fulfill this specific request gladly even though he may be eager to offer support. He may already have a long to-do list in preparation for the conference; he may have several errands to run; he may want to send an urgent e-mail about an unrelated matter. In other words, there might be other needs that have priority for him right now: a need for order, for efficiency, for connection. The other's power of choice (need for autonomy) is respected when the need and the request are clearly differentiated. The other is then free to acknowledge the importance of our need at the same time that he informs us which of his needs might make it difficult (or impossible) to fulfill our request. The clearer he is about his own needs, the easier it becomes to devise a strategy that will consider both sets of needs.

Learning to translate communications that mix together needs and strategies into clearly differentiated feelings and needs helps us to make connections with others that are mutually satisfying instead of contributing to painful disconnection. Consider the following list of confusing needs and strategies and see if you can translate it into an observation, a feeling, a need, and a request:

- I need you to be quiet.
- I need you to listen to me!
- I need you to love me.

- I want you to attend worship every week.
- I want you to do what I say.
- I want you to be on time.
- I need to show you who the pastor is.
- I need you to take care of me.
- I need you to get along with other people in the church.
- I need you to stop smoking (drinking, swearing, talking, yelling, arguing, procrastinating).[15]

For example, "I need you to be quiet," might be "translated" as follows:

- *Observation*: "When I hear whispering while I am giving the deacons instructions about their task . . ."
- *Feeling*: "I feel annoyed . . ."
- *Need*: "because I'd like everyone to hear what I am saying." (The need is to be heard.)
- *Request*: "Would you wait till I'm finished before making your comment or asking your question?"

Such a process of translation can also be helpful whenever someone makes demands of us, diagnoses us, offers us unwanted advice, or communicates with us in ways that we don't enjoy. Instead of getting annoyed with them, we can seek to understand what needs they might be trying to satisfy. We can train ourselves to empathically guess what their intentions might be. At the same time, we can also train ourselves not to react to blame with shame or counter-blame, to judgment with judgment, to anger with anger, but instead stay clear about our own intention to connect with both their needs and our own. In this way we are able not only to accept their humanity with compassion but our own as well.

How might you respond to a member of the church youth group who exclaims, "You can't tell me what to do!" Such a sentence might evoke something like the following from her pastor, youth group director, or other leader:

- "Actually, yes I can. That's part of my job."
- "You had better learn to be more respectful."
- "As long as you are part of this youth group, you'll follow the rules."
- "We'll see about *that* when you want to go on the youth group mission trip this summer."

None of these reactions pauses to consider the teenager's needs, nor, for that matter, your own needs as church leader. Yet, such a moment of reflection is essential if you are actually going to connect with this teen. If this teen (who is typically in a power-under position)[16] says, "You can't tell me what to do," what might she be feeling and needing? Perhaps she is feeling powerless and wanting her autonomy to be acknowledged. Perhaps she is angry because she desperately wants to be heard. Perhaps she is hopeless because she wants some sense of mutuality and reciprocity. The significant point to be made here is that taking the time to check out precisely what she might be feeling and needing communicates compassionate care and has the potential to transform the entire interaction. Not only does it avoid a power struggle, it shows that you care about her unmet needs and her distress.

Before responding, you may first need to translate your own judgments into feelings and needs by a process of self-empathy. Even if you don't respond with a power-over statement, you might be thinking, "This kid is totally obnoxious." Or, "How dare she talk to me in that tone of voice?" Translating such judgments into your own feelings and needs has a much greater chance of making a real connection in a moment like this. The judgment, "This kid is totally obnoxious," can be translated into, "I'm upset because I'd like to be treated with respect." Or, "When I hear that tone of voice, I'm upset because I'd like more mutual caring between us." Once you connect with your own needs for respect and caring, you can reach out to this member of the youth group either through honest expression or through empathic listening.

Notice that this translation project works in both directions. When you direct your attention outward, you focus on what the other's feelings and needs might be. Alternatively, when you direct your attention inward, you seek to discover feelings and needs of your own that might have been triggered by the other's comment. You take responsibility for your own feelings by connecting them with your underlying needs and expressing them honestly at the same time that you seek to understand the other through empathy.

Thinking about Needs in Christian Perspective

Compassionate communication's core commitment to consider all persons' needs as of equal value can be understood in the context of Jesus' injunction to "love your neighbor as yourself" (Mark 12:31). When we truly love our neighbors, we take their needs to heart as fully as we do our own. When we truly love ourselves, we will not sacrifice our own needs for the sake of our neighbor's because we trust that our needs matter to God. We also know that if we sacrifice our own needs without doing so gladly, it will likely contribute to feelings of resentment. Both the needs of others and our own needs matter.

When the apostle Paul exhorts the church at Philippi to: "Let each of you look not to your own interests, but to the interests of others" (Phil 2:4), he recognizes the human tendency to look only to one's own interests. He reminds his readers to take to heart the needs of the other, as Christ took to heart the needs of all. From a Christian standpoint, caring about the needs of others extends far beyond the Christian community to every human being made in the divine image as well as to every creature given the gift of life by God. Christians acknowledge the preciousness of every living thing when they seek to obey God's commandment "thou shalt not kill" as well as the Deuteronomic injunction to "choose life." Whatever truly serves life is the will of God.

From a Christian perspective, God created us not only to need God but also to need one another at the core of our being. To paraphrase St. Augustine, our hearts are restless in this life until they rest in God. We are essentially incomplete apart from our connection with God. God also created us to need our fellow human beings. Many of our needs are interdependent; we cannot meet them on our own. We depend on others in order to thrive. Though we can love and respect ourselves, we still need the love and respect of others if we are truly to flourish. In fact, we cannot grow to love and respect ourselves apart from first receiving it from another. The apostle Paul asks, "What do you have that you did not receive?" (1 Cor. 4:7). All human love is ultimately rooted and grounded in the love of God. "We love because he first loved us" (1 John 4:19).

When we are rooted and grounded in the love of God, we are strengthened in our inner being. We have the kind of self-acceptance and inner peace that enables us to reach out to others. We trust that a way forward can be found through impasses that we might have in our relationships with others. With our connection to God's love at the center of our being, we have a sense of spaciousness and possibility. We are less likely to give up in despair when things grow difficult. Filled with God's fullness, we have access to our own needs and care about the needs of others. We are not afraid to be vulnerable and to ask for what we need, even in the midst of high anxiety and conflict. When we are rooted and grounded in the love of Christ, we are eager to contribute to the needs of others.

We confess our radical dependence on God for meeting our basic needs every time we pray. "Cast all your anxiety on him, because he cares for you" (1 Pet. 5:7). God is the ground and source of every human need. We turn to God in prayer with our needs for courage, hope, faith, and wisdom. In acknowledging our pain, we turn to God with our need for consolation or comfort, forgiveness or reconciliation. When we are elated, we recognize God as the source of every good and perfect gift by turning to God with thanksgiving and praise. In the Lord's Prayer we identify the needs that are at the center of the church's common life: for God's name to be hallowed, for God's kingdom to come, for God's will to be done on earth as in heaven. We also acknowledge our dependence on God for something so basic as our daily bread, for the forgiveness of our sins, for the grace to forgive those who have hurt us, for protection from trials that are beyond our capacity to bear, and for deliverance from every kind of evil. In prayer, we acknowledge God as the source of all that promotes life: the source of love, mercy, kindness, justice, hope, faithfulness, patience, trust, and wisdom.

We pray to God about our needs. Jesus tells us not to be anxious about our needs because God knows them even before we ask: "Do not be afraid, little flock, for it is your Father's good pleasure to give you the kingdom" (Luke 12:32). Paul reminds us that God "will satisfy every need of yours according to his riches in glory in Christ Jesus" (Phil. 4:19). Scripture teaches that Jesus Christ is himself the fullness of life that we long for. As the light of the world, Jesus Christ fulfills our human need for illumination, guidance, and wisdom. As the bread of life, he sustains us body and soul with his own substance. Physical hunger cannot be separated from our hunger for spiritual food; thus depth of meaning is yoked with daily sustenance. As the water of life, Christ at once assuages and increases a thirst for justice. As the cup of salvation, Jesus Christ grants fullness of joy, reminding us that the wellspring of grace is sufficient for our every need.

Worship and prayer keep alive the longing of our hearts: for true knowledge of God, for lasting peace and reconciliation, for the healing balm of forgiveness, for the richness of life lived in community. Worship connects us with the love of God, both God's love for us and our love for God. Prayer gives us constant training in identifying our needs, giving them voice, truly connecting with them in the context of our faith in God. Their beauty becomes apparent when we see the integral connection between our needs and our longing for the kingdom of God. Faith actually magnifies our longings and focuses them when we are in prayer.

Jesus Christ instructs us to see the kingdom of God in our midst, near at hand, among us. He calls us to wake up, to see God's beauty all around us, the richness of God's gifts being poured out on all creation. When we connect with these gifts from God as the most basic needs of our souls, we acknowledge their inexpressible beauty. We see them as gifts from above that can be lived out here and now on earth.

When God is understood as the wellspring of our lives, we come to see every good and perfect need as a manifestation of God's grace. Paul exhorts us: "Finally, beloved, whatever is true, whatever is honorable, whatever is just, whatever is pure, whatever is pleasing, whatever is commendable, if there is any excellence and if there is anything worthy of praise, think about these things" (Phil. 4:8). When we ponder all these excellences, our thoughts naturally move toward God, for God alone wholly embodies truth, honor, justice, purity, loveliness, grace—all that is excellent and worthy of praise. As Scripture exhorts us to ponder the goodness of God, so compassionate communication encourages us to ponder the goodness of our universal human needs. We understand God as the source of all goodness; at the core of our life of prayer is a process of discernment in which we struggle to give voice to our heart's true needs.

From a Christian standpoint, when we connect with our needs, we are drawing from the wellspring of God's grace in a particular form. The kingdom of God (the focus of Christian longing) is a place of true freedom, a need essential to human thriving: "For freedom Christ has set us free" (Gal. 5:1). The kingdom of God is a place of safety and peace: "The wolf and the lamb shall feed together. . . . They shall not hurt or destroy on all my holy mountain, says the LORD" (Isa. 65:25). These, too, are fundamental human needs. The kingdom is a community where people treat each other with kindness, act with integrity, speak honestly, and hear each other with compassion: "[Love] does not rejoice in wrongdoing, but rejoices in the truth. It bears all things, believes all things, hopes all things, endures all things. Love never ends" (1 Cor. 13:6–8). When we live in a steady awareness of our true needs, we become acutely aware of our interdependence and rejoice in it. We receive it as a gift from God. We recognize that we are made in the image of God in order to love one another, pray for one another, uphold and support one another, and encourage one another in the life of faith. Because the image of God is relational by definition, we glorify God whenever we acknowledge our basic interdependence. The church as the body of Christ connects us to our intrinsic need for one another so that we can receive the gifts of every person who gathers in Christ's name. When the Holy Spirit works among us, not only are we deeply connected to each other but also to our own truest selves.

Our spiritual fellowship with one another manifests as a community of mutual care. Thus all of the ways that we depend on others in order to be fully human are celebrated. Rosenberg identifies many of these interdependent needs—acceptance, appreciation, closeness, community, consideration, contribution, love, respect, support, and understanding.[17] Each need contributes to the flourishing of our common life. Scripture affirms our interdependence again and again by its claim that it is not good for human beings to be alone, through its emphasis on God's own identity as being fully relational and interpersonal, and through the image of the body of Christ as an interdependent unit.

Ultimately, then, our "neediness" is one of the most basic signs of our dependence on God and one another, and is therefore to be affirmed. It is a sign of our sin when we pretend to have no need of God or of our fellow human beings. God's "power at work within us is able to accomplish abundantly far more than all we can ask or imagine" (Eph. 3:20). As we trust in these words of promise, we are able to seek the fulfillment of human need even in situations where we would otherwise be tempted to despair. Our continued failure of imagination as to how human needs might be fully met can be countered by faith in a God who wills our human thriving. When we humbly bring our needs before God each day, we acknowledge God alone as Lord of our lives. When we work toward the fulfillment of human need, whether our own or that of another, we are responding to God's grace in our lives: "Do not be afraid, little flock, for it is your Father's good pleasure to give you the kingdom" (Luke 12:32).

Chapter 3

Search Me and Know My Heart

Identifying and Expressing Feelings

Search me, O God, and know my heart;
test me and know my thoughts.

Psalm 139:23

The Church and Feelings

Following a five-year surge in membership, First Presbyterian Church began exploring the feasibility of a new building campaign. The session (church elders) appointed an eight-member task force to solicit information from congregation members and local contractors. After six months of interviews, the task force presented three plans to the pastoral staff and then to the elders, one focused on renovation and the other two on new construction. All three pastors agreed to promote one of the new construction plans at the session meeting. However, much to their surprise, nearly one-third of the session members argued vigorously against new construction, citing cost as the primary factor in their decision. The senior pastor and task force representative presented their talking points of seemingly rational reasons for a new facility, to no avail. The session tabled the discussion until its next meeting. In the meantime, the pastors and task force members consulted with a church growth specialist and compiled more data to support their proposal. They were confident that the elders would recognize their logic, especially since the calculations suggested that the congregation could confidently build a new facility without debt. But again, the same result. Five session members sat with their arms crossed and spoke very little. It seemed clear that they had dug in their heels. The task force and pastoral staff were frustrated and perplexed. Why were these five elders refusing to go forward with a building campaign that made so much sense? How could the task force open up conversation again?

In the last chapter, we learned that all human actions are attempts to meet basic universal needs. Perhaps these session members were trying to meet needs for security and stability. Perhaps the task force and pastors were trying to meet needs for growth, meaning, and contribution. If these two groups could identify the variety of needs underlying their differing strategies, they might move beyond their current impasse. A new strategy for the building campaign might emerge. If they were able to connect at the level of their needs, they would likely experience increased cooperation and meaning in fulfilling their common mission as leaders of this congregation. Yet identifying and connecting with needs is not part of typical decision-making patterns in the church. In fact, even personal awareness of our needs is uncommon. So how might this group of church leaders identify the needs motivating their decisions and construct an action plan based on those same needs?

To begin, they would learn to identify, experience, and express their feelings. Feelings provide a pathway for identifying needs. Naming and experiencing our feelings helps us to connect with our needs, because feelings emerge from needs. When our needs are met, we experience so-called positive feelings; when our needs are unmet, we experience so-called negative feelings. Feelings also emerge from interpretations of our situation. If one of the session members interprets the task force proposal as an attempt to undermine long-standing church traditions, she might feel angry, hurt, or resentful because she values those traditions and wants them to be respected (she has a need for respect). If a pastor interprets the elders as short-sighted and resistant to change, he might be feeling frustrated because he wants most to contribute to future generations. If the pastors, elders, and task force members could communicate their thoughts, feelings, and needs with this kind of clarity and without accusation and blame, then their life together might be transformed. Instead of being dead-locked in disagreement, they might move the church into faithful ministry in the world. They might find a way forward that would both respect the traditions of the past and also contribute to future generations; that is, a strategy that would take both sets of needs into account. Compassionate leaders who value others' needs as much as their own are intent on listening for the core values of those with whom they most disagree.

NVC teaches us practical skills to identify, experience, and express our feelings fully. It helps us to differentiate our thoughts from our feelings, to identify and feel our feelings fully, and then to connect to the life-serving needs underneath our feelings. In compassionate communication, our feelings are not merely instrumental, however. They are not, in other words, merely a means to connecting with needs. As the latest advances in brain research demonstrate, feelings are essential to life-giving relationships. For emotion moves us toward encounter with others and, when considered theologically, emotion moves us toward encounter with God.

Differentiating Feelings from Thoughts

One of the four basic skills in Nonviolent Communication is the capacity to differentiate our thoughts from our feelings. This can be somewhat challenging in an English-speaking context, given that we use the word *feel* to cognitively assess people, places, and events. That is, we often use the word *feel* to describe our interpretations, ideas, and opinions:

- "I feel *that* our pastor's decision is good for the church."
- "I feel *like* eating pizza tonight." Or the shorter (and more maddening to mavens of the English language), "I feel *like* pizza."

Sometimes we use the word 'feel' to evaluate ourselves or others:

- "I feel *like* a lazy bum."
- "I feel *like* she's a nice person."

Notice that none of these statements explicitly expresses a feeling. Instead they express thoughts, opinions, or ideas. As Marshall Rosenberg helpfully notes, whenever we follow the word *feel* with words such as *that*, *like*, or *it*, we are not expressing a feeling but rather a thought of some kind.[1]

Likewise, some of our words often masquerade as feelings.[2] They are *faux* feelings. These words are harder to distinguish from feelings because they are so closely linked to them. Faux feelings contain some kind of evaluation or judgment about ourselves or others. "I feel betrayed" communicates my belief that another person has done something to me, specifically that the other person has betrayed me and is therefore unworthy of my trust. "I feel manipulated" communicates my interpretation of the motives underlying another person's actions: that the other person is trying to bend my will to his own.

In compassionate communication, we differentiate our thoughts from our feelings so that we can take responsibility for our feelings and needs

Table 3.1 Common Faux Feelings

Abandoned	Neglected
Abused	Overworked
Attacked	Pressured
Betrayed	Put down
Bothered	Rejected
Cheated	Ridiculed
Coerced	Threatened
Disrupted	Unappreciated
Intimidated	Unheard
Let down	Unwanted
Manipulated	Unseen
Misunderstood	Used

rather than blaming others for them. To take responsibility means first to notice our evaluations rather than pronouncing them as truth on the one hand, or suppressing them on the other. Then we can translate our faux feelings or evaluations into actual expressions of emotion. For instance, if I believe that another person has betrayed me, I might be feeling hurt. If I believe that another person is manipulating me, I might be feeling confused and angry. Table 3.2 illustrates some further possible translations.

Table 3.2. Translating *Faux* Feelings into True Feelings

Statements that Communicate Thoughts	*Statements that Communicate Feelings*
I feel inadequate. (I am judging myself to be inadequate.)	I feel anxious when I spend less than ten hours in sermon preparation.
I feel manipulated. (I am judging him to be manipulating me.)	I feel distressed when my boss talks about me with my coworker rather than talking to me directly.
I feel that she's a nice person. (I am judging her as nice.)	I feel delighted by her presence in this group.
I feel like pizza. (I think I'd like to eat pizza for supper.)	I feel hungry, and I'd like to eat pizza.

While it is important to differentiate thoughts from feelings in compassionate communication, it is equally important that we do not create a false dichotomy between thinking and feeling. It has been our experience that proponents of NVC sometimes elevate emotion over thinking, in some cases even denigrating intellectual discourse. It also has been our experience that theologians and church leaders often elevate thought over emotion, denigrating the expression of feeling in the context of difficult conversations and debate. In contrast to both of these forms of dualism, we propose that thought and feeling are actually inseparable, even if it is helpful to differentiate them for the sake of clarity.

In his book, *The Developing Mind: How Relationships and the Brain Interact to Shape Who We Are*, psychiatrist Daniel Siegel presents an overview of the human brain, which discredits dualistic conceptions of thinking and feeling. Structurally, the brain consists of three interconnected parts: lower/deeper, middle, and higher/frontal regions. The lower/deeper structures regulate physiological responses. The frontal structures regulate complex thought processes. The middle structures coordinate the activity of the other two regions. Also called the limbic system, these middle structures "mediate emotion, motivation, and goal-directed behavior."[3] They directly process certain kinds of information such as emotional responses to social contexts. These three regions of the brain cannot be neatly dissected from one another. In fact, the limbic system seems to lack clearly definable boundaries. Moreover, all three regions are intricately woven together by a vast and complex spider-web-like system of neurons. Neurons transmit energy and information throughout the brain every second of every day. One hundred billion neurons stretch across the brain. Each neuron has approximately ten thousand connections that link it to other neurons. "Thus there are thought to be about one million, billion of these connections, making [the brain] 'the most complex structure, natural or artificial, on earth.'"[4]

A basic understanding of the human brain shows the conceptual inadequacy of dichotomizing thinking and feeling.[5] There are no two parts of the brain referred to as the "emotional mind" and the "rational mind." Thought and emotion are not even separable, let alone intrinsically at odds with each other. If the limbic system regulates both emotion and social processes, and if it also stretches throughout the brain, then "the entire brain can be considered 'emotional.'" Put another way, "emotions are everywhere in the processes of the mind"; they are "ubiquitous."[6]

Multiple Dimensions of Emotion

The latest advances in neurobiology demonstrate that feelings are central to our daily functioning. Emotions are everywhere in the functions of our brain and our bodies. They move us toward action. Moreover, emotions exist at varying levels of development: primary emotions, categorical emotions, moods, and temperaments (technically called "self-states").

At the simplest level, feelings "are fluctuations in the energy and informational flow of the mind."[7] Siegel calls these primary emotions. They are activated by a stimulus. For instance, if you are driving in two-lane traffic and a car suddenly lurches into your lane, you might automatically swerve, slam on your brakes, or yell something that you would avoid saying in public. In this scenario, the lurching car is the stimulus that your brain appraises as harmful to your well-being. The primary emotion is the surge of energy rushing through your body, which enables you to change your course with lightning speed. The primary emotion directs the flow of information in your mind so that you can focus intently, exclusively, and perhaps in a hypervigilant manner on taking action.

While we may or may not be conscious of our primary emotions, they nevertheless engage our whole person.[8] They are expressed bodily through muscle changes in our face and limbs and in the function of our heart, lungs, or intestines. In the above scenario, the primary emotion might manifest itself through an increased heart rate, perspiration, and shaky hands.

In order to practice compassionate communication, we give these surges of energy a feeling name such as anger, fear, sadness, and happiness. Siegel calls these categorical emotions—"specific classifications of emotion"[9] that we experience and consciously acknowledge. While there is no universally agreed upon system for classifying emotions, Daniel Goleman suggests that there are basic families of categorical emotion: anger, sadness, fear, enjoyment, love, surprise, disgust, and shame. Each of these emotions has a variety of nuances. We might consider each to be a core emotion with manifold variations. Anger, for instance, has many variations: irritation, annoyance, frustration, resentment, indignation, outrage, and fury.

Feelings are often fleeting. One moment you may be feeling sad, and the next you may be feeling surprised or even happy. Our emotions change when our evaluation of our context changes. Filmmakers know this well. With a quick twist in the plot, an audience's evaluation of a character can change from positive to negative (or vice versa), leading to a dramatic change in emotion, perhaps from contented to agitated. It is important to remember that the evaluation and emotional change happen in less than a second, so we experience the evaluation and the feeling simultaneously.

At other times, feelings are anything but fleeting. They seem to linger over us. We may experience ourselves as stuck in particular feeling states. Often we refer to this as a "mood." "Mood can be thought of as a bias in the system toward certain categorical emotions. Mood shapes the interpretation of perceptual processing and gives a 'slant' to thinking, self-reflection, and recollections."[10] Moods may be characterized by any emotion ranging from despondency to elation. Consider the actor and filmmaker, Woody Allen. Anyone who watches his movies anticipates that the character played by Woody Allen will likely be sardonic, pessimistic, or even morose. At times, this mood hovers over the character and becomes a continual state of mind. A state of mind is simply a pattern of brain activity that predisposes us to think and act in a particular manner. In a state of mind, neurons connect to each other in a given pattern. Once a pattern has been established, it is likely to be repeated in the future. As Siegel explains, neurons that fire together, wire together.[11]

Like feelings, states of mind come and go. Our state of mind at any given moment is influenced significantly by our context and our history. Consider this example. A friend describes his feelings of relief, peace, and relaxation that cluster together each year as he boards the ferry from Cape Cod to Martha's Vineyard. All of a sudden, where there was struggle, there is now ease. Where there was frustration, there is now hope. He and his wife have been traveling to Martha's Vineyard for nearly ten years now, riding that same ferry, leaving behind the cares of pastoral ministry. He experiences this state of mind annually because states of mind, like feelings, are recursive. Because neurons that fire together wire together, states of mind that occur frequently are likely to keep recurring. Recurring states of mind can become self-states, or temperaments, that characterize our personality and our way of being in the world.[12]

To summarize, we can conceptualize the multi-dimensions of emotion in concentric circles.[13] At the core is the basic emotional nucleus, such as sadness. The next circle outward includes all the nuances of the basic emotional nucleus. The next circle represents moods, states of mind in which one repeatedly experiences the nuances of the basic emotion. Beyond moods are temperaments.

Understanding the differences among these various dimensions of emotion gives us insight into the various types of responses to the commonly asked question, "How are you feeling?" As Siegel explains, your answer might reflect a general response to a particular stimulus, to a primary emotion, a categorical emotion, a mood, or temperament. If you are only generally aware that something has affected you, you might say, "I'm feeling good or bad or so-so." If answering at the level of primary emotion, you might say, "I'm feeling aroused,

Illustration 3.1 The Multiple Dimensions of Emotion

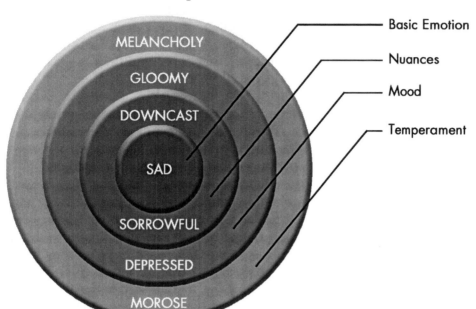

alert, or energetic." At the level of categorical emotion, you might say, "I'm feeling disappointed, delighted, or irritated." We can track our typical responses to this question and thereby identify the degree to which we are aware of and able to express our emotions.

Enhancing Emotional Intelligence

Emotional intelligence is central to compassionate leadership. Indeed, it is central to success in any kind of leadership. As Daniel Goleman and others have demonstrated, high-level executives and foreign diplomats who influence and inspire collaborative, complex work toward common goals demonstrate significant levels of emotional intelligence. These leaders are able to empathize with others and manage interpersonal relationships with grace. The five elements of emotional intelligence, according to Goleman, are "self-awareness, motivation, self-regulation, empathy, and adeptness in relationships."[14] Of these five elements, self-awareness is the most basic. It is the foundation for all other emotional capacities and thus the fundamental prerequisite for compassionate communication in leadership. Goleman writes,

> The ability to monitor feelings from moment to moment is cru-
> cial to psychological insight and self-understanding. An inability to
> notice our true feelings leaves us at their mercy. People with greater
> certainty about their feelings are better pilots of their lives, having
> a surer sense of how they really feel about personal decisions from
> whom to marry to what job to take.[15]

Similarly Siegel writes, "Without the involvement of consciousness and
the capacity to perceive others' and one's own emotions, there may be an
inability to plan actively for the future, to alter engrained patterns of behavior, or to engage in emotionally meaningful connections with others."[16]

While nearly all of us experience moments in which we are unaware
of our feelings, some people are significantly disconnected from and
chronically unaware of their feelings. Some claim not to experience certain emotions, such as shame, grief, anger, or fear. Siegel refers to those
who are almost completely unconscious of their feelings as suffering from
"emotional blankness," which is a manifestation of "a lack of binding of
emotion to consciousness."[17] In emotional blankness, emotional processing gets short-circuited so that the person may not be conscious of any
dimension of his feelings. In other cases, a person may have minimal emotional awareness, such as only being aware of her primary emotion. But
she may not be able to identify or articulate clearly what she is feeling.[18]

Shame can contribute to this kind of disconnection. Often confused
with guilt in which a person regrets her choices or actions, shame is a
feeling of embarrassment combined with a strong belief that one is defective, flawed, and perhaps even unlovable. A shame-state emerges when a
person, especially in the earliest years of life, receives little or no empathic
connection with others in the midst of intense feelings, whether negative
or positive. The lack of emotional resonance, the experience of "feeling
felt,"[19] leads to a negative evaluation of emotion, which in turn leads to
its suppression. Emotional resonance, however, can be achieved through
new attachment relationships, for example with a counselor, pastor,
friend, or partner. The attachment relationship would provide space for
both acknowledgment and exploration of the shame, especially the negative self-evaluations. The experience of being heard with understanding
would facilitate the process of bringing feelings into consciousness, experiencing them, and expressing them fully.

Though some feelings are painful to identify and experience, suppressing
them does not make them go away. Whenever we try to eliminate our feelings, we merely give them more power. For example, if we have negatively

evaluated our anger and suppressed it, either consciously or unconsciously, we are in greater danger of acting it out or turning it inward against ourselves. Whether we are disconnected completely (at the conscious level) or unable to articulate our feelings fully, they nevertheless press for acknowledgment and expression. Identifying and experiencing them does not give them power over us, as some perceive to be the case; rather it gives us access to what we already are enduring unconsciously. As Eugene Gendlin writes, "What is true is already so. Owning up to it doesn't make it worse. Not being open about it doesn't make it go away. And because it's true, it is what *is* there to be interacted with. Anything untrue isn't there to be lived. People can stand what is true, for they are already enduring it."[20]

One way to enhance awareness of our feelings is to pay attention to our bodies. Research of emotional expression in isolated cultures suggests that human beings experience a common range of feelings that are expressed in similar facial expressions. For instance, in all cultures, a wide grin conveys gladness or some variant of it; a frown conveys displeasure or sadness.[21] Our affect, our facial expression, conveys our feelings to others. Our affect may also trigger our own awareness of our feelings. If you notice that you are scowling, you might become aware that you are feeling irritated. If you notice a knot in your stomach, you might become aware of your anxiety. Likewise, we can turn our attention to our whole bodies in order to identify our feelings. Particular feelings often manifest themselves in physiological responses. We may clench our teeth when we feel angry; incessantly tap our foot when nervous; roll our eyes when annoyed; smile broadly or leap into the air when ecstatic. We can become aware of the ways that we typically embody certain emotions. When we are having trouble identifying what we are feeling, we can turn our attention to our bodies, noting a lump in the throat, tightness in the chest, or energy coursing through our legs, all of which provide clues to our emotional state.

There are a number of group exercises that can help us identify our feelings by paying attention to our bodies. In one exercise, group members break into pairs. One member of the pair thinks of a feeling and then expresses it bodily (without words). The other person tries to empathically guess the feeling. This exercise can also be played as a form of charades, with group members trying to guess the feeling acted out by one person. Another exercise asks participants to pay attention to the physiological and emotional changes they experience in relation to perceived changes in their context. In this exercise, group members are instructed to mill around the room. As they are meandering through the room, the group facilitator periodically asks them to imagine changes in their context, for example that the others in the room are members of their congregation or their family of origin; that the others in the room are former terrorists; or that they are now on their elementary school's playground. With each change in context, group members are asked to notice what happens in their bodies and what they are feeling. At the end of the exercise, group members gather together to share their discoveries. The group facilitator also can ask them to identify their thoughts as they imagined these changes in context. What did they tell themselves about their family members, their peers, the "terrorists," their fellow congregants? How did these thoughts or opinions influence their feelings? If they have learned to connect feelings to needs, as discussed in the next section of this chapter, the group facilitator could take them a step further, asking what needs were stimulated by their thoughts and feelings.

Connecting Feelings to Needs

Compassionate leadership, as we are defining it, flows from connecting to the beauty, or full life-giving quality, of our needs. When we speak and act on the basis of our needs, we enhance our capacity to live in humanizing encounter with others. Judgments can be transformed into acceptance and respect; misunderstanding can be transformed into mutual knowing and being known; and conflict can be transformed into new vision for congregational mission.

Feelings are the gateway to connecting with the fullness of our needs and others' needs. First we learn to differentiate our feelings from our thoughts. We identify and experience our feelings fully. And then we connect to the life-giving quality of our needs underneath our thoughts and feelings.

As Marshall Rosenberg teaches, our feelings emerge from our needs. To put it another way, our needs are the source and cause of our feelings. For example, if our needs for celebration and play are being met, we might feel happy, delighted, or invigorated. If our needs for celebration and play are not being met, we might feel cranky, stressed, or down. It is crucial to recognize that feelings are not caused by another person's choices or actions. Another's words or actions may *trigger* our feelings, but they do not *cause* them. Our feelings, whether positive or negative, arise out of our needs. Because we have not been socialized to think about our needs, we tend to be less conscious of them. While we are more likely to be conscious of our feelings, we might only be aware of our primary emotions or initial orienting responses to a situation or person. That is, we might only be able to identify whether we like, dislike, or feel neutral toward a situation or person.

Compassionate communication gives us tools for noticing how our interpretations of ourselves or others give rise to a variety of feelings. This also is because our thoughts are connected to our needs. When we lack the skill to speak of our needs directly, we often express them through our beliefs or opinions. If I think, "My colleague will never understand me on this issue," I might be feeling discouraged because I need understanding. If I hold onto the belief that my colleague "will never understand me," the discouragement will remain. If, however, I become conscious of this interpretation, I can "translate" the thought directly into feelings and needs: "I'm very discouraged because I long for understanding in my relationships." To demonstrate this further, we can build table 3.3.

Table 3.3 Translating Thoughts and Judgments into Feelings and Needs

Statements that Communicate Thoughts	*Statements that Communicate Feelings*	*Statements that Communicate both Feelings and Needs*
I feel inadequate. (I am judging myself to be inadequate.)	I feel anxious when I spend less than ten hours in sermon preparation.	When I spend less than ten hours in sermon preparation, I feel anxious because I need competence.
I feel manipulated. (I am judging him to be manipulating me.)	I feel distressed when my boss talks about me with my coworker rather than talking to me directly.	When my boss talks about me with my coworker rather than talking to me directly, I feel distressed because I need openness and trust.
I feel that she's a nice person. (I am judging her as nice.)	I feel delighted by her presence in this group.	When she participates in this group, I feel delighted because it meets my need for playfulness.
I feel like pizza. (I think I'd like to eat pizza for supper.)	I feel hungry, and I'd like to eat pizza.	I'd like to order pizza, because I feel hungry and need to eat.

Here it is important to note that *both* the situation in which we find ourselves *and* our interpretation of that situation can clue us in to the needs underneath our feelings. Perhaps you have presented a lecture and a member of the audience says to you, "That didn't make much sense to me." You might feel discouraged because you need appreciation. Or perhaps you have asked one of your colleagues to join a local church task force and his response was, "No way!" Here you might feel discouraged because you need support. In both situations, you experience the same feeling but related to different needs. If your interpretation of those scenarios changed, then your feelings and needs likely would change as well. Perhaps in response to the audience member's comment, you think, "He's clueless!" Now you might be feeling annoyed, because you need understanding. If in response to your colleague's "No way," you think, "Wow! He must be overwhelmed with a lot of work right now," then you might feel concerned because you value wholeness and self-care.

These examples highlight the interlocking relationships among thoughts, feelings, and needs. As recent brain studies (as well as other psychological theories) teach us, feelings are the consequences of our interpretations of events and contexts in our lives. And as NVC teaches us, feelings are the consequences of our needs—met or unmet. Particular beliefs about a situation may lead to our needs being met or unmet, which in turn may trigger so-called positive or negative feelings respectively. Particular events combined with beliefs about those events yield emotional consequences because the combination of the context and our belief about it either meets our needs or does not meet our needs.[22] Related beliefs and feelings mutually reinforce one another so that they become more likely to be experienced in the future. They can even spiral into either debilitating or life-enhancing patterns. In the former, we remain disconnected from our needs. In the latter, we are connected to our needs even if those needs are unmet in a given situation.

To explain further, let's return to the case study from the beginning of this chapter. One of the task force members might feel so angry and dejected that he rants for weeks to his wife about the five elders and the church in general. He seriously considers resigning from his leadership position. His feelings and actions are related to a series of reinforcing, spiraling beliefs. These are conclusions that he has drawn based on high levels of ongoing frustration. He tells himself repeatedly that (1) the elders do not respect or trust his research into the feasibility of a new building campaign; (2) they care more about saving the past than preparing for the future; (3) the church never "gets it" until it's too late; and (4) it is pointless to try to make a difference by serving as an elder anymore. These beliefs perpetuate his feelings of frustration, despondency, and even hopelessness. By ruminating on these beliefs, he stays stuck in these feelings and remains unaware of his needs. (1) The action of the five elders to vote against new construction plus (2) his interpretations of their actions and his interpretation of the church's past actions (3) have triggered levels of intense frustration, despondency and even hopelessness (4) because he has not fully recognized and connected with his needs for respect, trust, purpose, and making a meaningful contribution. If he could slow down his own internal reactions, then he could differentiate his interpretations from his feelings. He then could connect to the needs that he values so highly, needs that are not being met in this situation. For instance, he could identify the underlying feelings and needs in each of his four deeply held interpretations as depicted in table 3.4.

**Table 3.4 From Static Evaluations
to the Living Energy of Feelings and Needs**

Evaluation	*Translation into Feelings and Needs*
The elders do not respect or trust my research.	I'm discouraged because I need trust in our working relationship.
The elders care more about saving the past than preparing for the future.	I am worried because I long to prepare future generations for church leadership.
The church never gets it.	I feel distressed because I long for our church to understand the needs of its members.
It is pointless to serve as an elder.	I feel hopeless because I need a sense of purpose in what we are doing.

In other words, this elder could translate into feelings and needs the sentences that are now paralyzing him as they go round and round in his mind. This process would diminish the debilitating power of his interpretations over him. It might enable him to move toward strategies to meet his needs. It might enable him to express himself honestly and authentically, without blame or judgment, to other church leaders. Expressing his feelings and needs directly holds the potential for opening up the discussion to fruitful dialogue. If other members of the church council could go through a similar process, together they would increase the chances of moving out of their current impasse and toward more creative ways of dialogue and decision-making. They might even discover an unexpected new strategy for building construction, a strategy that meets more needs for more people in the congregation.

To summarize, connecting with others at the level of our feelings enables our brains to develop throughout life. It enables us to understand one another and to appreciate how intimately intertwined our lives are. Contrary to popular expressions that pit heart against head or vice versa, feelings are everywhere in the processes of the mind and in relationships. Differentiating our feelings from our thoughts enables us to express our feelings with greater accuracy, thereby contributing to the mutual speech and hearing that characterize our common life-in-encounter. Connecting feelings to our needs, we are freed to enact life-giving strategies that contribute to our own flourishing as well as that of others. Once we become aware of our underlying needs, we experience a great deal of relief and a shift in our emotions. Once we recognize the source of our agitation, we are free to respond to the other in a clear and balanced way. No longer reactive, we can take into account the needs that are at work in us (and in the other). Whether or not we find a strategy to meet those needs, our capacity to identify, experience, and express our feelings and needs fosters connection and understanding in the midst of disagreement, difference, and dissension. For when we are connected to the fullness of our needs, we can speak with non-anxious, nonreactive honesty. Such honesty is a crucial component of transforming church conflict.

Feelings in Christian Perspective

Unfortunately churches rarely discuss feelings from a theological, let alone any other, perspective. When referenced in sermons or Sunday school classes, feelings are often presented in a negative light. Feelings are to be controlled, suppressed, and even denied. This attitude toward emotion is not new in the church. It extends at least as far back as the eighteenth-century Enlightenment. During this time, philosophers and theologians exalted rationality over against emotion, creating a dualism that still pervades our culture. Logic is pitted against emotion, head against heart, soul against body, and the masculine against the feminine. These dichotomies, even if they exist only at the subconscious level, shape our attitudes, experiences, and expression of feelings.

The scriptural presentation of emotion challenges this dualistic thinking and the accompanying denigration of the emotional life. In his careful interpretation of Scripture, pastoral theologian Ray Anderson demonstrates that "feelings are something located at the core of the self in its orientation toward God and the other."[23] As he writes, the Hebrew word translated as "heart" encompasses both rationality and emotion. Moreover, rationality is not equivalent to the English word "to think." Reason, from a biblical point of view, is not detached, emotionless, or abstract thought. Instead it is wisdom infused by both thought and feeling. "When feeling becomes separate from intellect, and intellect from feeling, a split has occurred within the self which must be overcome for reason to be restored."[24] Such a split leads to folly, the antithesis of wisdom. Anderson writes,

> The most dangerous of all folly is not created by following one's emotions, but by giving over one's mind to a way of thinking that is impenetrable by the logic of feeling. This kind of thinking produces folly at the sociological, political, and religious level. Racism, sexism, demagoguery, and persecution in the name of God all reflect a kind of folly that is grounded in a "truth" that has become inhuman and devoid of feeling.[25]

Both the Old Testament and New Testament portray God as emotive. In the Old Testament, God expresses pleasure, anger, and sorrow in response to the actions of Israel. Jewish philosopher Abraham J. Heschel writes, "God does not reveal himself in an abstract absoluteness, but in a personal and intimate relation to the world. He does not simply command and expect obedience; He is also moved and affected by what happens in the world, and reacts accordingly. Events and human actions arouse in Him joy or sorrow, pleasure or wrath."[26] When Israel rebels, God feels grief (Isa. 63:10). When God's people open themselves to God's providential care, the Lord rejoices (Zeph. 3:17).

Likewise in the New Testament, Jesus Christ, who is both fully God and fully human, expresses a wide range of emotion. Jesus acts with passion. The Gospels unashamedly portray him as angry, sorrowful, dismayed, torn, exhausted, peaceful, joyous, and delighted. As the self-revelation of God to humanity, Jesus Christ reveals that emotion is integral to the life of God. As the revelation of true humanity, Jesus Christ also reveals that emotion is an essential and blessed aspect of human existence.

Just as Jesus' life teaches us that feelings are a core aspect of person-hood, so also it demonstrates how feelings move us to prayer and other forms of ministry. When his friend Lazarus died, Jesus wept with sorrow and then raised him from the dead (John 11:33–44). When a leper begged him for mercy, Jesus felt pity, touched him, and healed him (Mark 1:40–42). On the night of his arrest, in the Garden of Gethsemane, Jesus felt distressed, agitated, and grieved (Mark 14:32–34). He then poured out his heart to God in what we now call his "Great High Priestly Prayer" (John 17). And in his last hours of life, in the throes of physical, emo-tional, and spiritual anguish, Jesus cried out in lament to God: "My God, my God, why have you forsaken me?" (Mark 15:34). In all these instances (and more), Jesus experienced and expressed his feelings fully; his feelings moved him to prayer and to action.

More precisely, the Holy Spirit worked in and with Jesus' feelings (not against Jesus' feelings and not in spite of Jesus' feelings). The Spirit enabled Jesus to see people as God sees people; the Spirit stirred up Jesus to action, enabling Jesus to act with the compassion of God in response to the sin and suffering of those around him.[27] The Spirit also spurs us to prayer and to action. The Spirit joins us to Christ and through Christ to God. Feelings are essential to this life of koinonia—to our union and communion with God and each other—for emotion moves us toward encounter with others and with God. As Wolfhart Pannenberg wrote, "On our journey to God the affects [emotions] are the feet that either lead us closer to God or carry us farther from him; but without them we cannot travel the way at all."[28]

In prayer, we are caught up in this union and communion with Christ and through Christ with God by the power of the Holy Spirit. As the Spirit opens our hearts—that is, our feelings and thoughts—to suffering and brokenness in the church and in the world, we are moved by compas-sion to pray. "When persons join together in prayer, they are emotion-ally vulnerable. . . . They are not detached; they take the emotional risks involved. When pastoral caregivers pray with complete strangers (as they do in hospice and hospital chaplaincy), they too open themselves up to an unusual degree of emotional intimacy."[29] Likewise, in the midst of church conflict, we intercede for and with others in Christ's name, by the power of the Holy Spirit, and from a place of emotional connectedness. Authentic expression of emotion in prayer is no less necessary in the midst of church conflict than it is in pastoral care. In fact, the honest expression of feelings and needs in corporate prayer may be the one thing needed when persons, groups, and congregations find themselves immobilized by disagreement and distrust. Expression of our deepest longings and most intense feelings in prayer supports our fellowship with one another and with God. In prayer we beseech God to make us one as Jesus and the Father are one; we acknowledge our dependence on the Spirit's work of peace and unity; and we place our trust in Christ, the head of the body and the one in whom all things hold together (Col. 1:17).

Chapter 4

Do Not Judge

Making Observations and Requests

"Do not judge, so that you may not be judged. For with the judgment you make you will be judged, and the measure you give will be the measure you get. Why do you see the speck in your neighbor's eye, but do not notice the log in your own eye? Or how can you say to your neighbor, 'Let me take the speck out of your eye,' while the log is in your own eye? You hypocrite, first take the log out of your own eye, and then you will see clearly to take the speck out of your neighbor's eye."

Matthew 7:1–5

Most mainline Protestant denominations in North America have been rent apart by sexuality debates over the past thirty years. Special interest groups represent the various sides of this debate. Tempers flare and accusations fly, especially at denominational gatherings. Judgments, spoken and unspoken alike, keep factions well-defended against each other. The strategies of these factions for meeting their own needs seem to be ineffective; their ability to devise creative strategies to meet the needs of all those involved is hindered. As we write this book, two denominations—the Evangelical Lutheran Church of America and the Presbyterian Church (U.S.A.)—teeter on the brink of schism because they have not been able to find ways to live together faithfully in Christ in the midst of their disagreements.

This widespread, intractable conflict exists at the congregational level as well as the denominational level. Not only are congregations being severed from one another, but also individual congregations are being torn asunder. Numerous churches have split into two, with one group choosing to stay in their denomination and another group choosing to leave it. Families who once worshiped together are now set at odds and cut off from each other.

Far-reaching conflict calls for compassionate leadership at every level of the church's existence—denominational, congregational, and interpersonal. It calls for leaders who are committed to communicating with empathy and honesty in the midst of high anxiety. Such communication, especially in the context of dissension, requires a high level of skill in translating our judgments into our basic values or needs. As NVC teaches us, all those involved in these debates are seeking to meet fundamental human needs—such as justice, compassion, and integrity—that reflect their understanding of the Christian faith. Yet rarely do members of denominational interest groups or factions within congregations learn to connect with those with whom they disagree at the level of the core needs that they hold in common. If those on opposing sides could see the needs that bind them together, then they could work together toward developing strategies that would contribute to the flourishing of the whole.

These two basic skills in NVC—making observations and requests—are essential to transforming conflict. Though not sufficient in and of themselves to reunite splintered denominations or to prevent congregational splits, they enable church leaders and members to move toward more authentic encounters in which they gain courage to speak honestly about their core values. By refusing to make moralistic judgments about one another's faithfulness, but instead translating their judgments into their core values again and again, church leaders would keep their hearts open not only to their fellow members of the body of Christ but also to Christ himself who admonishes us to "judge not." Perseverance in seeing others as Christ sees them can change the tenor and tone of the most acrimonious debates. Commitment to making observations and requests (instead of judgments and demands) supports the whole church in living faithfully in correspondence to Jesus Christ, the True Human. Instead of contradicting their identity in Christ—by denouncing one another or denying their interdependence—church leaders and members would see and hear one another with compassion and love. They may disagree, even vehemently at times. But equipped with the skills of compassionate communication, they could keep their hearts open toward one another and pray for one another. While such communication cannot usher in the kingdom of God, it can sustain the church in keeping hope alive when it cannot see any way beyond its current impasses.

Making Clear Observations

Compassionate communication is honest and life-enriching communication. It expresses what we are observing, feeling, and needing, often in relation to another person's words or actions. The intention driving such honesty, from a Christian perspective, is a profound commitment to living out the interdependence of Christ's body. It is willing to hold onto one's own beliefs and values while reaching toward the other with openness. All too often, our honesty contributes to disconnection, cutoffs, chronic conflict, and relational impasses. Telling others what we think of them frequently alienates us from each other as well as from our own core values and needs. Life-alienating communication, as Marshall Rosenberg notes, is riddled with evaluations and judgments. When we learn to translate our evaluations and judgments into observations, we find a way to connect with those with whom we disagree, which is a basic prerequisite for transforming conflict.

Differentiating Observations from Evaluations

In NVC, an observation is a concrete statement or thought that reflects what we are hearing, seeing, smelling, tasting, or remembering in reference to a specific context, event, or interaction. By very definition, then, observations are distinct from our interpretations, evaluations, and judgments about what we perceive with our senses.

Evaluations can take many forms: interpretations of one's actions, labels denoting one's character, or diagnoses of one's personhood.[1] In all instances, evaluations are stories that we tell ourselves. These stories may be circumscribed, focusing on particular actions or events, or they may be all-encompassing, such as a totalizing assessment of someone's identity (or even our own). Totalizing evaluations may also focus more generally on the way the world works, so to speak. Such evaluations often include the words *always, never, everyone, no one,* and so forth, as indicated in table 4.1.

Evaluations can also take the form of moralistic judgments, which are static assessments of persons or groups. They typically classify others as wrong and bad and ourselves as right and good. Moralistic judgments usually increase defensiveness and resistance in the person whose actions concern us. They prevent mutual understanding and hinder ongoing dialogue. In contrast, value judgments support mutual understanding and perseverance in working through conflict. Value

Table 4.1 Life-Alienating Interpretations, Labels, and Diagnoses

Interpretations of Actions	*Labels*	*Diagnoses*
He always tries to dominate	He's manipulative	He's narcissistic
She wants attention all the time	She's needy	She's histrionic
They don't care about work	They're irresponsible	They're dependent
I'm easy to get along with	I'm good-natured	I'm sanguine
He excels in academics	He's brilliant	He's a genius
She never worries about status	She's humble	She's got high self-esteem
No one's polite anymore	People are rude	Our culture is low-brow

judgments name what matters most to us, that is, the needs that we care about in any particular instance. They identify whether particular actions are consonant with our values or whether particular actions contribute to our needs in a given situation.[2] Value judgments emerge from self-awareness, from a capacity to identify and connect with our needs. Value judgments also maintain our connection to the needs most precious to us. From a Christian perspective, they connect us to those qualities of life in the kingdom of God that we long for, such as justice, peace, trust, freedom, integrity, and so forth.

As demonstrated in tables 4.1 and 4.2, evaluations and moralistic judgments can be framed in positive or negative terms. Positive evaluations may be a form of flattery, an attempt to ingratiate oneself with another person through excessive praise. Or they may simply be a judgment about another person. While our culture appraises flattery as problematic, it encourages us to share our positive labels and diagnoses openly. Yet from the perspective of compassionate communication, such positive interpretations can be life-alienating, though in more subtle ways than negative interpretations.

Table 4.2. Moralistic Judgments vs. Value Judgments

Moralistic Judgment	*Value Judgment*
The CEO of that corporation is power-hungry and materialistic. He obviously doesn't care about the plight of those working in his factories.	When I read in the news that factory workers are making less than minimum wage without health benefits, I feel distressed because I want financial and physical security for all people.
She's an amazing pianist—way better than me!	I so enjoy hearing her play the piano; I am inspired by her creativity and dexterity.
Mainline Protestant denominations are irrelevant and dying.	When I hear that membership in my denomination has dropped by nearly 20,000 people this year, I feel discouraged because I want the church to flourish.

Imagine that a number of congregants approach the pastor after a church service and say, "That was an awesome sermon," "That was your best sermon ever," or "I loved it!" The pastor might feel elated, or she might feel embarrassed. She might wonder, "What was different in comparison to my other sermons? What exactly did they appreciate?" Then when preparing her sermon the following week, she might feel anxious because she doesn't know how she can possibly do as stellar a job as she did last week. Now she tells herself that she has to live up to their expectations. She begins to worry about disappointing them. What is more, she has no idea what her congregants found to be so meaningful in last week's sermon because she did not receive a single concrete observation about what they noticed and appreciated. If, by contrast, her congregants had said something like, "Pastor White, I appreciated the story you told at the end of the sermon because it helped me to be more at peace about my mother's death," or "I loved this sermon because it helped me understand a passage in Scripture that I could never relate to," they would have given her valuable feedback. By specifying both the concrete part of the sermon they appreciated (observation) and the need it served (peace or understanding), the congregants would have communicated clearly how the pastor contributed to their well-being.

Differentiating observations from evaluations, whether positive or negative, helps transform conflict for several reasons.

1. Negative evaluations tend to evoke defensiveness and lead to disconnection between people.
2. Ironically, positive evaluations can also evoke defensiveness. If I enjoy your praise this week, I might resent the fact that it is not forthcoming next week. I might also take offense at your presumption that you are in a position to judge me at all.
3. Clearly stating observations without evaluations acknowledges our human fallibility, our complete inability to judge others (or ourselves) with full accuracy. God alone knows the human heart and God alone is judge. We are not even to judge ourselves (1 Cor. 4:3).
4. Differentiating observations from evaluations helps to establish a common understanding of what has triggered us either positively or negatively. It helps us to be clear about what is happening within us.

Expressing Observations with Clarity

How then do we differentiate observations from evaluations in order to communicate with honesty and clarity? When initiating an exchange, we begin with a concrete observation about what is happening that is or isn't enriching our life. In this way, we offer important information to another person about *the exact actions or words that are affecting us.* We express only what we are hearing, seeing, remembering, or otherwise sensing specific to time and place, taking care to leave out any judgments, evaluations, or words that imply rightness or wrongness. We want to remember four things about this style of communication:

1. **Be specific.** In compassionate communication, it is important to be specific about the time or place of an event or the actual aspects of an event or conversation. Instead of saying, "in our last conversation," we might say, "When you said that you just wanted to go to bed and stay there for three days . . . ." Instead of saying, "No one on this church board is willing to take any responsibility," we might say, "In the last three church board meetings, I have asked for volunteers to teach an adult Sunday School class. Five of the board members told me that they are unable to teach the class. I have not heard from the other four members."

2. ***Differentiate observations from evaluations.*** A video camera could record our observations—a person walks across the room, throws a book on the floor, and says, "I've had it!" An evaluation of this action would be the thoughts or judgments of the person using the video camera about what he has just witnessed: that person is throwing a fit; that is one angry person; that person stormed into the room, shouted, and threw around a bunch of books.

In classical NVC, an observation often begins with "When I see/hear . . . ." But simply starting a statement with this phrase does not guarantee that we are making an observation without evaluation. "When I saw you dominate the church council meeting . . ." is an interpretation of the elder's behavior. The elder's specific actions have not been identified. "When I heard you talk for fifteen minutes during tonight's church council meeting . . ." is an observation, a clear and specific expression of what the speaker heard.

3. ***Own your evaluations, interpretations, and judgments.*** Differentiating observations from evaluations does not mean that we never make evaluations or express our evaluations and interpretations. Rather it means that we do not conflate our observations and evaluations and it means that we take responsibility for our evaluations and interpretations. If we express an evaluation, we acknowledge it as our own story or interpretation about the other person, the situation, or ourselves. Moreover, we express our evaluations only when we have some confidence that it will contribute to the other person's understanding and ability to connect with us. Note the examples in table 4.3 that demonstrate how to own our evaluations.

Table 4.3. Taking Responsibility for Our Evaluations

Evaluations Mixed with Observations	*Evaluations Differentiated and Owned*
When you don't care about my needs by saying "it doesn't matter what you think"	When you say "it doesn't matter what you think" and I tell myself that this means you don't care about my needs
When you derail our small-group meeting by telling us the latest jokes you heard at work	When you tell jokes during our small-group discussion time and I tell myself that you are derailing our conversation

4. *Appreciate your judgments and evaluations.* When first practicing compassionate communication, many people feel surprised, even shocked, to discover how often their thoughts and words contain moralistic judgments. Consequently, they judge their own judgments and try to suppress them or shut them down. However, when we suppress these thoughts, we also detach ourselves from the feelings and needs embedded within them. Instead of suppressing our moralistic judgments because they fail to reflect our values, NVC teaches us to *listen to* our judging and blaming. Like a pain signal sent out by our nervous system to alert us to a physical ailment calling for intervention, so our moralistic judgments, evaluations, diagnoses, and blaming reveal that some of our needs are unmet at a given moment. Rather than avoiding these thoughts, we aim to explore them in order to identify the needs underneath them. We can receive our judgments and evaluations as indicators of core needs that are important to us, values that we believe contribute to the kind of life portrayed in the New Testament description of the kingdom of God. We may even rant to ourselves or a trusted friend until we can identify our unmet needs in the situation. Afterward we can speak with honesty and clarity, differentiating our observations from our evaluations, identifying and expressing our feelings, and connecting with the beauty of our needs.

Observations and Evaluations in Theological Perspective

When we look at church history, it is not surprising that persons and groups today remain mired in mutual recrimination and blame. In the early church councils, theologians anathematized—cursed—each other in the midst of debating the divine and human natures of Jesus Christ. During the Reformation, Martin Luther referred to the pope as an ass, a tyrant, and the antichrist.[3] Under the leadership of John Calvin, the Geneva Council burned Michael Servetus at the stake for his denial of the Trinity. In the twentieth century, Karl Barth and Emil Brunner were estranged for decades as a result of their disagreements about natural theology. Throughout the entire history of the church, revered leaders have blamed "the Jews" for killing the Son of God and have supported violence against them.[4]

Jesus' admonitions in the Sermon on the Mount seem to go unheard and unheeded. In this sermon, Jesus claims that peacemakers are blessed and are called children of God (Matt. 5:9); he sternly warns against calling another person "fool" (Matt. 5:22); he tells us to love and pray for our enemies (Matt. 5:43–48; Luke 6:27–36), to forgive (Matt. 6:14–15), and not to judge others (Matt. 7:1–5; Luke 6:37–42). As New Testament scholar Ulrich Mauser points out, in the Lukan writings (Luke and Acts), "the word 'peace' comes close to becoming a theological term that captures the whole meaning of the Christ event."[5] This peace includes health and healing as well as forgiveness and reconciliation. The entire Gospel of Matthew addresses a more specific aspect of peace. It seeks to eradicate judgments and factions in the early church. It warns against those who "will cause dissension and conflict in the community, instilling hatred and betrayal in its midst."[6] The gospel of peace pronounced by Jesus and fulfilled in his life, death, and resurrection is meant to utterly eradicate any "us versus them" thinking and "the compulsion to divide the human race into the good and the bad."[7]

Jesus' own life seems to go unheeded as well. When arrested under false accusations, Jesus eschewed violence as a means of protecting himself (Matt. 26:52–54). In response to those who judged him, mocked him, fled from him in his moment of greatest need, or executed him, Jesus prayed, "Father, forgive them for they know not what they do" (Luke 23:34). When he looked at others, he saw their needs for redemption, reconciliation, and well-being and had compassion on them.

At this point, it is important to acknowledge two apparent contradictions to these claims about the word and work of God in Jesus Christ. First, the New Testament identifies human sin as the cause of broken relationships between humanity and God and among persons and groups. Jesus told his followers to "go and sin no more." The apostle Paul wrote, "All have sinned and fallen short of the glory of God" (Rom. 3:23). Is it a moralistic judgment to speak of sin? Can Christians practice compassionate communication while understanding themselves and all human beings as sinners? To put it more starkly, is the concept of sin a stumbling block to those who desire to adopt the practices of NVC? Is the Christian concept of sin an irreconcilable difference between NVC and Christian faith?

In order to answer these questions, let's consider a paradigmatic case: Jesus' interaction with the woman caught in adultery (John 8). After finding her in *the very act* of adultery, religious leaders forcibly brought this woman before Jesus, asking him whether or not they should follow the "law of Moses" and stone her to death. Jesus knelt down and wrote in the sand, averting his eyes and thereby refusing to participate in this public humiliation. He then announced that anyone in the crowd who was without sin could cast the first stone. His listeners, instead of hurling stones at the woman, "went away, one by one, beginning with the eldest." They understood that as sinners themselves they were in no position to judge another. Thus Jesus effectively rejected violence as an acceptable form of punishment, challenged the categorization of people into good and bad, and subverted the implicit double standard inherent in this law: Where was the man who participated in this act of adultery? Moreover, Jesus refused to exploit another person in order to prove a theological point. When the crowd dispersed, he urged the woman to "go and sin no more." The plain meaning of the text suggests that he considered adultery—married people having sexual relations with someone other than their spouse—to be a sin, a contradiction of the life that God intended for this woman. From the standpoint of NVC, her choice to engage in sexual relations with someone other than her husband would fail to meet a number of needs: faithfulness, trust, respect, consideration, honesty, and integrity. From a Christian perspective, her choice disrupted her connection with God, with her husband, and with her community.

In this narrative, the religious leaders have made a moralistic judgment about this woman: she has engaged in a wrong that deserves condemnation and punishment. Jesus' use of sin language to describe her action, however, is not a moralistic judgment. It includes an ethical judgment or value judgment about life in the kingdom of God, but it does not condemn or dehumanize her. By forgiving her sin, he restores her to her true self and gives her the opportunity to make new choices that will enrich her relationships with God and others. In this regard, Jesus transformed the language of sin common in his day.

Here and elsewhere in the New Testament, sin language functions like a value judgment. It refers to choices, attitudes, actions, and inactions that are contrary to the life of freedom that God has called us to. Sin refers to our proclivity to live in contradiction to the persons we were created to be. It points to how we are caught in an "impossible possibility," as Karl Barth calls it, an unfathomable spiral of choosing against connection to God and others and thus against that which brings us life, love, peace, and wholeness. In other words, it describes the human predicament.[8]

Sin as a category is not used in the New Testament to create two classes of people: those who are sinners and those who are not. "All have sinned and fall short of the glory of God" (Rom. 3:23). We are all simultaneously sinners and saints, *simul justus et peccator*. This Latin phrase was used in the Reformation to indicate that even as believers in God, we are simultaneously both justified and sinners. We have been reconciled to God through Jesus Christ. In Christ, we are a new creation. At the same time, we frequently choose that which contradicts God's reign of peace and therefore that which contradicts our new identity in Christ. The fact that we so often choose such a contradiction, even when we long to live differently (Rom. 7:15–20), signals the depth of our estrangement from God's intention for our lives. Yet even while acknowledging this, the New Testament refuses to grant sin a definitive status for our identity as children of God (Rom. 8:2). Sin does not eradicate the created goodness of humanity. It does not ultimately define us, for God in Jesus Christ has destroyed sin and its effects.

While the Gospels portray Jesus as transforming sin language, they also portray him as making what NVC would consider moralistic judgments about the religious leaders of his day. He pronounced a series of "woes" on the religious leaders, calling them "foolish," "hypocrites,"[9] and "white-washed tombs" (Matt. 23; Luke 11:37–52). Ironically, he calls them hypocrites in the same breath that he warns them against judging others. Additionally, Matthew reports Jesus as declaring, "Do not think that I have come to bring peace to the earth; I have not come to bring peace but a sword" (10:34).

These troubling contradictions have been the source of significant scholarly debate. Mauser takes on the challenge posed by Matthew 10:34 and convincingly interprets it as an apocalyptic text. It refers not to relations within the church, or between the church and the world, but to the relationship between Jesus Christ and evil. He writes,

> The enemy is superhuman; the peace that is meant is the undisturbed authority of Satan over the affairs of the world, which authority Jesus is destroying; and the sword refers to the battle for the inauguration of God's rule in the end time. The saying exhibits, therefore, an altogether essential and necessary association of Jesus with the "sword."[10]

According to Mauser, the usual meaning of "sword" is subverted in this passage. Jesus is the sword that inaugurates God's reign of peace. He is radically different from any human sword as he defeats evil not by violence but by radical trust in God. He refuses to respond to evil with evil. He opposes any supposed peace that turns a blind eye to human need.[11] Therefore this statement in Matthew's Gospel does not provide justification for violence in any setting. Like the rest of the Gospel, it seeks to deter those in the Matthean community who were tempted to take up arms or adopt a revolutionary ideology.

Still, there are times when the scriptural witness attributes moralistic judgments to Jesus, and we are left with the question of application to our own context. We suggest neither excising nor harmonizing these portions of Scripture. Instead we propose the following hermeneutical principles as a means of navigating our way through this maze:

- The Gospel narratives state that Jesus saw people as they were; he saw them clearly and truly (John 2:25).
- Among humans, only Jesus has the capacity to see others without his own prejudice distorting his view.
- Jesus' ministry involved seeing, welcoming, and healing those who were marginalized in society. He directed his harshest judgments at established religious leaders.
- The Christian tradition has always given more weight to some aspects of Jesus' teaching than others, particularly the Sermon on the Mount and his words and deeds during his passion and crucifixion.
- What is allowable for the God-Man Jesus may not be allowable for Christians. Our knowledge of ourselves and others is always tainted by our sin and finitude. We cannot judge ourselves or others perfectly.

If we acknowledge a radical distinction between our knowledge and God's knowledge, then we will form and express any evaluation or judgment with a healthy dose of trepidation. One way to practice this concretely is to differentiate our evaluations from our observations. If we seek to live in correspondence to Jesus' teaching and life as a whole, we will avoid judgments that dehumanize those created in God's image. And, when discussing and confessing sin in the church, we can follow these guidelines:

- Faithful understanding of sin does not eclipse the goodness of God's creation—human beings. It acknowledges that those who sin nevertheless continue to bear God's image.
- Faithful understanding of sin sees it as an aberration of human nature, a contradiction of our true humanity.
- Faithful understanding of sin leads us toward, rather than away from, connection with ourselves and others. In a communal context, faithful confession of sin involves honest speech and hearing and opens up new avenues of mutual assisting with gladness.

- Faithful confession of sin describes our actions, feelings, and needs before a gracious God. Thus the basic skills of compassionate communication may enhance our authenticity in our prayers of confession, lament, petition, and thanksgiving.
- Faithful confession of sin deepens the possibility of human connection and solidarity because it acknowledges that "all have sinned and fallen short" (Rom. 3:23) of God's intention for humanity. No one is in a position to judge another.
- God's grace sets the context for discussing and confessing sin. Because grace triumphs over sin, the church's witness in the world takes the form of grace, not condemnation.

Making Effective Requests

Compassionate communication empowers us to make and receive requests that contribute to the life-giving needs at work in a particular situation, relationship, or context. It opens up space for creative strategies to emerge from a shared commitment to identified needs. Valuing both our needs and the needs of others *equally* enables us to move into the fourth step of NVC: making clear and effective requests. Requests are strategies that seek to contribute to universal human needs. Though particularly helpful whenever we are caught in an interpersonal or communal conflict, the skill of making requests can contribute to collaboration in any situation.

Differentiating Requests from Needs

At the heart of many interpersonal impasses and power struggles lies a failure to differentiate requests from needs. Typically we argue about the effectiveness or validity of competing strategies without ever identifying or connecting with the needs that such strategies seek to meet. In other words, we bypass that which has the potential to connect us at the level of our common humanity, that is our needs and values. We also squelch the creativity that can emerge when we *jointly* seek to meet the needs at stake in any given situation, relationship, or context. And we forfeit the opportunity to acknowledge the value of everyone's needs.

Therefore it is important that we clearly distinguish requests from needs. As discussed in chapter 2, needs are shared human values that sustain us in living a physically, emotionally, and spiritually fulfilled life. While we may at any particular time be more or less aware of certain needs, needs themselves are constant, timeless, and universal; they are independent of any action, person, place, or thing. Requests are the means of meeting needs and thereby enriching our life in encounter. Needs do not conflict, though strategies can and often do conflict, especially when disconnected from needs. While we may be unable to imagine any other strategy to meet our needs, in reality there are countless strategies to satisfy any particular need.

Table 4.4. Differentiating Needs from Requests

Statements that Express Needs	*Requests/Strategies Based on Needs*
I really need some support.	Would you be willing to moderate tomorrow night's worship committee meeting for me?
I'd like some comfort and affection.	Would you be willing to hold me close for a minute right now?
I want to be heard and understood.	Would you be willing to tell me how you understand what I've been saying?

Criteria for Effective Requests

Clear and effective requests in compassionate communication fulfill three criteria: (1) they are context-specific; (2) they are stated in positive action language; and (3) they are not demands. While requests (or strategies) contribute to common, universally experienced needs, they must be specific in order to be clear and effective. In other words, requests are context-dependent. They emerge from and seek to address particular situations and relationships. Like observations, requests are specific to time and place so that they are doable.

For example, if a personnel committee is concerned because the church secretary lacks the computer skills necessary to create aesthetically pleasing bulletins and newsletters and to distribute them in a timely manner, the committee members might be tempted to ask her directly to strengthen her computer skills. Or they might ask her to refrain from using the electric typewriter when creating the church bulletin. Neither one of these requests is likely to be effective because they don't specify the actions that would contribute to everyone's needs in this situation. If, on the other hand, the personnel committee asked her to take a course about using Microsoft Publisher, which is being offered next month at the local community college, they would be making a specific request that would likely meet multiple needs: for ease, efficiency, order, beauty, and reliability in church communications. Such a strategy might also contribute to the secretary's needs for support and learning. If they followed the OFNR template in their communication with the secretary, they would further enhance the likelihood of compassionate connection: "When I heard you say that it takes about ten hours each week to type up the church bulletin, I became concerned because I'd like you to have more ease at your job. At the same time, when I see our newsletters without any photos or illustrations, I find myself longing for a way to bring more beauty and interest to our newsletters. I wonder whether you would be willing to take the course on how to use Microsoft Publisher that is being offered next month at the community college?"

Notice in this example that the chair of the personnel committee has not made any demands. Requests in compassionate communication are not demands. Requests are grounded in respect for human choice, freedom, and autonomy. If another person says no to our request, there is no punishment, no silent treatment, no attempt to induce guilt, no withdrawal or withholding of love, no refusal to contribute to that person's needs out of a desire for retribution. Conversely, if another person says no to our request, we can choose to hear the implicit yes embedded within that no. Knowing that every choice represents an attempt to meet a basic need, we trust that the other person is saying yes to other strategies that he or she believes will contribute to needs that are more pressing at the time.

In contrast, a demand uses some sort of threat or punishment to force another person to meet our needs in a specific way. Some demands seek to induce guilt: "If you don't clean the kitchen, I'll feel very disappointed." Other demands threaten punishment: "If you won't clean the kitchen, I won't cook dinner." Demands might be disguised as a request, beginning with the phrase, "Would you be willing to . . . ." In these instances, our tone of voice may reveal that our true intention is simply to get the other person to do what we want. The true test comes when the other person says no. How will we respond? Will we resort to life-alienating communication to get our needs met at the expense of the other's needs? Or will we empathize with the other person, seeking to understand the needs that are preventing her from saying yes? Is our overall intention to foster connection and open communication or to get our own way?

Respecting the other's autonomy does not imply that we ought to give up on our needs. A particular strategy might not be effective in meeting our needs even if that strategy fits the criteria for a request in compassionate communication. NVC teaches us to hold our *requests (strategies) lightly but our needs tightly*. We are to remain unattached to specific strategies but committed to meeting our needs. If, in the above example, the church secretary told the personnel committee that she wasn't willing to take the computer class, the members could engage her in conversation (listen with empathy) in order to better understand her needs. They could consider other strategies that would meet her needs as well as theirs. Even if they weren't able to find a common, agreed-on strategy, they could mourn the unmet needs in this situation before making any official personnel decisions. In other words, even if our requests are not received with gladness, we can still connect with the other person through empathy and with ourselves in self-empathy. In the next two chapters, we will show how shifting our focus to the beauty of needs (both our own and those of others) enables us to continue to seek connection rather than insisting on our own way.

Types of Requests

In compassionate communication, there are at least three distinct types of requests: connecting requests, action requests, and strategizing requests. Connecting requests seek to maintain or foster connection, communication, and understanding between persons and groups. They are particularly helpful in the midst of discussing hot topics.

Connecting requests ask for reflection on what another person heard us say or for feedback about the other's experience in response to what he has heard us say. If we want clarity that the message we intended to communicate is the same as the message that was received, we might ask, "Could you tell me what you just heard me say?" If we want to know the other person's reaction, particularly his feelings and needs, we might ask, "What comes up for you when you hear this?" or "How do you feel, hearing that?" We might want to know what the other person thinks about what we said, as in "Do you think this is a fruitful way for me to proceed? I'd like your perspective on this situation." These kinds of connecting requests slow down the conversation, and in this regard, they go against our cultural predilection for immediate efficiency. Yet in the long run, they contribute to the kind of mutual understanding that allows for trust to grow in our personal and professional relationships.

Action requests can be posed to ourselves or others. We can request of ourselves or another person a specific, concrete, doable action that would contribute to our need(s). If we identified our needs for our physical well-being and support, we might request of ourselves to "call a friend tonight and ask him to drive me to my doctor's appointment on Tuesday." We might then call that friend and ask, "Would you be willing to drive me to my doctor's appointment on Tuesday at 10:00 a.m.?" Sometimes action requests may be less obviously active or physical, as in "Would you be willing to tell me what kept you from calling Friday night when you had said that you would?"

Strategizing requests blend together components of connecting and action requests. They mobilize persons and groups to persevere in the midst of misunderstanding or disagreement rather than cutting off from each other. Strategizing requests are especially helpful when we are unable to move past an interpersonal impasse or when we experience ourselves as stuck in conflict with another. In this type of request, we ask the other person or group to enter into strategic dialogue about how to meet the various pressing needs in any given situation. I might ask my spouse, "Can we schedule an hour next Saturday morning to work on a strategy for our summer vacation? I want to create a vacation plan together that will truly give you the rest and relaxation you need *and* the exercise and fun that I am longing for." In leading a conflicted church education committee, I might state, "Since we haven't found a curriculum that meets all of these needs—needs for theological integrity, meaningfulness, and relevance to our particular context—I'd like to suggest that we meet twice during the next two months in order to review three different curricula. Is there anyone whose needs would not be met with this strategy?"

Requests in Theological Perspective

Just as members of the church sometimes exhibit negative attitudes toward explicitly expressing our feelings and needs, so we are also sometimes resistant to making requests of others. Some of this resistance emerges from the cultural norms of self-sufficiency and individualism through which we unconsciously filter our faith.

Two complementary cultural myths that tend to undermine the capacity to make a direct request of others are the "hero myth" and the myth of the "good mother."[12] Whether a cowboy or human being imbued with extraordinary power, the hero's life is one of isolation and life-alienating sacrifice. The hero denies his own needs—in particular needs for community and understanding—in order to contribute to the safety and well-being of others. When others seek intimacy with him, the hero assumes that such closeness would threaten the safety of both himself and his loved ones. So he "nobly" separates himself and functions independently.

Similarly, the "good mother" denies her own needs for the sake of her family. She "goes without." She sacrifices her physical and emotional well-being in order to take care of others. She suppresses her needs for learning, adventure, and autonomy because she assumes that her family's needs for support and nurture are more important. Instead of taking a weekend away with friends, she stays at home so that her husband can go on a golfing trip. Instead of pursuing her self-defined goals, she finds a well-paying but unsatisfying job in order to earn money for their children's college education. If the hero denies his need for connection, the good mother denies her need for autonomy. Such denial prevents both of them from experiencing the joy of true interdependence. Lacking mutuality, they fail to experience the gladness that a shared life brings.

The church often unwittingly baptizes these cultural myths with an uncritical appropriation of Scripture. Jesus' admonitions to "take up your cross and follow me" (Matt. 16:24) and "lose your life so you will gain it" (Matt. 16:25), coupled with Paul's affirmation of "being content in all circumstances" (Phil. 4:11)—as well as other similar texts—can become justification for self-abnegation, workaholism, or a passive acceptance of injustice. Counterbalancing texts—for example, "Come to me, all who labor and are heavy laden, and I will give you rest. Take my yoke upon you, and learn from me. . . . For my yoke is easy, and my burden is light;" (Matt. 11:28–30); or "Ask and it will be given you; search and you will find; knock and the door will be opened for you" (Matt. 7:9; Luke 11:9)— are eclipsed. Overemphasizing the former texts and neglecting the latter encourage Christians to be motivated more by fear or "shoulds" than by the beauty of life in the kingdom of God. It leads people to live with an inverted ordering of divine and human action, believing that the kingdom of God depends on them for its consummation. Stress, burnout, and depression ensue.

The vision of the church set forth in various New Testament texts confronts these cultural myths and misappropriations of Scripture. The members of the church are to exist in mutual service, mutual dependence, and mutual support. *Together* they participate in the mission of God in the world. *Together* they represent true humanity. They bear each other's burdens; they suffer *together* and rejoice *together*. They may interpret their experiences of persecution, suffering, or temptation as a participation in the cross of Christ. They bear this cross through the power of the Holy Spirit *in and with* the community of faith, *not separate* from it.[13] For there is no such thing as an isolated Christian. To exist in isolation and independence is to contradict one's true humanity and neglect the church's mission to represent this humanity to the world.[14]

When church leaders and members respond to each other's requests with gladness, they live out one aspect of God's intention for our lives: giving and receiving assistance from one another in full mutuality. Making and receiving requests, however, cannot be based on a demand that one live according to God's intent for human life. Demands inherently contradict the freedom and gladness that also mark true humanity. Moreover, demands emerge from a scarcity mentality rather than an abundance mentality. A scarcity mentality believes that there are not enough resources to meet everyone's needs and that one person, group, or nation's needs can be met only at the expense of another's. The scarcity mentality yields desperation and conniving rather than trust and faith in God's provision. Jesus' disciples exhibit this mentality when they see a meager two loaves and a few fish rather than the Bread of Heaven who feeds the world; when they interpret children and beggars as an energy drain; and when they become anxious about money. In contrast, Jesus trusts in his heavenly Father who feeds the masses. He sees the marginalized as harbingers of the kingdom of God. He celebrates authentic giving and receiving wherever it occurs, but particularly when it cuts across social, ethnic, or economic differences that often divide humanity.

Compassionate leadership in the church is based not on a scarcity mentality but an abundance mentality—the twin beliefs that everyone's needs matter and that there are enough resources and creativity to find a way to meet everyone's needs. As they seek to transform conflict, congregations can put their trust in the Good Shepherd who came to bring abundant life (John 10:10), the One in whom and through whom these words have been fulfilled, are being fulfilled, and will be fulfilled:

> The LORD is my Shepherd, I shall not want. He makes me lie down in green pastures; he leads me beside still waters; he restores my soul . . . . Even though I walk through the darkest valley I fear no evil; for you are with me; your rod and your staff—they comfort me.

You prepare a table before me in the presence of my enemies; you anoint my head with oil; my cup overflows. Surely goodness and mercy shall follow me all the days of my life, and I shall dwell in the house of the Lord my whole life long. (Ps. 23)

We endeavor to trust that the kingdom of God has come, is coming, and will come even when we fail to experience its manifestation in our midst. This is what it means to live in eschatological hope. Our requests of ourselves, one another, and God emerge from this hope and trust at all times, but especially in the midst of difference and disagreement. As we request what we believe will contribute to the needs of all those mired in conflict, we wait for the full manifestation of God's grace to transform all our relationships.

Part 2

Skill Sets:
Empathy, Self-Empathy, and Honesty

Chapter 5

God's Compassion Is over All

Listening with an Open Heart

The LORD is good to all, and his compassion is over all that he has made.

Psalm 145:9

God's love is the wellspring from which we draw when we need compassion for ourselves or another. It is noteworthy that throughout the Gospels the word compassion is used only to describe Jesus or the God-figure in Jesus' parables.[1] The New Testament witness thus affirms God alone as the source of all compassion. Jesus Christ as the only Son of the Father reveals both the depth and breadth of divine compassion. His life-story shapes our understanding of its very meaning. We remember his compassion toward each human soul who cries out to him for help: the blind, the deaf, the lame, those stricken by disease or burdened with grief. We remember his lament over the city of Jerusalem as he perceives the blindness and wretchedness of its inhabitants. We recall his compassion for the thousands who are hungry not only for bread but for the smallest morsel of hope. When we contemplate his compassion toward those who crucify him, we ask, who *is* this one praying for his tormentors? What immeasurable compassion resides in this human breast?

"Compassion," writes Andrew Purves, "reveals the inner nature of God."[2] Christ's compassion becomes "a window of access into the nature of . . . God's vulnerability and willingness to suffer with us."[3] The Lord who has compassion over all that he has made does not leave us to suffer alone the anguish of our mortal condition, nor the consequences of our sin, but actively wills to share it.

> The mercy of God lies in his readiness to share in sympathy the distress of another, a readiness which springs from his inmost nature and stamps all his being and doing. It lies, therefore, in his will, springing from the depths of his nature and characterizing it, to take the initiative himself for the removal of this distress. . . . The personal God has a heart. He can feel and be affected. . . . God is moved and stirred . . . in his innermost being . . . open, ready, inclined . . . to compassion with another's suffering and therefore to assistance.[4]

Though we cannot fathom the depth of such love, nor comprehend the mystery of Christ's atoning sacrifice, his life story enables us to envision a transcendent ground for hope, which is a vision nothing short of the redemption of the entire world for the kingdom of God to come on earth as it is in heaven.

The church is both called and enabled to "participate in God's continuing compassion for the world."[5] When our compassion is grounded in God's own love, we connect to a transcendent source, which enables us to keep our hearts open in trying situations rather than close ourselves off in self-protection. Though compassion cannot be sustained over the long haul by means of our own meager resources, it can be renewed daily by means of our connection to the core of God's love. While Nonviolent Communication emphasizes the importance of our listening to others with compassion, Bonhoeffer grounds it as a spiritual practice of the church by showing its foundation in God's listening to us. Just as God shows his love for us by listening to our prayers, so we are to demonstrate our love for others by listening to them.

> The first service that one owes to others in the community involves listening to them. Just as our love for God begins with listening to God's Word, the beginning of love for other Christians is learning to listen to them. God's love for us is shown by the fact that God not only gives us God's Word but also lends us God's ear. We do God's work for our brothers and sisters when we learn to listen to them.[6]

Listening to our brothers and sisters in Christ is one way that we are invited and enabled to participate in Christ's work. Learning to hear the cry of another's heart is not only a gift to be cherished, it is also a skill to be honed.

Compassion, Sympathy, and Empathy

Let us make some distinctions among several closely related concepts: compassion, sympathy, and empathy.

Compassion

Compassion, as we understand it, is first of all an attribute of God. Indeed, it is descriptive of a central aspect of God's character, the steadfast love that is merciful toward all that God has made.

> Bless the LORD, O my soul,
> and all that is within me,
> bless his holy name.
> Bless the LORD, O my soul,
> and do not forget all his benefits—
> who forgives all your iniquity,
> who heals all your diseases,
> who redeems your life from the Pit,
> who crowns you with steadfast love and mercy,
> who satisfies you with good as long as you live
> so that your youth is renewed like the eagle's.
> . . . .
> As a father has compassion for his children,
> so the Lord has compassion for those who fear him.
> For he knows how we were made;
> he remembers that we are dust. (Ps. 103:1–5, 13–14)

The psalm speaks of multiple aspects of God's compassionate nature: it is forgiving, healing, and redemptive in character. God's mercy crowns our lives; his goodness renews it. The compassion of God reaches out toward those who are poor and needy; here it is compared to the love of a father for his children. Throughout both the Old and New Testaments, God's compassion toward the widow, the orphan, the slave, and the oppressed, indeed anyone especially in need, is repeatedly attested. The scriptural terms, *rahamim* in Hebrew (related to "womb") and *splagchna* in Greek (related to "bowels"), "carry the thought of yearning over another with great feeling."[7] As Christians, we believe that in so far as someone has true compassion for others, it is ultimately derived from this transcendent source.

In his Letter to the Romans, the apostle Paul speaks of the special gifts of the saints, each one of which is needed for the body of Christ to function properly. After naming prophecy, ministry, teaching, exhortation, giving, and leading, he speaks of the gift of compassion. "We have gifts that differ according to the grace given to us: prophecy, in proportion to faith; ministry, in ministering; the teacher, in teaching; the exhorter, in exhortation; the giver, in generosity; the leader, in diligence; the compassionate, in cheerfulness" (Rom. 12:6–8). When compassion is a gift of the Spirit, it shines forth with special luminosity. Certain saints of the church come to mind. We think of someone like Marietta Jaeger-Lane, a woman whose seven-year-old daughter was abducted and murdered. Jaeger-Lane not only became a founding member of Murder Victims' Families for Reconciliation, but also has spent her entire life since the tragedy working for the abolition of the death penalty. We think also of Bishop Desmond Tutu, Martin Luther King Jr. and Nelson Mandela, who have inspired generations of those working for reconciliation among people of different races. In *No Future Without Forgiveness*, Tutu speaks of the costliness of bringing healing to a traumatized nation. It is a cost that he and thousands of others have borne; to do so with an affirmation of their common humanity with those who have harmed them is a compelling witness to the God who has sustained them.[8]

Sympathy

The second, closely related word is sympathy. By sympathy, we mean the feelings that are evoked in us when we listen to or observe the feelings of another. In sympathy we find ourselves spontaneously sharing another's feelings. If she expresses sadness and despondency, we may sympathetically notice similar feelings arising in us. Alternatively, we might begin to feel joyful as we hear about the joyful, expansive feelings of another. If he is in acute pain, we might become aware of an analogous pain in ourselves, sometimes to the point of feeling it viscerally. Judith Jordan recounts an especially vivid moment witnessing such sympathetic feeling in a child only eighteen months old.

> A mother inadvertently jammed her hand in the door of the playroom and was in obvious pain. Her 18-month-old daughter immediately picked up a soft, cuddly toy with which she had been comforting herself earlier and took it to the mother, standing close to her, looking worried and rubbing it against her mother's cheek. When the mother smiled and said she was all right, the child's face lit up.[9]

From what Jordan observes, we imagine that the child experienced some sort of anguish analogous to her mother's and moved swiftly to alleviate her mother's pain. She could not be at peace until she knew that her mother was comforted.

Because the brain is hard-wired for relationship, such sympathetic feelings can arise quite early in life. Siegel states: "Within the brain are clusters of cells that are designed to fire in response to eye contact and facial expressions. . . . For example, seeking proximity to a caregiver and attaining face-to-face communication with eye gaze contact is hard-wired into the brain from birth. It is not learned."[10] The child observed by Jordan had the capacity to "feel with" her mother and express it (though without words) at a year and a half. That she was able to share her mother's feelings in this way indicates a prior history of a secure attachment.

> Attachment at its core is based on parental sensitivity and responsivity to the child's signals, which allow for collaborative parent-child communication. Contingent communication gives rise to secure attachment and is characterized by a collaborative give-and-take of signals between the members of the pair. Contingent communication relies on the alignment of internal experiences, or states of mind, between child and caregiver. This mutually sharing, mutually influencing set of interactions—this emotional attunement or mental state resonance—is the essence of healthy secure attachment.[11]

Though a capacity for sympathy may be innate, it flourishes in an environment characterized by a secure attachment with a caring parent.

Sympathy often arises in the context of sharing a common loss. Although each person's grief is uniquely her own (and thus needs to be understood in its particularity), shared feelings of sadness often bring consolation. At funerals we sometimes find comfort in hearing the qualities of our loved one praised by another; even to have his foibles described can bring unexpected delight. At the same time, a sense of isolation can arise if the particularity of our own loss is not acknowledged. When someone says *sympathetically*, "I know *just* how you feel," we want to protest that she simply does not, indeed, cannot, know how we feel, for our pain is unique.[12]

Empathy

Sharing similar feelings may be healing, but empathy provides a depth of understanding that sympathy typically cannot reach. Empathy recognizes and acknowledges difference in the midst of similarity. Paradoxically, we have a greater sense of companionship when the uniqueness of each person's grief is acknowledged. Empathy is a disciplined undertaking in which one momentarily sets aside one's own unique feelings and needs to connect with the other's unique feelings and needs. The focus in empathy is on fully connecting with the other person, whereas in sympathy we are often more connected with our own feelings than we are with the other's. The boundary or distinction between your feelings and mine is blurred.

Psychotherapists have endeavored for years to capture the distinctive character of empathy. Heinz Kohut considers it the "single most essential quality that enable[s] emotional well being."[13] The human being, he said, "can no more survive in a psychological milieu that does not respond empathically to him than he can survive physically in an atmosphere that contains no oxygen."[14] Carl Rogers, one of Marshall Rosenberg's mentors, describes empathy in this way:

> To sense the client's private world as if it were your own, but without ever losing the "as if" quality—this is empathy, and this seems essential to therapy. To sense the client's anger, fear, or confusion as if it were your own, yet without your own anger, fear, or confusion getting bound up with it, is the condition we are endeavoring to describe.[15]

With this definition, note that Rogers also distinguishes between empathy and sympathy. If one's own anger, fear, or confusion get bound up with the anger, fear, or confusion of the speaker, one is responding sympathetically rather than empathetically.

When there is a sturdy empathic connection between persons, the listener is able to sense the other's feelings and needs even if they are not explicitly stated. When we observe parents who are receptive to the needs of their newborn, for instance, we see how they seek to understand the child from within, sensitively attuning themselves to a range of nonverbal signals. They attend to the quality of the child's cries, to its facial expressions, tone of voice, and bodily movements as they attempt to discern the child's needs. This kind of exquisite attention to the other also underlies effective psychotherapy, which is frequently described as a kind of reparenting process.

> Responding to the patient's nonverbal signals, including tone of voice, facial expressions, eye gaze, and bodily motion, can reveal the otherwise hidden shifts in states of mind. Resonating with these expressions of primary emotions requires that the therapist feel the feelings,

not merely understand them conceptually. Resonance involves the alignment of psychobiological states between patient and therapist.[16]

This kind of resonance enables a person to "feel felt" which may well be "an essential ingredient in attachment relationships . . . [and] vital to close relationships of all sorts throughout the lifespan."[17]

Resonating with another "requires that the therapist feel the feelings, not merely understand them conceptually."[18] How does this statement square with Rogers's insistence that the therapist's own feelings are not bound up with those of the client's? What actually happens when the listener seeks to empathize with another? Is she feeling what the other feels? Or is she simply seeking to understand her conceptually? Theorists at the Jean Baker Miller Training Institute (formerly the Stone Center) of Wellesley College insist that both cognitive and affective components are actively engaged in effective empathy. On a feeling level, there is a profound sense of connection between two people that has a physiological basis. This quality is akin to the sympathetic sharing of a feeling that we described above. "In part they [genuine empathic moments] have a physiological quality in which our posture, our teary eyes, our tense muscles unconsciously reflect the state of the patient, thereby transmitting to us a kind of visceral experience of the patient's emotional state."[19] In these instances, we are not feeling grief or anxiety related to our own life experiences (as in sympathy) as much as we are experiencing the effect of being attuned to the experience of the person sitting before us. In other words, as we resonate with another's feelings, we find ourselves mirroring them, usually unconsciously. As we physically mirror the other, our own body imparts information about what the other might be feeling. Siegel explains: "The signals from the body also directly shape our emotions. Our awareness of bodily state changes—such as tension in our muscles, shifts in our facial expressions, or signals from our heart or intestines— lets us know how we feel, though bodily feedback occurs even without awareness."[20] We thus get a sense of the other's feelings by raising into awareness the feedback our own body is giving us.

Another dimension of the affective component of empathy has to do with the personal associations that enable the listener to guess at the other's feelings and needs. Alexandra Kaplan calls it "associative empathy."[21] The listener associates something comparable from her own experience as she listens. These associations come effortlessly to mind, like the "free-floating attentiveness" recommended by Freud.[22] The ability of the listener to notice these associations and then to detect their emotional impact assists her in guessing the other's feelings and needs. She uses these memories as a reference point for connecting with what the other might be feeling and needing in the present. But the central focus of her attention is not on her own experiences; it is on the experience of the other. She notes her own feelings and needs, not in order to explore them or to share them, but as possible clues about what the other might be experiencing.

Simultaneous with these essentially affective dimensions of empathy are cognitive components that go in a different direction. While one may feel an intense sense of connection with the other, there is at the same time clarity about one's own distinct identity. As Kaplan explains, "The cognitive component of empathy follows a different, essentially contradictory, course from that of the affective. Specifically, while there may be an interpenetration of affect, identity remains differentiated. The therapist, throughout, never loses sight of herself as a distinct being; at the same time, she is emotionally joined with another."[23] Clarity about her own differentiated identity enables her simultaneously to connect with others emotionally, understand their feelings and needs as if from the inside, while holding a completely different point of view. For this reason, accurate empathy does not imply agreement. One can understand another and yet have quite different feelings and needs in relation to the matter at hand. One is "affectively connected and cognitively differentiated at the same time."[24]

While a vast amount of literature on empathy has originated either in infant studies or in assessing therapeutic effectiveness, empathy is a vital quality in all our relationships throughout life if we are to thrive. Indeed, any relationship characterized by empathic attunement inherently fosters emotional growth. It provides an environment in which persons feel fully alive, connected to themselves and others, with a felt sense of belonging. Jean Baker Miller and her colleagues identify five features that arise out of such relationships: zest, action, knowledge, self-worth, and connection.[25] The feeling of zest is the energetic, expansive feeling that comes in the wake of "feeling felt." A surge of vitality accompanies the sense of emotional connectedness. When one has little sense of emotional connection, by contrast, this feeling of zest is noticeably absent. As one experiences oneself being fully heard and gains a greater sense of self-connection, one is also empowered to act. One feels less stuck and has more of an internal sense of freedom to take action in any situation.

Empathy also expands one's knowledge. As one is given the freedom to explore many facets of one's life situation, one becomes aware of components that previously had remained hidden from view. A more comprehensive picture emerges. Previously unconscious feelings rise to the surface and one is able to articulate needs that were previously unacknowledged. At the same time, one grows in feelings of self-worth. A caring attitude on the part of the listener conveys to the speaker that she is worthy of another's time and attention, which increases the sense that she matters. Inevitably, the experience of connection fosters a desire for even more connection. Enduring emotional bonds are forged over time in relationships that have empathy at their core.

In conclusion, compassion, as we are using the term, is a spiritual gift, sympathy a learned behavior, and empathy a finely honed skill. When the apostle Paul exhorts the Christians in Rome to "rejoice with those who rejoice and to weep with those who weep" (Rom. 12:15), he sees them as joined together as one body in their love for Jesus Christ. That love is the source of their compassion for one another. Whenever we share a common feeling or strongly identify with another's feelings, we give voice to feelings of sympathy. And finally, when we seek in a disciplined way to understand the particularity of each person's feelings and needs, we are practicing the skill of empathy.

Developing Empathic Skill

NVC has devised a number of concrete practices to help us develop empathic skill. At their heart is the aim simply to connect with the other. There is a quality of presence that communicates, "I'm here for you." Whether there is silence or talk, whether laughter or tears, does not seem to matter as much as conveying that the listener is there for whatever comes up. The skilled listener communicates a precious sense of spaciousness, of having all the time in the world. Empathy cannot be hurried. When we take the time to be present in this way, however, things are often surprisingly resolved with greater efficiency and ease. Whenever we really seek to connect with another, things begin to fall into place. In large part, this is due to our clarity of focus. In compassionate communication, we pay attention to feelings and needs. In empathizing, we aim to assist others in fully connecting with what they might be feeling and needing in any concrete situation. We do this with empathetic guesses.

There are three levels involved as we listen empathically to another, each level building on the one before it. As we gain more skill, we can practice the deeper forms of empathy, which means keeping our focus almost exclusively on the other's needs. Reflecting content, reflecting feelings, and connecting feelings with the underlying needs represent three levels of mastery, each of which takes the connection to a deeper level. Consider this pastoral care conversation:

Parishioner: Yesterday when I told my husband where I was hoping we could go on vacation next summer, he got intensely frustrated and started yelling at me. I was so frightened that I was unable to think. It's just like when I was girl and Daddy went into one of his rages. I would get so completely bewildered about why he was mad and felt really scared. I would just hide.

Now imagine three different responses to the parishioner, first, reflecting content; second, feelings; and third, full empathy that focuses on connecting the feelings and the needs.

Response 1:   (Reflecting *content*) So yesterday when you were making plans for your summer vacation, your husband got angry and yelled at you. This reminds you of childhood memories when your Dad would get mad at you and you would feel scared and confused.

Response 2:   (Reflecting *feelings*) So when your husband yelled at you yesterday, you got really scared and also bewildered, not understanding what triggered his anger.

Response 3:   (Connecting *feelings* with *needs*) So when you recall your husband yelling at you yesterday, are you feeling frightened because you need to trust that you are physically safe with him?

What is the significance of these three different responses? Response 1 shows that the pastor understands the content of what has been said. This kind of reflection can be important particularly in situations where it is difficult for one person to understand the other's actual words. It can also be helpful when many details are shared in an intensely emotional or confusing way in order to clarify what the speaker saw, heard, thought, and felt. In compassionate communication, we want to ground our listening in concrete observations as much as possible. Response 2 shows that the pastor has a basic understanding of the parishioner's feelings. By responding in this way, she indicates her interest in those feelings, which tacitly encourages the parishioner to focus her attention there. Response 3 focuses entirely on connecting the parishioner's feelings with her underlying needs. The pastor brings the feelings into the present (when you reflect now on what happened yesterday), "are you feeling" (*present tense*) "frightened because you need" (*again, the present tense*) "to trust that you are physically safe?" This empathy guess takes all the information and integrates it. The pastor hears the comment about Daddy and "one of his rages" but does not place her focus there. Taking the relevant information from the past and putting it into the present helps the parishioner to sense right now what is still alive in her. The past lives on in the present, but the focus of attention is what she needs right now in relation to her husband.[26]

Let's imagine the dialogue further with response 3, as the pastor continues to listen solely for how her parishioner's feelings might be connected to possible underlying needs:

Parishioner: No, I do trust that I am physically safe. I know he won't hit me. It is more like a visceral response to a raised voice. I just get scared.

Pastor: Are you afraid because you'd like some trust that the two of you can stay connected in the midst of such intense emotions?

Parishioner: Yes, I get so upset when he gets mad at me and I don't know what I did wrong.

Pastor: Are you perplexed and sad because you'd like some understanding and acceptance?

Notice how the pastor has no investment in "being right" in her guesses. The fact that her first guess (about physical safety) was "wrong" does nothing to disturb the connection between the speaker and the listener. Instead, it actually prompts the parishioner to look inward and explore her own feelings further. The pastor keeps her focus on her parishioner's feelings as they point to underlying needs. She connects fear with trust. Yet, this is not an intellectual exercise in which she thinks about the logical relationship between fear and trust; rather, it is an intuitive resonance with what she might need when her husband expresses anger. How can she stay connected with him when he is angry? This guess also takes into account the earlier statement that she "would just hide" whenever her father was angry. Perhaps a similar disconnection happens with her husband.

The empathic guessing is a process where the pastor might ask herself, "How am I feeling right now as I imagine myself in her situation? When I am afraid, what am I needing? What clues does she give me?" When the parishioner says that she doesn't know what she did wrong, it sounds like she is returning to her feelings of bewilderment over what triggered her husband's intense feelings. She also seems to be taking responsibility for her husband's anger because she wonders what she did wrong. Instead of seeing herself merely as the *trigger* for his anger, she speaks as if she is the *cause*. As the pastor turns her attention toward that statement, she asks herself, "What might this woman need?" Perhaps she needs not only understanding (related to her perplexity) but also acceptance (related to her feeling of having "done something wrong"). With each guess, the pastor focuses on the most recent sentence.

In summary, the three levels are: reflection of content, reflection of feeling, and connecting feelings with the underlying needs. Simple reflection of content contributes to clarity about what has been said. Reflecting feelings conveys a greater sense of connection that may help the speaker to explore further the various facets of what she is feeling. But only the third listener actually gets the depth of connection that is facilitated by empathy. By focusing her attention on the parishioner's needs, the pastor helps her to become much more aware of why the interaction was so upsetting to her. What does she actually need when her husband expresses his anger with intensity? The empathy enables the parishioner to become conscious of several dimensions. She is not afraid of being hit. Instead, she wants increased understanding of her husband. What actually happens in him when he suddenly becomes furious? She is also becoming aware of a sense of panic that grows whenever she fears disconnection from him. Sadness begins to well up with the final empathy guess, which connects her to her need for acceptance. Since she describes herself as having done something wrong, it sounds like she may also need self-acceptance. By focusing on how her feelings are connected with underlying needs, the pastor helps her to gain access to her deeper longings.

Dian Killian and Jane Connor, two certified NVC trainers and authors, emphasize the transforming power of empathy when needs are accurately identified and brought into full awareness. They write, "Among those who practice Nonviolent Communication, there is the belief that 90% of the power of empathy is associated with empathizing with needs, and 10% associated with empathizing with feelings."[27] When we empathize with feelings or simply reflect the content of someone's story, the connection with the other is not as sturdy or deep. Nor does the parishioner get the clarity she needs about what is really at stake for her. Only when we plumb the depths of the need underneath the feeling do we assist the other in getting the kind of self-understanding that will enable her to take action. Making an explicit connection between feelings and needs is the key.

Simply paraphrasing content can have the disadvantage of reinforcing the person's story, which may prevent her from envisioning a different way of acting. If we simply paraphrase the content without helping her to focus on her needs, we may inadvertently reinforce her belief that the past is being repeated in the present, unchanged. While understanding the connection between the past and the present may be illuminating, it doesn't actually change the dynamic between them now. The parishioner needs to find a way to do something different with her husband than she did with her father. Even if she understands how her husband's anger triggers old fear and pain, it doesn't transform it. The story from the past may help explain why she is triggered in the present, but it doesn't help her find a way to bring about the change she wants.

This can be done only by helping her identify her actual present need. Once she is fully connected to it, she can make a request that will assist her in taking action. If she identifies a need for understanding her husband, for example, she can craft a request that they spend some time together exploring what he was feeling and needing when he suddenly expressed his anger. Alternatively, her focus might be on her longing for a sense of internal peace whenever her husband raises his voice. Her true need may be to stay connected with herself in the midst of emotional intensity. Something will shift when she connects fully with her actual, present need. She may even breathe an audible sigh of relief. Even though she may not yet have a strategy for getting what she wants, she has clarity about what needs she is trying to meet. Empathy helps her get that clarity.

Notice that at no point does the pastor start to analyze the woman's statements; she does not intellectually ponder the connection between the childhood reaction to her father's rage and her husband's current anger. Nor does she analyze the husband or suggest strategies over how to influence his future behavior. Her focus is exclusively on connecting with what her parishioner is feeling and needing in the present. There are obviously many other ways to respond to someone's personal sharing. Sometimes called the "typical twelve," they are familiar, often habitual, responses to a story of personal distress.[28]

Advising:	I think you should leave the room the second he raises his voice.
One-upping:	You think that's bad? Let me tell you about the rages *my* husband gets into.
Educating:	I can recommend a really good book that describes what happens in the brain when you've been traumatized as a child.
Analyzing:	It sounds like you have internalized your father's rages so that your husband's raised voice triggers that old fear.
Storytelling:	Did I ever tell you what I did on my honeymoon when my husband yelled at me?
Minimizing:	Well, at least he doesn't hit you the way your father did.
Sympathizing:	I feel frightened when I hear how angry he gets.
Interrogating:	How often does he go into one of these rages?
Reassuring:	I'm confident that you'll find a way to resolve this together; the two of you have been through a lot.
Avoiding:	Let's talk about something else, OK? This topic is quite upsetting.
Diagnosing:	It sounds like you have some typical codependent personality traits. OR It sounds like he has dysfunctional anger syndrome.
Judging:	It sounds like you've made a poor choice in a spouse.

It can be helpful to identify one's habitual patterns of response. Perhaps there are particular situations that typically evoke one of the above responses. One might recognize, for instance, that one can listen with ease to one's spouse most of the time, but when she speaks in a whiny tone of voice, one will typically reassure or educate. Alternatively, one might habitually try to gather all the facts before focusing on feelings and needs. It is worth pondering one's default mode: does one habitually tell an inspiring story or give sound advice, diagnose the speaker, or analyze the situation? In some cases, of course, what is actually sought is advice. It can be annoying to receive empathy when one is seeking information. Empathy is the preferred mode of responding when a deeper connection and mutual understanding is the desired aim.

Just as music is not simply a matter of playing the right notes, so empathy is not a matter of guessing right. Instead, it is a practice that is deeply rooted in the soul of the listener. When we hear music, we hear the presence of a human soul. The pianist, for example, has her heart connected to every finger. And yet, the breathtaking recital comes only after countless hours of practice. While empathy is not a mechanical process, developing skill in empathy is something like practicing scales. NVC offers a variety of skill-building exercises that will one day enable us to make music. Several exercises are described below:

1. Attuning oneself to the other physically. Empathic listeners can practice attuning themselves to the facial expressions and body language of others. Because our feelings and needs reside in our bodies, mirroring exercises can assist us in guessing another's felt experience. If you divide the group into pairs, one partner can recall a feeling and allow his face to express the feeling without words. The listener imitates the speaker by acting as a mirror of the other's facial expression. After imitating it, the listener guesses what the speaker might be feeling. Alternatively, the listener can mirror the body language of the speaker. Are the legs crossed? The shoulders slumped? The chest caved in? The empathic listener gets clues about the other's emotional state by mirroring exactly what he sees in the other's body language.

2. Ability to empathically guess the observation. Scenarios for practice might include the following:

   • A deacon comes into the church kitchen and says in an irritated tone, "I just can't believe the mess in here." How might an empathic church member respond? Not having a clear observation from this deacon, he might guess what she is reacting to: "Are you upset because of the dishes piled in the sink?" Or, "Are you reacting to the empty pizza boxes piled on the counter?" Or, "Are you distressed when you see the dirt all over the floor?" In each guess, he is seeking to assess empathically what observation has triggered her reaction.

   • A mother says in an exasperated tone of voice, "I never know how to reach you!" To get clarity about the observation, the teen might say, "Are you frustrated because you called my cell phone last night and didn't get an answer?" Or, "Are you upset because you didn't know I was spending the night at Sam's last night?"

- Ability to guess feelings and needs when they are expressed as judgments. There are a number of feeling words that actually express a thought or judgment about someone. For example, "I feel manipulated," or "I feel betrayed," communicate the judgment that I believe another person is manipulating me or has betrayed me. Empathic listeners can practice translating such statements into feelings and needs. For example: "Are you angry because you would like to have a choice in this matter?" Or, "Are you distraught because you'd like to be able to trust your friend?" If one "feels manipulated," the underlying need might be for choice and a sense of agency. If one "feels betrayed," one may be needing trust. In order to heal a sense of betrayal, one first removes the implicit judgment of the other by expressing one's need for trust. Someone skilled in empathic listening will know how to translate such faux feelings into real feelings and needs.

Consider the faux feelings in table 5.1 and their translations into honest expression of feelings and needs, and the empathic reception of feelings and needs expressed as judgments in table 5.2.

Table 5.1. From Faux Feelings to an Honest Expression of Feelings and Needs

Faux Feelings	*Feelings and Needs*
I feel misunderstood.	I feel frustrated because I'd like to be heard for my intentions.
I feel rejected.	I feel hurt because I need acceptance.
I feel taken for granted.	I am upset because I'd like some appreciation for my contribution.
I feel threatened.	I am feeling scared and want to be safe.
I feel intimidated.	I am wary because I want to trust that my words will be received with understanding.
I feel pressured.	I feel irritated because I need more time and space to make up my mind.

Table 5.2 Empathic Responses to Expressed Judgments

Expressed Judgments	*Empathic Reception*
The kids are driving me crazy!	Are you feeling overwhelmed and wanting some peace and cooperation at home?
You're always sitting in front of the television!	Are you frustrated because you'd like to spend some time together?
You will never get into college if you don't study more!	Are you worried because you want me to succeed in life?
I can't believe you did something so stupid!	Are you upset because you want to trust my judgment?
How come everyone in this family always tells me what to do?	Are you frustrated because you'd like your choices to be heard and respected?

The goal of these exercises is to build skill around one's use of compassionate communication. No matter what is said, one develops facility and ease in responding empathically, just as one builds ease by practicing scales over and over again.[29]

Empathy is an incomparable gift that we can offer to those around us each day. The key question as we seek to empathize is: what is the life-serving need that is longing to be fulfilled? As we focus on this question, we imagine the other person's life predicament and try to connect with their simple human needs. We do this with empathic guesses. It doesn't matter if our guesses are right or not. What matters is the quality of the attention and presence that we bring. As we focus our attention on others, we convey our longing to understand and connect with where they are right now in their lives. If we are fortunate, we will experience the joyful sense of connection that is so life-giving. At the end of his book on how our minds develop, Siegel captures the experience well:

> Connections between minds . . . involve a dyadic form of resonance in which energy and information are free to flow across two brains. When such a process is in full activation, the vital feeling of connection is exhilarating. When interpersonal communication is "fully engaged"—when the joining of minds is in full force—there

is an overwhelming sense of immediacy, clarity, and authenticity. It is in these heightened moments of engagement, these dyadic states of resonance, that one can appreciate the power of relationships to nurture and to heal the mind.[30]

It is worth reiterating that empathic relationships not only nurture us but also can actually heal the mind. They give us the sense that life is worth living and the experience of its being lived with zest and joy. When our minds are joined in this way with others, we feel fully alive.

Finely honed skill in empathic listening is the sine qua non not only of pastoral care but also of pastoral leadership, especially when conflict is brewing. Those church leaders who can empathetically connect with dissatisfied or critical parishioners will be able to reduce the level of anxiety (both the parishioners' and the one being criticized) quite dramatically. Issues that are creating tension can be identified and parishioners will trust that they can speak their mind openly without threatening those in leadership. Those who are skilled with empathy typically have another basic skill set integrated into their functioning. They will know how to offer themselves empathy, which means that they will be able to respond, rather than react, to whatever their parishioners have to say. We turn to that crucial skill in the next chapter.

Chapter 6

Loving Your Neighbor as Yourself

The Art of Self-Empathy

You shall love your neighbor as yourself.

Matthew 22:39

In chapter 22 of Matthew, Jesus says that "the great and first command-ment" (v. 38) is: "'You shall love the Lord your God with all your heart, and with all your soul, and with all your mind'" (v. 37). He then goes on to say that a second is like it: "You shall love your neighbor as yourself. On these two commandments," says Jesus, "hang all the law and the prophets" (vv. 39–40). It is an astonishing summary for its clarity and economy. We are to love God with everything that we are, single-mindedly and wholeheartedly, with all-out passion from the depths of our being. And we are to love our neighbors as we love ourselves, to care about their welfare and take their longings to heart in the same way that we care about our own well-being. In saying this, Jesus assumes a love of oneself as the basis for illuminating what he means by loving one's neighbor. As we love and care for our own bodies and souls, so we are to love and care for our neighbors'. We are to regard our neighbors' needs as having the same importance as our own.

Yet how are we to understand what it means to love ourselves in light of other New Testament injunctions to deny ourselves? Is self-love less honorable than love of neighbor or, even worse, intrinsically sinful? Numerous biblical passages can be brought to bear on such an inter-pretation: that we ought to "deny ourselves," (Matt. 16:24), "hate even life itself" (Luke 14:26), and "put to death the deeds of the body" (Rom. 8:13). Similarly, we must "do nothing from selfishness or conceit, but in humility count others better than [ourselves]" (Phil. 2:3).[1]

A theologically adequate understanding of self-love becomes even more difficult when we consider the Bible's denunciations of human sin. Old and New Testaments alike speak of the pervasiveness of sin. "Indeed I was born guilty, a sinner when my mother conceived me" (Ps. 51:5). "All have sinned and fall short of God's glory" (Rom. 3:23). "For I know that nothing good dwells within me, that is, in my flesh" (Rom. 7:18). Entire theological traditions, specifically those stemming from John Calvin's thought, affirm the "total depravity" of human nature. Some have claimed that the self is inherently evil. They have argued that God calls us to a life of self-abnegation. Anything less is selfish and sinful. So we are left wondering, does Scripture teach us to hold ourselves in contempt?

Perhaps surprisingly, Calvin's own theology helps us answer these questions. In the *Institutes of the Christian Religion*, Calvin defines "the sum of the Christian life" as "self-denial." By this, he means the setting aside of "the yearning to possess, the desire for power," as well as "arrogance, ostentation, . . . [and] avarice."[2] Self-denial resists the tendency to exaggerate the faults of others, enabling us to relate to others with "true gentleness"[3] and "to look upon the image of God in all men, to which we owe all honor and love."[4] In other words, juxtaposed with this emphasis on human sin is the affirmation of the goodness of humanity, which is made in the image of God. Scripture teaches us to value our life, body and soul, as a precious gift from God. It teaches us to honor our bodies as temples of the Holy Spirit and to know that we are beloved children of our maker. Passages that emphasize self-denial, humility, and even hatred toward our own lives are meant to counteract the human tendency to think only of ourselves. As in the injunction to "love our neighbor as ourselves," self-love is the assumed point of reference. It is taken for granted that we will cherish our lives and the needs of our bodies and souls. What we need to hear is that our neighbors' lives deserve the same kind of tender solicitude as our own.

The tradition of interpretation that portrays human beings in a completely negative light wants to emphasize that there is no aspect of human nature untouched by sin. However, the Calvinistic affirmation of "total depravity" does not mean that there is nothing lovable or worthy about human beings, but rather that human beings are incapable of acting or even willing the good apart from God's grace. Such a confession does not negate the affirmation of our having been created in God's own image. Though sin corrupts or distorts the image of God, it does not destroy it. Scripture states that after God created the world and all its creatures, including human beings, "God saw everything that he had made, and indeed, it was very good" (Gen. 1:31). Indeed, God creates human beings in God's own image and honors us by calling us to a life of love, witness, and service. Though we sin, God continues to extend steadfast love toward human beings. In an effort to see our true situation before God, especially the gravity and pervasiveness of sin, we are not to lose sight of the fact that God loves and cherishes us as beloved children. If we are the object of the Lord's compassionate care in spite of our sin, then we also ought to have compassion on ourselves. We are to care for ourselves in correspondence to the tenderness that God extends toward us.

It is paradoxically the case that we cannot love either God or others if we do not love ourselves. Love of self is intrinsically tied to love of neighbor. Even the golden rule makes no sense without a proper regard for the self. We must respect ourselves and cherish our own lives if we are to respect and cherish others. As Ray Anderson observes, "Love of self and neighbor, as grounded in God's love of both, is not two separate commands to love, nor two kinds of love. Rather, this command to love includes three aspects: God, the neighbor, and the self. One cannot despise oneself and truly love God or the neighbor."[5] When Paul admonishes husbands to love their wives, his reasoning also proceeds from the basic assumption of a proper love of self.[6] "In the same way, husbands should love their wives as they do their own bodies. He who loves his wife loves himself. For no one ever hates his own body, but he nourishes and tenderly cares for it, just as Christ does for the church, because we are members of his body" (Eph. 5:28-30). Because we are equally members of Christ's body, so Paul seems to say, we are to cherish every member equally. All have worth and value, including ourselves. Love of self and neighbor is one love that flows in both directions. Everything depends on the mutual and reciprocal care between our neighbor and ourselves.

We come to esteem ourselves only as we are cherished by others, by our parents or early caregivers, and by friends and family thereafter. We are deluded if we believe that we can manufacture a sense of self-worth simply by ourselves. Writing ourselves notes of self-affirmation, giving ourselves hugs, or asserting our own value fail to convince us of our worthiness. Rather, "we love because [God] first loved us" (1 John 4:19). Human love is radically dependent on divine love for its very existence. Parents cannot sustain love for their children apart from a sense of being loved themselves. Ultimately all love comes from God. We cannot grow truly to value ourselves simply by willing ourselves to do so. Love is always a gift. It comes to us through the actual experience of others loving us. As we are loved and respected by others, we learn to love and respect ourselves.

Though we are to love ourselves, we are not to elevate ourselves or others in such a way that displaces God. God remains the center of our lives; God alone is to be loved with all our heart, soul, and mind. We are called not simply to meet our own needs, as if those needs were the only ones that mattered, but to glorify God by caring for all that God has created. We are to take to heart the needs of our neighbor (and indeed all of creation) with the same care with which we take our own needs to heart. Here is where the biblical injunction to deny ourselves has its place. In so far as we elevate our own needs above others or look only to our own interests and fail to take the interests of others into account, precisely then we are to honor and love others as made in the image of God, as others whose very being matters as much as our own.

Jesus always spoke specifically to each person's heart. Longing for healing, the woman with the flow of blood audaciously crept up behind Jesus and touched the hem of his robe. But Jesus did not rebuke her; on the contrary, he praised her for acting in faith (Matt. 9:20–23). Similarly, blind Bartimaeus, though reprimanded by the crowd, was rewarded for his crying out for healing (Mark 10:46–51). However, those intent on justifying themselves, such as the rich young ruler or the publican who prayed his self-satisfied prayer, are exhorted to consider the needs of others or to count others as better than themselves.

There is no uniform rule that can be applied in all contexts. Indeed, whether to focus primarily on another's need or to assert my own is a matter of daily (or even hourly) discernment. Should I assert my own need here? Or should I pay more attention to the needs of the other? What is God calling me to do in this particular situation? Compassionate communication not only gives us tools for discerning our own needs and those of others, but also gives guidance toward choosing strategies that take into account all those whose needs are unmet in any given situation. The point is that everyone's needs matter, including one's own.

On a practical level this means caring for ourselves as we would care for others. It is as important to know about caring for ourselves as it is to know about justification by faith alone. Indeed, justification by faith alone entails self-care at a practical level. If we believe that Jesus Christ is the one who justifies our lives, then we know that we cannot earn our salvation. We see that we don't have to prove ourselves to anybody, least of all to ourselves and the tyrannical shoulds that drive us mercilessly toward an idealized version of ourselves.[7] We don't have to live up to the idealized self because we know that our real selves are loved and accepted by God. If God knows our worst and nevertheless forgives us and cherishes us, then we can rest secure in God's love. If God honors us by calling us to participate in the work of witness, service, and prayer, then we ought to treat ourselves with the same honor that God has already granted us.

Yet there are those in the church who seem utterly to disregard their own needs as they pour themselves out for the sake of others. In doing so, they endanger their own health and well-being. Some exhaust themselves to the point of burnout. Others act out, seeking to fulfill needs that they don't even know are there, clamoring for attention. In either case, they are disconnected from their own needs. Such situations are tragic. Years and years of prayerful discernment, community encouragement, diligent study, financial resources, and hard work all come to naught. They either leave the ministry discouraged and disillusioned or are forced to leave by a community reeling from a sense of betrayed trust. If they only knew how to identify their needs, the tragedy could be averted. For in and of themselves their needs are precious and worthy of fulfillment. If the persons involved are able consciously to connect with all their needs, they can seek to meet them in ways that are in harmony with their basic values. If instead, they remain disconnected from their needs, they either ignore them or act on them unconsciously, to the hurt and detriment of both neighbor and self. Lives are shattered, gifts wasted, and the splendor of God's glory lies shrouded in darkness.

Self-Pity Compared to Self-Empathy

Some people object to taking the time to pay attention to their own feelings and needs because they consider it a waste of time. In many cases they are confusing self-empathy with self-pity. It is important to differentiate between them for they lead in diametrically opposed directions. When we engage in self-pity, we see ourselves essentially as victims. We tell ourselves that we can't do whatever is asked of us and that we are powerless to initiate change on our own. We often have a story that justifies our sense of helplessness: others have power over us and they are to blame for our disempowered state. So we feel sorry for ourselves. Self-pity is a closed down, turned inward sort of stance. Self-empathy, by contrast, is healing and empowering, an opening up to possibility and growth. In self-empathy, we focus on our core needs. In so doing, we are able to take responsibility for ourselves. Options become apparent as we more deeply connect with what matters most to us in any particular situation. Because we are self-connected, we are able to make choices aligned with our values. In addition, the process of self-empathy itself meets our needs for self-care and compassion, as well as self-understanding. Even if our needs are not met in any particular instance, we are still able to be at peace. We trust that with time other options will open up. Because we are not wedded to any particular strategy, we remain open to what might unfold. We may feel profound sorrow that things have not turned out as we wanted, but self-connected mourning over unmet needs is deeply healing. Instead of feeling sorry for ourselves, we feel true sorrow as we connect fully with the precious value of what we have lost. Such mourning is life-giving because it renews in us a deeper commitment to living out our values in the world. In chapter 8 we discuss the healing nature of the work of mourning.

The Importance of Self-Empathy in Pastoral Care

It is a paradoxical fact that listening well to others is intimately tied to knowing how to listen to ourselves. In pastoral care, we need to be attentive to our own anxiety because whenever our anxiety increases, our ability to hear another decreases. As Margaret Kornfeld puts it, anxiety creates "static" in our listening.[8] When our anxiety lies outside our awareness we are likely to fall into old habits; we might offer advice or reassurance or assume a "teaching" rather than a "listening" mode. Indeed, we are vulnerable to all the "typical twelve" that we listed in chapter 5 (advising, one-upping, educating, analyzing, storytelling, minimizing, sympathizing, interrogating, reassuring, avoiding, diagnosing, or judging). Whenever we hear ourselves resorting to one of these modes of responding in a pastoral care encounter, it is likely a sign that our anxiety has been triggered. Our anxiety is a signal of an unmet need that wants our attention. *If we are unable to empathize with another person, it is a sign that we ourselves need empathy.* We can get the empathy we need either by reaching out to a trusted friend or colleague for help or by practicing the specific skill of self-empathy. If we start to feel angry, frustrated, helpless, or fearful, it is a sign of our own unmet needs.

In order to create a trustworthy environment for others, we need to acknowledge and address the source of our anxiety. Kornfeld notes that anxiety is often created by self-doubt. Self-doubt indeed seems to be an expression of anxiety, but knowing this is not sufficient. We need to take the next step and identify the unmet needs that fuel the self-doubt. What are the circumstances under which our self-doubt arises, and what do we need? When we are first learning the empathic skills involved in pastoral listening, for example, anxious self-doubt often arises from a need to contribute to the well-being of others while we ourselves are unsure about how to proceed. We might also identify needs for contribution, competence, and confidence. The spiritual challenge is to find a measure of self-acceptance as we slowly learn how to meet these important needs. It is often difficult to have compassion for ourselves as we experience the awkwardness of learning new skills.

Attitudes Toward Self and Others

It is a curious fact that our attitudes toward ourselves and our attitudes toward others are often deeply entwined. For example, some people drive themselves anxiously to accomplish task after task, while seldom letting themselves simply enjoy what they are doing in the moment. It is as if they are rushing ten feet ahead of themselves. Yet, if you were to observe them closely, you might see them driving their children in a similar way, constantly reminding them to do this or that, hardly allowing them a minute to relax. Or to choose another example, some people have a "fix it" attitude toward others, rattling off solutions to a problem before the problem has been fully described. If you listen closely, however, you might notice that they also become impatient with themselves whenever they are unclear about what direction to take. They don't know how to check in with themselves and accurately assess the full range of the needs they are trying to meet with any given decision. They simply want to decide and be done with it.

Sometimes, however, a person will speak to others with the utmost consideration and respect, yet speak to himself as if he were the most despicable creature alive. If he makes a mistake, he immediately berates himself with scathing judgments or calls himself an idiot. The more he regrets a decision, the more he treats himself with scorn. He would be horrified at the thought of speaking to another in this manner, yet he speaks to himself as if he were of no value. If he were to analyze his self-talk, he might be able to recognize its origins in childhood. Perhaps a parent spoke to him in such a disparaging way, or perhaps a beloved older brother spoke of himself in this way. It may be a learned pattern; in other words, something picked up long before he became fully conscious of what he was internalizing.

Such analyses may be provisionally helpful, yet ultimately they do little actually to change the pattern. Only self-empathy can give us the skill that we need to learn how to treat ourselves with the same consideration and respect that we want to accord others. Just as we do not want to judge or blame others, so now we strive to identify the needs that are underlying any self-judgment or blame. Just as we help others to translate their negative interpretation of themselves when they compare themselves to others, so we now seek to catch ourselves in the act of comparing ourselves. When we translate the comparison into our own feelings and needs, we may experience pain, but we will also discover a hidden treasure: a bundle of unacknowledged needs that we are longing to find a way to live out fully. The others are carrying personal values of ours that we ourselves need to become more fully conscious of. In self-empathy, we learn to notice when we feel overwhelmed, sad, anxious, or distressed so that we can take the time to be with ourselves in a loving way, to listen to ourselves with the kind of compassion we would give a frightened child. When we listen to ourselves in this way, we learn to make choices that truly reflect our values, which typically gives us a sense of satisfaction and even joy.

Being Triggered and Asking Ourselves: What Is the Need?

Self-empathy usually begins with a trigger. We hear, see, or remember something that brings up strong negative feelings in us. We might feel a sharp stab of hurt, the boiling up of anger, intense anxiety, or a feeling of being overwhelmed. The more powerful the emotion, the more urgent the underlying need or value. If I experience only mild anxiety about an upcoming interview, for example, it may be because I have a sense of confidence or it may be that the interview is simply not that important to me. If I experience intense anxiety, by contrast, it may be because much is at stake. I anticipate that some vital need will be met (or not) as the outcome of the interview. The process of self-empathy would help me to assess precisely which needs of mine—and there may be many—are generating such intense feelings.

In self-empathy we strive to stay attuned to ourselves in a bodily way. In other words, we don't think about the problem so much as feel into it. We don't analyze our anxiety with our rational capacities, but rather we pay attention to what happens in our bodies when we ask ourselves what it is about this concrete situation that matters to us. Such a process is described in vivid detail in Eugene Gendlin's groundbreaking book,

Focusing. Developed in the 1970s at the University of Chicago, *Focusing* teaches a process of paying attention to our physiological responses in order to connect with feelings that generally lie outside of our awareness. Working with the "felt sense" in the body, Gendlin teaches us to notice when the body relaxes. When we accurately identify our feelings, there is a noticeable shift on a bodily level. For example, when we strain to remember a name that is on the tip of our tongue, there is a distinct tension that dissipates the moment the name is recalled. Calling the body a kind of "biological computer," Gendlin reminds us that, "the equivalent of hundreds of thousands of cognitive operations are done in a split second by the body."[9]

When we find a word that matches the felt sense in the body, a letting go or relaxation is experienced, sometimes accompanied by a literal sigh of relief. "Ah yes, that's it! That word captures the feeling exactly," we might exclaim. At this point, Gendlin would recommend probing further to elicit even more information from the body's felt sense. Previously unconscious feelings may now begin to rise up into awareness. Gendlin suggests that as we pay close attention to the felt sense in our bodies, we might ask ourselves several questions: "What is it about this whole issue that makes it so . . .? What is the worst thing about this problem? How would I feel inside if it were solved? What do I need for me not to feel so . . . 'anxious' or 'jumpy' or 'frightened,' or whatever word seems to fit the felt sense?"[10] After asking, we wait for the body to answer; we do not fill in the blanks with our conscious ideas or thoughts. Instead, we trust the inner wisdom of our body to speak.

The last question that Gendlin asks connects feelings with needs. Though the significance of connecting with one's needs remains implicit in focusing, in compassionate communication it is the master key to the whole process. Asking myself "What do I need in this particular situation?" is the fundamental question that is able to bring about the distinct shift that Gendlin describes. What would relieve me of the anger or constriction or shame that I have identified? What need am I longing to fulfill? What need, if it were fulfilled, would bring me to a place of relaxation and peace? Focusing and compassionate communication both work with the felt sense of the body; in other words, only compassionate communication emphasizes the pivotal role that fully connecting with one's needs plays in the process. When we inquire into our needs in the same way that Gendlin suggests that we ask about our feelings—by attending to what goes on in our bodies—we are not simply connecting to words in our head. We are testing to see if the words in our minds correspond to the feelings in our bodies. Indeed, we actually pay attention to our bodies (especially to the viscera, where we find our "gut" feelings) to find our needs. The process, in other words, entails a deep integration of the cognitive, affective, and bodily components of our being.

A Simple Example of Self-Empathy

On a recent plane trip, I had fallen asleep when the flight attendant was serving drinks. Immediately upon waking, I noticed that she was collecting the cups to prepare for landing. Since I was quite thirsty, I asked for some water, explaining that I had been asleep earlier. In what sounded like an annoyed tone of voice, she replied that it was too late since the plane was about to land. She walked on by, collecting the cups. She then took them to the front to dispose of them. I was upset. It was apparent that she was not going to bring me any water. I thought to myself: "How difficult would it be to get me a cup of water? I'm really thirsty. We aren't landing now anyway. Surely you have enough time." This line of thought offered no relief at all. I then switched tactics and tried to empathize with what I imagined as her feelings and needs: "Perhaps she is annoyed because she wants ease in completing all her tasks before landing." The attempt to connect empathically with her brought a slight shift but not enough to give any real relief. I was still upset.

However, when I asked myself what I needed in order to be at peace, I realized at once that my thirst was not the essential thing. I was indeed quite thirsty, but even more than water was my need for caring. I interpreted her tone of voice and her lack of action as a lack of caring. I was upset because it seemed to me that she did not care whether or not I was thirsty. When I heard myself accuse her (inwardly) of not caring, I asked myself whether caring was my deeper need. My body responded instantly with a dramatic release of inner tension. The shift was unmistakable. Caring was indeed my need. I was longing for some kind of care in her response. I thought further: "Even if she can't get me the water, if she would convey some care about my need, I could accept it. I could be at peace, if only she had said: 'I'm sorry, Ma'am, but I'm unable to get you some water right now. We are about to land and I need to return to my seat for the sake of safety.'"

To anchor myself more securely in the beauty of this need, I focused on how much I value caring. I meditated not only on how I strive to convey it in my relationships with others but also on how it feeds my soul when others convey care toward me. The longer I focused on the quality of the need itself (rather than on its absence in this particular instance), the more I felt at peace. Though still thirsty, I was no longer angry or agitated. I had connected with a value that mattered a great deal to me, one that was clamoring for attention through my feelings of distress.

Jane Connor, a certified NVC trainer, has developed a simple process for noticing what her common triggers are.[11] She carries a little notebook in which she jots down the exact observation (what she sees, hears, remembers, and so forth) throughout the day that triggers any kind of distress or unease. At the end of the day, she meditates on each of the triggers, asking herself what her feelings and needs were in each situation. In a single day, she might discover many unmet needs: for contribution, respect, understanding, meaning, acknowledgment, collaboration, choice, support, community. For example, she may observe one colleague speaking brusquely to another or refusing to answer the other's question. The moment she notices her anger flaring up, she writes down exactly what she has seen and heard. That evening when she meditates on the incident, she asks herself what she was thinking when her anger flared. By following her thoughts and attending carefully to her needs, she might discover that her unmet need is for respect. She would like her colleagues to treat each other with respect. Even when there are disagreements or different ways of viewing the world, she longs for each person to be treated respectfully.

If we make such a "trigger translation journal" a daily practice, we will become intimately acquainted with our core values. In addition, we may find places of vulnerability where we especially need healing. If our reaction is extreme, it may be that we have unresolved grief in relation to a core value. Over time, we can become acquainted with the patterns of thoughts, feelings, and needs that are repeated again and again. These patterns represent primal pathways in the brain that can be healed and transformed by empathy and self-empathy. Though the needs themselves are universal, each of us experiences them in a way peculiar to our unique makeup and history. In cases where chronic needs have remained unmet (and often unacknowledged) for years, our triggers will be correspondingly intense. Therefore, when we are intensely reactive, something of great value is at stake. Remembering this helps us to slow down and use all our skill to pay attention to the life-giving needs that are longing for acknowledgment.

Transforming Self-Judgments

In his book, *Nonviolent Communication: A Language of Life*, Marshall Rosenberg states the basic premise that lies behind the work of translating self-judgments: "Self-judgments, like all judgments, are tragic expressions of unmet needs."[12] Whenever we judge or blame ourselves, we are demonstrating that we have failed to act in harmony with our own values and needs. But it does little good to berate ourselves. That only deepens our sense of guilt, shame, powerlessness, or depression. It also perpetuates the cycle of keeping ourselves disconnected from our true needs. However, if we practice self-empathy, we can discover precisely what our needs are and look for satisfying ways to meet them.

It is an axiom in compassionate communication that all our actions are motivated by needs. If we find ourselves judging or blaming ourselves for an action we have taken, it is likely that we have failed to take into account all of our needs. For example, in ending a phone call quickly I may meet my need for efficiency, only to regret it later when I hear that my parishioner was hurt because she had hoped for a deeper connection with me. Now my need for caring may come to the fore. As I acknowledge the regret I feel when hearing about her disappointment in response to my action, I recognize that it emerges because I value caring in all my relationships. At the same time, however, I want to identify what need I was trying to meet with the action I took. Why did I end the conversation so abruptly? Oh yes, it was because I had a long list of tasks I was trying to accomplish before I left town for a week. I had felt a great need to be efficient in completing my checklist. Once I am fully connected to both sets of needs (in this example, both caring and efficiency), the self-judgment begins to fall away. While I may mourn the fact that I did not anticipate my parishioner's unexpressed need, I no longer would judge myself as inadequate or uncaring. By connecting fully with *both* sets of needs—the need I was trying to meet as well as the need I did not meet—I am able to meet another crucial need: the need for self-acceptance.

Notice that in both examples (the example of my wanting a glass of water on the plane and the example of my ending a call abruptly) my need was the same. In both cases I identified the unmet need of caring. One of the benefits of a regular practice of self-empathy is the discovery that my need for caring entails both receiving and giving care. Self-empathy demonstrates clearly that the love of self and love of other are truly intertwined. If I value caring, its absence will trigger pain whether I am the one who fails to live it out or whether someone else fails to offer it to me. I might also be triggered when I hear a mother speaking in an exasperated tone to her children as they enter the sanctuary on Sunday morning. I may feel sad, and through self-empathy, identify caring once again as my unmet need.

Though these simple examples may seem trivial, it is helpful to practice self-empathy with relatively uncomplicated situations. Then when we are triggered about major events in which there are whole clusters of unmet needs to be identified, we will have the basic skill mastered: the skill of connecting with all the needs at play. Once we see the self-judgments falling away in these relatively simple examples, we will be motivated to keep practicing.

People who are prone to shame and depression have self-judgments swirling about their minds almost constantly. In such cases the work of transforming self-judgments becomes a means of liberation. Those who have been taught to judge themselves as children (either through the explicit teaching or the modeling of a cherished other, usually a parent) often judge themselves harshly and repeatedly. They believe the self-judgments to be true and get little relief from the nearly constant inner barrage. In chapter 1, we summarized the four ways that a message can be heard: first, we can hear it as blame or judgment. To defend ourselves we are quick to blame the other back. Second, we can hear the message as judgment and then agree with its essence. With this choice, we basically join the other in criticizing ourselves. Third, we can empathize with the sender of the message by attempting to discern his feelings and needs. Fourth, we can empathize with ourselves by seeking to identify our own feelings and needs in light of what has just triggered pain. In depression, the ingrained habit of mind is typically option two. Self-empathy (option four) becomes a lifeline for those who struggle with depression or significant self-judgment as they learn to identify and connect with chronically unmet needs.

Deepening Needs Consciousness

As we work to identify clusters of chronically unmet needs, we have found that the need for acceptance and self-acceptance are often closely entwined. When we fear someone else's judgment it is frequently the case that what we need even more than the other's acceptance is our own self-acceptance. Self-judgments are far more treacherous than the judgment of others because we so often believe them. We believe that these judgments are the truth. And because we believe that they are true, we also believe that others must hold them as well. Because they go on autonomously in our minds, they are difficult to catch. One pastor, for example, constantly told herself that she was lacking in basic integrity. These self-accusations would typically arise in situations in which someone would say something that she disagreed with. Rather than openly stating her disagreement, she would remain silent about her reaction and keep her opinions to herself. Even in matters of great importance to herself and the church she would hesitate to speak up. Then she would berate herself for lacking the courage of her convictions. She told herself that she was simply hiding out, lacking in basic integrity. Not only was she being inauthentic by keeping her opinions to herself, she was also hiding her talents and not giving others the benefit of any possible insight that a differing perspective might impart.

Paradoxically, the action of judging herself is itself an attempt to meet a need. The act of self-judgment alerts her to the fact that at least one of her needs has not been met. What unmet needs did these judgments point to? Her overriding need corresponded to the loudest and most frequent judgment resounding in her mind: a need for integrity. She wanted her actions to reflect her deepest values. She wanted the freedom to express her thoughts in the church even when they might be unpopular. She wanted to be more open, to make the contribution that might come from stating what she thought and why. She wanted to be authentically and fully herself. The cluster of unmet needs she identified as I assisted her in a process of self-empathy were integrity, openness, freedom, contribution, authenticity, and then, surprisingly, simple connection. The need for connection took her by surprise. She had the sudden insight that by hiding her true thoughts and opinions, she had gone through life feeling lonely, not fully connecting with others because she was not revealing her authentic self.

In seeking to transform these judgments, she sought first to connect with the range of feelings that arose whenever she failed to speak up. The feelings were intense frustration, sorrow, and fear, each surfacing as she worked through the previous feeling. First, there was great frustration that no matter how much she coached herself to speak up, she remained silent and let the significant moment pass by. After exploring this frustration she discovered a well of sadness about all the relationships in which she had failed to speak up because she didn't have the trust to say what she really thought. Once she felt the sadness fully and saw how huge her unmet need for trust really was, she became aware of the depth of her fear.

That fear needed further exploration. By asking herself about the needs connected to these feelings she began to have compassion toward herself regarding her choice to remain silent over all these years. Though she clearly suffered from many unmet needs with this strategy, she also saw how she experienced a sense of safety by staying silent. She enjoyed relative harmony in her interpersonal and work relationships because she seldom rocked the boat. Her coworkers found her pleasant to be around, little knowing that fear of conflict kept her from speaking honestly about what she really thought and felt. At this point in the process she took the time to consider both needs—the need to be herself and express herself fully as well as the need to have compassion on herself when she chose to stay silent. As she did this, the childhood roots of her fear filtered up into awareness, in particular the emotional chaos and violence that had reigned in her family home. Her mother would erupt into terrifying rages out of nowhere; her sister would slap her if she said or did things that the sister didn't like. Hiding her thoughts and feelings became a strategy for survival in a home where it seemed unsafe to assert herself in any way.

As she remembered these scenes concretely, even more compassion welled up within her for herself and for the frightened child who was afraid of her mother's rage and her sister's aggression. She could now appreciate the needs she was meeting through her strategy of keeping her true thoughts and feelings to herself. If she made herself as invisible as possible she seemed able to avoid triggering irrational anger in her mother; if she kept her opinions to herself she was able to keep her sister from slapping her. Hiding out became a way of keeping herself relatively safe in a home that seemed unsafe. Her needs for safety and harmony were so overriding that she believed it was impossible to express herself honestly in that setting.

In self-empathy, she was able to find a way to affirm, even to love, both sets of needs: the needs she was trying to meet by hiding (namely, safety and harmony) as well as the needs that she could not meet with this strategy (integrity, authenticity, freedom, contribution, and connection). By connecting with all the needs involved, she was able gradually to find ways to take new risks, to stand by herself with compassion when she feared someone's displeasure. She discovered strategies, in other words, that met both sets of needs: the needs that were met by hiding her true thoughts as well as the needs that would be met by speaking up. Slowly but surely, as she sought and received the support that she lacked as a child, she was able to find more freedom in speaking her mind fully. With that came much joy not only from the deepened connection that she had with others but also from the self-respect that came from meeting her own need for integrity.[13]

This example shows how core beliefs about herself and others kept this pastor from engaging her congregants and colleagues with honesty and security. She had developed a number of stories about herself that were reinforced every time she kept silent about something that mattered to her. Concretely, these beliefs could be summarized as follows: "I will be hurt if I say what I really think. . . . The only way that I can stay safe is by hiding out, by becoming as invisible as possible." In a more extreme state, the belief was "If I say what I really think, I will be killed." This unconscious belief was reinforced by the larger context of multiple assassinations of national figures in her childhood. These national events seem to have reinforced the neural pathways that had developed by growing up in her family of origin. The process of self-empathy enabled her to become aware of beliefs that essentially kept her stuck in old patterns. As she took more risks in which she questioned these beliefs, she found greater freedom and joy of self-expression.

Self-Empathy and Prayer

Those who use self-empathy as a practical spiritual discipline sometimes find that it leads directly to prayer: to asking God for what they need. In this way, self-empathy can deepen our connection with God. When we turn to God in prayer having already gone through a process of self-empathy, we are unlikely simply to rattle off requests. Instead, we are likely to pray about the true nature of our need and to offer up our requests haltingly, trusting that God, the searcher of hearts, will hear our hidden cry. "Likewise the Spirit helps us in our weakness; for we do not know how to pray as we ought, but that very Spirit intercedes with sighs too deep for words" (Rom. 8:26). Though we can sometimes be badly mistaken in assessing our true need, prayer keeps us aware of our most fundamental need: our need for God and for God's grace in its rich multiplicity of forms. Indeed, Scripture teaches us that God is the author of "every perfect gift" (Jas. 1:17) who will supply us with whatever we need for our life and wellbeing. "And my God will fully satisfy every need of yours according to his riches in glory in Christ Jesus" (Phil. 4:19). "Rejoice in the Lord always; again I will say, rejoice. . . . Do not worry about anything, but in everything by prayer and supplication with thanksgiving let your requests be made known to God" (Phil. 4:4, 6). Prayer connects us to God and to all the needs fulfilled in God.

Needs, from within a Christian understanding, are all finally rooted and grounded in God. They are not ultimately understood as human qualities but rather as gifts from above. In prayer we connect to God as the source of our needs, to Christ as the one in whom all our needs are fulfilled, and to the Spirit who searches our hearts and enables us to pray from the depths of our need. When we are discouraged, we need patience or courage. We access that patience or courage through our koinonia with God in prayer. If we are disappointed in ourselves we may identify our need as integrity or honesty. Once again, we find our center of integrity by reference to our relationship with God. At another point we may recognize a need for trust. When we discover, again and again, that we are united to Christ and the communion of saints, we become grounded in a source of faith far greater than our own. As we confess our sins to God and each other, our needs for restoration and wholeness are met. As we lament the injustice all around us, our despair turns to hope. We are empowered to live in the already-but-not yet—in this time of waiting for the fullness of God's kingdom to come.

To put it another way, self-empathy that leads to prayer supports our capacity to live compassionately. Connecting to God, the transcendent source of compassion, gives us the ability to keep our hearts open when we would otherwise be tempted to shut down. When we are overwhelmed with anxiety or despair, we have One to whom we can turn for strength. Indeed, the New Testament presents Jesus Christ as One who has taken the suffering of the entire world into his own heart. He does not leave us alone to suffer the anguish of loss and death, nor the consequences of our sin, but actively intercedes on our behalf. Self-empathy that leads to prayer will not only become a means for preventing what is commonly called "compassion fatigue," but also can become a vital discipline for revitalizing faith.

Transforming Self-Judgments and the Forgiveness of Sin

From a Christian point of view, we are taught to seek God's forgiveness when we have not lived according to the values of our faith. Through the Holy Spirit, our conscience signals to us that we have failed to act with integrity or be fully honest. In Christian theology, when we fail to live up to God's commandments, we are counseled to confess our sin, receive God's forgiveness, make amends toward those we have hurt, and live in grateful acknowledgment of God's mercy. Transforming self-judgments, as taught by Rosenberg, is not synonymous with confession of sin. Nor is it a replacement for it. While NVC lacks (and likely rejects) a concept of sin, Christian theology cannot do without it. As we discussed in chapter 4, the concept of sin, so closely tied to our understanding of our need for God and the salvation accomplished in Jesus Christ, is indispensable to our entire understanding of the life of faith. However, transforming our self-judgments gives us a deeper understanding of ourselves, which in turn transforms our practice of confession and repentance. For it enables us to encounter God with a depth of authenticity frequently lacking in our corporate prayers of confession.

When Rosenberg acknowledges that there are times when we fail to live according to our most cherished values, he is seeking to develop a concrete tool for recognizing the dynamics at work in those situations. What he has developed is especially helpful for Christians when they get caught in cycles of self-blame and self-judgment, even when they believe that God has forgiven their sin. Though they know that they should let themselves be at peace under the mercy of God, they are unable to rest in that knowledge. Practicing self-empathy and striving to identify the unmet needs at work in their choices gives them a practical tool for bringing their behavior into alignment with their deepest Christian beliefs. Here are the essential steps:[14]

1. Write down something you said or did that you now regret.
2. Write down all the thoughts and judgments you have about yourself regarding your behavior. Don't move into detached analysis or personal memories. Stay connected to the energy, the variety, and the intensity of all the self-judgments that come into your awareness.
3. Notice what you feel in your body. Try to identify what feelings are most alive. There might be a number of feelings connected to a single judgment or a number of judgments that bring up the same feeling.
4. Connect each feeling to an underlying need. When you notice a release or relaxation in your body, that means that you have connected with a true need.
5. Now stay connected to that need and deepen the empathy for yourself by imagining that need being fully met. Notice how your body feels when you imagine that the need is met.
6. This is the quality of life you are longing for. In other words, focus on the *presence* of the need as a personal value of yours, not on its *absence* in this particular instance.
7. Notice how the need is an attribute of God's goodness and a gift from God's hand. Pray about this need and how much you long for it to be fulfilled. Meditate on its beauty and on the promise of God for this need to be satisfied when God's kingdom is fully lived out on earth as it is in heaven.

Self-Empathy as a Vital Practice for Church Leaders

Among pastors, caring for others is too frequently accompanied by neglecting self-care. Clergy suffer from high levels of stress, burnout, and depression. In fact, the statistics are alarming. A 2006 Episcopal Clergy Wellness Report found that stress is an emotional health risk for 73 percent of Episcopal priests and that Episcopal clergy experience significantly higher rates of depression than the overall population.[15] A 2002 study by Austin Seminary, which is affiliated with the Presbyterian Church (U.S.A.), found that nearly 20 percent of their graduates in pastoral ministry are not satisfied with their work. Forty-seven percent often feel drained in fulfilling their functions in their congregations, particularly in their attempts to manage interpersonal conflict. And 36 percent frequently experience stress from conflicting or ambiguous expectations at work.[16] Gwen W. Halaas, who has written extensively about the need for self-care among clergy within the Evangelical Lutheran Church of America, summarizes current research on clergy wellness:

> Other studies of religious professionals found that Protestant clergy had the highest overall work-related stress and were next to the lowest in having personal resources to cope with the occupational strain. A study in 1987 found that the top three stressors for clergy were congregational conflicts and church conservatism, difficulties involved in parish commitments, and the emotional and time demands of crisis counseling. Researchers have found that one in three pastors leaving ordained ministry had family difficulties, and that clergy rank third among professionals who are divorced. A study of male clergy and their wives found work-related stress on the family in two areas: the lack of available social support and the intrusion on family life. Finally, although clergy rank in the top 10 percent of the population in terms of education, their salaries rank only 325 out of 432 occupations.[17]

Self-empathy and the process of transforming self-judgments, though not a panacea for all the problems related to clergy wellness (or lack thereof), can support ministers and others in choosing a healthy life. After identifying and connecting with our own needs in self-empathy, we can make requests of ourselves or others to meet those needs. When deciding how to allocate our time and resources, we can weigh our needs, noticing which ones are most pressing at any given moment. As we'll see in the next chapter, we can learn to say no without guilt and yes without resentment. These capacities can sustain church leaders in the midst of their daily activities. In the midst of conflict, when anxiety runs high, self-empathy can help us stay grounded in our most cherished values. When criticism comes our way we can connect with our unmet needs—for understanding, support, appreciation, and so forth—rather than blaming others, creating factions, or spiraling down into shame. In prayer we can bring our needs to God, the source of all love. God's compassion then becomes the transcendent basis of our ability to have compassion on ourselves and others. God's forgiveness, mercy, and grace become the bedrock on which our self-acceptance rests.

Chapter 7

Speaking the Truth in Love

Honest Expression

But speaking the truth in love, we must grow up in every way into him who is the head, into Christ, from whom the whole body, joined and knitted together by every ligament with which it is equipped, as each part is working properly, promotes the body's growth in building itself up in love. . . . So then, putting away falsehood, let all of us speak the truth to our neighbors, for we are members of one another. Be angry but do not sin; do not let the sun go down on your anger, and do not make room for the devil. Let no evil talk come out of your mouths, but only what is useful for building up, as there is need, so that your words may give grace to those who hear.

Ephesians 4:15–16, 25–26, 29

Not all honesty is compassionate. Most of us can recall times when we have spoken our opinions honestly and then regretted it later. Perhaps we spoke passionately but without consideration for those to whom we were speaking. Their crestfallen or stony affect may have been the first clue that our words diminished rather than enhanced our relational connection. Some of us hold our tongues until we can't take anymore, and then we blast the unsuspecting person with our pent-up tirade. Any momentary sense of release that comes from finally speaking our minds gets overshadowed by pangs of regret for failing to speak in a caring manner. And if we have ever been on the receiving end of such honest expression, we know the feelings of shock, dismay, confusion, or anger that may result. Our defenses go up and we start judging either the other person or ourselves with severity. Our needs for trust, respect, and consideration may be so unmet that we put up an impenetrable barrier that the other cannot cross. Or we may spiral down into self-blame and shame.

From an NVC perspective, this kind of honesty is life-alienating. It does not contribute to mutual understanding. It may be assertive but it is neither empowering nor authentic. It is not empowering because it doesn't encourage the other person to speak and act with openness and trust. It is not authentic because the speaker is disconnected from his or her needs or values. Authenticity involves discovering and articulating our deepest values (what matters most to us), while simultaneously regarding the other as highly as ourselves. True authenticity flows from the knowledge that our own well-being and purpose in life depend on relationship with others.[1]

Similarly, from a Christian perspective, life-alienating honesty stands in stark contrast to "speaking the truth in love." Speaking the truth in love, as Ephesians 4 so clearly depicts, is founded on the knowledge of our koinonia with one another. Koinonia, among other things, means that Christians belong to one another, that our lives are woven together in Christ, and that there is no such thing as spiritual growth outside of our relationship with other members of the body of Christ. To speak harsh judgment against another or to engage in vitriolic, polarizing discourse with another is an attack on Christ's body. Indeed it is an act against both the other and ourselves, for we are all part of the same body. If I demean my arms (e.g., for not being as toned as I would like), I am demeaning myself for I don't exist separate from my arms. So it is in the body of Christ. When we engage in life-alienating honesty we contradict our own identity as members of Christ's body. We act as though we are not connected to each other for all eternity.

By contrast, compassionate honesty is life-serving. It acknowledges interdependence and contributes to mutual understanding, support, peace, and trust (to a name a few needs). It is grounded in an intention to connect with the other and to remain connected to oneself. As such, compassionate honesty is refreshingly assertive; it is not nice; and it is not passive. It is authentic; it flows from our connection to our most cherished values and needs. It is empowering. Simple expressions of compassionate honesty, especially when they follow empathic reception, have a way of inspiring, even freeing, others to risk opening their hearts (and mouths) so that they can be seen and known more fully. In this sense, assertive, authentic, and empowering speech builds community.

Speaking in OFNR

Like empathy and self-empathy, honesty is an NVC skill set. It brings together the four basic skills of compassionate communication: **O** (making observations rather than evaluations); **F** (identifying and expressing feelings); **N** (connecting to needs); and **R** (making requests rather than demands). The more facility we have with each of these basic skills, the more likely we will be able to speak compassionately when we are triggered emotionally in relationship to others. Instead of reacting—for instance, by judging and blaming, by trying to persuade with ideas, by making threats, or by inducing guilt—we can choose to slow down our own internal processes and translate our judgments into observations, our opinions into feelings and needs, and our demands into requests. In this way, we transform life-alienating honesty into life-enriching honesty.

When we are first learning compassionate communication or when we find ourselves being reactive,[2] it is helpful to use the four basic skills (OFNR) in the following pattern:

> When I hear, see, observe, remember . . .
> I feel . . .
> Because I need . . .
> Would you be willing to . . .

To illustrate, let's return to the vignette in chapter 5 about the ongoing pain and animosity surrounding the sexuality debates in most mainline Protestant denominations. How can people whose convictions place them on opposite sides of these debates learn to speak compassionately with each other? If you want to share your perspective compassionately, you might say, "When I read the latest decision of our denomination to ordain gays and lesbians in committed partnerships (observation), I feel completely distressed (feeling), because I need to belong to a community of faith marked by theological integrity (needs). Would you be willing to share how you feel about what I've said? (connecting request)." How can people who refuse to choose sides actually contribute to respect and peace among their family, friends, colleagues, and fellow church members? If you are distressed and longing for unity in the body of Christ, you might say to a fellow church leader, "When I hear various groups in our denomination labeling each other as apostate, on the one hand, and mean-spirited, on the other hand (observation), I feel disheartened (feeling), because I am longing for more mutual consideration, respect, and understanding (needs). Would you be willing to attend a Nonviolent Communication workshop with me next month in order to learn new ways to communicate? (action request)."

The capacity to speak in this way begins with translating life-alienating honesty into life-enriching honesty. Some examples to illustrate this process can be found in table 7.1.

Table 7.1. Life-Alienating vs. Life-Enriching Honesty Using OFNR

Life-Alienating Honesty	*Life-Enriching Honesty Using OFNR*
Your room is a pigsty! If you don't clean it up, you're not going out tonight.	When I see dirty clothes on the floor and your bed unmade and remember that you agreed to clean up your room yesterday, I feel exasperated because I need order and beauty in our home. Would you be willing to pick up your clothes and make your bed before you go to the movies tonight?
He's completely inconsiderate; let's get him removed from the personnel committee.	When I hear him say that the pastor should be working more hours, I feel irritated because I want our community to be marked by consideration for the needs of others. Would you be willing to set up an appointment for next month so that the three of us can talk openly about this?
You are so disconnected. Will you just tell me what's going on inside of you?	When I ask you how your day went and you say "Fine," I feel disappointed because I want to connect with you. Would you be willing to tell me about one or two specific events from your day and how they affected you?

Admittedly, these examples sound mechanical and awkward. Few (if any) of us communicate using the OFNR pattern on a regular basis. Speaking this way with those unfamiliar with NVC might trigger suspicion, annoyance, or distrust. As one of our seminary students said in the second week of an NVC class, "I tried this on my wife last week and she glared at me and told me not to manipulate her!" The entire class, including the professor, burst into laughter because we could imagine how shocked and irritated his wife felt after hearing her husband speaking in OFNR about his in-laws' upcoming visit! For this reason, it can be helpful to explain to family and friends that we are learning compassionate communication, that we want to practice it in conversation with them, and that our intent is to learn to express ourselves in a more life-serving way. We can invite their feedback and responses to our new language, taking a playful attitude toward our own growth and learning.

Learning compassionate communication is analogous to learning a foreign language. Initially it is important to understand the basics, to learn the grammatical and syntactical rules of the language by following them with precision. Like any language, we will internalize it best if we are immersed in a culture of NVC. Therefore we recommend that those learning compassionate communication first follow the formulas set forth above. Just as cultural immersion fosters quicker assimilation of the language and ease in communication, practicing NVC in community speeds up the developmental process of learning. In NVC practice groups, workshops, retreats, and courses, we can learn the mechanics of compassionate communication so that we eventually can adopt colloquial forms of compassionate speech. In a supportive community we can begin to move through the natural developmental stages of compassionate communication. NVC trainers describe these stages as:[3]

1. *Life-Alienating Communication (pre-NVC):* honesty is marked by evaluations, denial of choice, failure to own one's feelings, and disconnection from one's needs.
2. *Mechanical NVC:* honest expression follows basic formulas of the four skills of compassionate communication without a single-minded, open-hearted intention to connect. Desperation and distrust fuel this speech.
3. *Mechanical and Connected NVC:* honest expression follows basic formulas of the four skills with single-minded, open-hearted intention to connect to the other.

4. *Colloquial and Connected NVC:* honest expression is grounded in commitment to connection, is based on internalization of the four skills, and is communicated using ordinary, colloquial language.

In light of these stages, the honest expressions in table 7.1 represent mechanical and connected NVC. Table 7.2 shows how to move from mechanical NVC to colloquial NVC.

Table 7.2. From Mechanical to Colloquial NVC

Mechanical, Connected NVC	*Colloquial, Connected NVC*
When I see dirty clothes on your floor and your bed unmade and I remember that you agreed to clean up your room yesterday, I feel exasperated because I need order and beauty in our home. Would you be willing to pick up your clothes and make your bed before you go to the movies tonight?	Hey, John, your bed isn't made and your dirty clothes are still lying on the floor. I'm remembering that yesterday you said you'd clean it up. I'm curious about what kept you from following through on our agreement. Did you have a particularly stressful day?
When I hear him say that the pastor should be working more hours, I feel irritated because I want our community to be marked by consideration for the needs of others. Would you be willing to set up an appointment for next month so that the three of us can talk openly about this?	I got so irritated when he said that the pastor should be working more hours. I want us to care for our pastor's health and well-being in light of the stresses that she's facing right now. I think I'd like to talk to him about this. Wanna join me for a meeting with him next month?
When I ask you how your day at work went and you say "Fine," I feel disappointed because I want to connect with you. Would you be willing to tell me about one or two specific events from your day and how they affected you?	I'd really like to connect with you right now. Could you give me some more information about what happened at work today and how it affected you?

Saying No

"Just say no!" is not so easy to do. Consider Jim, a recent seminary graduate. During his first two years of serving as a youth minister, Jim focused on building relationships and developing a solid youth program. He attended special school events in order to support the kids in his youth group. He spent hours empowering adults in the congregation to become assistant leaders of the youth group. He sponsored at least two special youth events each month. Parents and kids alike loved Jim's presence and leadership. In his third year at the church, he and his wife had their second child. With the increased responsibility of raising two small children, Jim's wife wanted him to spend more time at home in the evenings and on Saturdays. Jim agreed. He knew that he was called to be a faithful minister and also a faithful husband and father. Both were important. So in his fourth year, he asked the assistant leaders to attend some of the kids' special events at school, and he reduced the number of special youth events to one per month. Not surprisingly, some of the parents were disappointed with his choices. When they pressed him to increase the events or to be more present at school functions, he sometimes gave in. He wanted to say no but didn't know how (or at least that is what he thought). He felt guilty, stressed, and torn between his church and his family.

Jim is not alone in this kind of predicament. Pastors and church leaders (indeed many of us) struggle to say no in response to the requests of others. We see the many needs around us, and, forgetting the important distinction between us and God, we overcommit. When this happens, resentment, stress, and burnout ensue. Or if we do say no, we experience the pang of guilt, wondering if we are being selfish.

Compassionate communication teaches us to say no without guilt or yes without resentment. How? By connecting to what matters most to us in any given circumstance and then making choices on that basis by aligning our choices with our needs. It is often necessary to practice self-empathy in order to know what to say no to, or in order to say no with clarity about our intentions and values. It is especially important to practice self-empathy before honest expression if we are feeling anxious or guilty about saying no. If we say no without having first connected with our needs, our anxiety and guilt will muddy the waters of communication. Our own uncertainty or unease may be heard as some kind of aggression. Moreover, such anxiety or guilt is driven by unexamined internal beliefs and demands that function as self-judgments. If we empathize with ourselves and move from self-criticism to self-connection (connection to our needs), then we can become clear about what needs are most pertinent in any given situation. We then can make choices on the basis of those needs. We can say no without guilt and avoid the pitfalls of stress and burnout so common among church leaders.

Jim recognized that he was paralyzed by his own internal set of demands combined with the real expectations that others had of him as a youth pastor and father. In order to say no without a guilty conscience, he entered into a process of self-empathy. He began with observations: (1) listing the choices that he had made at church to decrease his workload; (2) noting the precise comments spoken to him by parents and youth; and (3) recalling his wife's request. Then he identified the internalized beliefs that were driving him: (1) that he had to be considerate of all the people in his life; (2) that he should figure out how to better to balance work and home life; (3) that he had to live up to everyone's expectations of him; and (4) that he essentially had to keep everyone happy. He moved back and forth between the actual observations and the evaluations and beliefs about himself and his situation. As he did this, particular feeling states began to emerge. He felt confused, frustrated, tired, afraid, and most profoundly, sad. Underneath each of these feelings, he identified particular needs— needs to contribute, to be seen and acknowledged for his work, to rest and relax. But when he felt his sadness, something shifted. He realized how much he values quality connection with his family. He remembered fully (mentally, emotionally, bodily) how much joy, energy, and delight he experiences when he spends time with his children. He also remembered how much he had longed for this from his own father and hadn't gotten it. By moving through this process, being present to his judgments, feelings, and needs, Jim became clear about what to do. Most pressing for him was the need for intimacy with his wife and children. By dwelling in the beauty of this need, he prepared himself to say no to his parishioners without guilt and regret. And that is precisely what he did.

The next day, Jim met with two of the parents who had expressed concern about the decreased number of activities for the youth group. By staying connected to his need for intimacy, he was able to use honest expression to set a clear boundary, in this case, to say no to the request to organize more activities for youth group. In essence, he used OFNR: I have been reflecting on your disappointment over the decreased number of youth group activities. I made this change because I now have two children under five at home. When I work two or three nights a week, I don't have the kind of quality time with them that I really want. For this reason, it's important to me to keep the special youth group activities to once a month. At this point in time, I'm not willing to add the extra events that you requested. I'm wondering how you feel, hearing me say that.

Because Jim spent time in self-empathy, he was able to say no non-defensively, even compassionately. Though the details of the conversation are not included here, Jim was able then to empathize with these parents' disappointment in response to his decision. Most relevant to our current discussion, saying no actually enabled him to say yes to himself, to his wife, and to his children. As Rosenberg points out, whenever we say no in NVC, we are saying yes simultaneously.[4] We make choices, we say no, so that we can live according to our deepest values and meet the needs that are most pressing for us in any given moment. What this means practically is that every time we want to say no, we ask ourselves what we are saying yes to. Such a procedure gets us immediately in touch with the needs that we believe would be unmet if we were to say yes to the request. We also know that if we say yes with anything less than a glad heart, we will eventually feel resentful.

Failure to say no may be a symptom of over-functioning, a common relational pattern in anxious families and congregations. Anxiety, from the perspective of family systems theory, is a belief (often unconscious) that one is vulnerable, at risk, or threatened in some way. When our anxiety increases, we frequently focus on situations, events, and people outside of ourselves. We try to fix externals in order to relieve our internal upheaval. This fixing gets manifest in particular relational patterns, one of which is over-functioning.[5] Signs of over-functioning include: advice giving, doing things for others that they could do themselves, worrying about others constantly, believing that you are responsible for others, thinking you know what is best for others, talking more than listening, and having goals for others' lives. Conversely, signs of under-functioning include: asking for advice instead of thinking through things on your own, seeking help when help is not needed, listening more than talking, tending to become addicted to substances, and not setting goals, (or setting goals and not following through on them).[6]

In Jim's situation, both he and the parents were anxious. Jim unconsciously believed that he was at risk—that his relationships with the youth and their parents would be undermined and that their displeasure with him could negatively affect his job, a primary source of meaning and security in his life. The parents feared for their teenagers' well-being, spiritual connection, and integrity. Instead of identifying and connecting to their own needs, they scrambled to get the youth program and the youth minister to meet their needs. They were both over-functioning (trying to fix the youth program as a means of fixing their kids) and under-functioning (trying to get Jim to increase his youth program activities instead of processing their own feelings and needs). Jim over-functioned when he worried about the parents' opinions of him and when he failed to refuse their requests. He potentially changed the overall pattern of both over- and under-functioning when he finally said no.

From a family systems perspective, saying no compassionately is a concrete means of becoming more self-differentiated by acting with greater autonomy, openness, and equality. Self-differentiated people are not ruled by anxiety—theirs or others'. They do not complete themselves by fusing with other people or by taking responsibility for others' feelings and needs. They balance autonomy and connection. They communicate with clarity and invite mutuality. They are able to share personal beliefs, opinions, feelings, and needs without a paralyzing fear of rejection.[7] Rather than exacerbating anxiety by adopting relational postures such as over-functioning, they maintain a centered presence in crisis situations. They can make decisions on the basis of their cherished values. In contrast to people who cannot say no, self-differentiated people are more likely to be able to collaborate effectively with others on common tasks. Teamwork and team leadership depend on free and glad (rather than compulsory and guilt-ridden) participation.

Responding to Criticism

In spite of Jesus' exhortation to "judge not lest ye be judged" (Matt. 7:1) or "to take the log out of your own eye before trying to remove the splinter from another's eye" (Matt. 7:5), criticism is rather common in the church. The pastor's sermons, the soprano's solos, the secretary's work on the bulletin, the church council's decisions: none of these is immune from critique. When the criticism occurs behind closed doors it is a form of triangulation—two or more people talking about their annoyance with another person rather than addressing it with that person directly. When parishioners take the risk to address their concerns directly with the pastor, soprano, secretary, or church council members, they take a step toward honest expression. But without the skills of compassionate communication, they likely will express themselves in life-alienating ways.

When we are on the receiving end of such life-alienating honesty, we have four options for responding (as we have mentioned elsewhere): blaming self, blaming the other, self-empathy, and empathy. Most of us have been socialized to respond to criticism either by internalizing or externalizing it. If the former is our typical pattern, we doubt and judge ourselves. Criticism from the outside ignites our own, fierce inner critic. We "should" on ourselves: "I should have remembered to _____. I should have known this would happen. I shouldn't have said that." We may scramble to appease the other person, to demonstrate our competence, to somehow fix it so that everyone is happy again. If, on the other hand, externalizing is our typical pattern, we judge or dismiss the other person. We label her as a troublemaker, as resistant to change, as critical and judgmental, and ironically we become that which we hate. Perhaps we vacillate from self-blame to blaming the other and back again. Whether we lash in or lash out, we decrease the possibility for an authentic encounter. We reduce the chance for honest expression because we are disconnected from our needs and the other person's needs.

Compassionate communication provides two alternate responses to criticism that can lead toward assertive, empowering, authentic honesty. First, we can choose to empathize with ourselves. We go through the basic steps of self-empathy: noticing our judgments of ourselves; differentiating our self-evaluations from what we actually heard (making an observation); experiencing our feelings and identifying our unmet needs in this situation. Second, we can choose to empathize with the other person, attempting to hear their feelings and needs with an open heart. If on the way out of church a parishioner says, "I sure miss our old pastor. He was an incredible preacher. I hope you get to be that good someday," we might practice some emergency self-empathy. In the moment, we might tell ourselves, "That hurts. I'd really like more consideration and appreciation." Even a quick internal response such as this can keep us from sliding into self-deprecation and help us to hear what matters most to the one standing before us. We then might say, "I'm wondering if you're disappointed because you'd like more meaningful connection to God when you listen to a sermon. Is that what you're saying?" Even if our empathic guess is not quite accurate, our attempt to hear the other person's needs reframes the entire conversation. No longer is it about blaming self or other but rather about attempting to arrive at some sort of mutual understanding.

Persistence in hearing the other fully may lead to insight and compassion. Perhaps in response to our empathic guess, the parishioner says,

"No. I know God is here. I just miss Pastor Tom." If so, then we've learned that the content or style of our sermon is not what is triggering this person as much as it is Pastor Tom's absence. We might follow up by saying, "I can imagine that my preaching reminds you of Pastor Tom and how much you value him and would like to reconnect with him." Instead of judging either ourselves or the parishioner, now we feel compassion. We see the parishioner in his grief. By empathizing with him, we help him to connect to his deeper self. Responding to his criticism with open-heartedness potentially facilitates his self-understanding and provides a space for him to acknowledge a very real loss in his life.

In other instances, self-empathy and empathy can transform criticism into constructive feedback. When First Presbyterian Church changed the format of its Sunday morning services by adding contemplative prayer and silence, a number of long-time parishioners vehemently complained to one another behind closed doors for six months. Then during a congregational meeting, eight church members stood up and declared, "We can't stand the new worship service. We've lost our church. And we're not the only ones who are unhappy about this." Positively, this brought the criticism out into the open where the pastor and elders could respond to it constructively. Negatively, discontent had simmered under the surface long enough for the church leaders to feel shocked, dismayed, and hurt, because their needs for consideration, appreciation, and open communication were not being met. After practicing some self-empathy and receiving some empathy from each other, a group of the church leaders met with these congregants to attempt to hear them fully. They discovered that a number of congregants missed the traditional passing of the peace, the sharing of announcements in the middle of the service, and the collective presentation of prayer concerns by passing a microphone throughout the sanctuary. Most importantly, the church leaders identified an important need embedded in these concerns: a need for connection to the whole community of faith during the worship service. Now they could hear the criticism as constructive feedback. And they could do something about it! In consultation with the worship committee, the pastor and elders added new elements in the worship service aimed at fostering greater communal connection.

Not only do self-empathy and empathy transform criticism into compassion and constructive feedback, but they also pave the way for honest expression. Now we can openly share our own feelings and needs that have been triggered by hard-to-hear messages. We might say to the parishioner who is grieving the loss of his former pastor, "You know, when you said that you hoped I would be as good a preacher as Pastor Tom, I felt discouraged because I'd like to be seen and valued for who I am rather than being compared to someone else." To those who are longing for more communal connection in the worship services, we might say, "When eight people stood up at the congregational meeting and said, 'We can't stand the new worship service,' I felt shocked and dismayed because I want to have ongoing open communication in our church. I also felt disheartened because I want our worship services to contribute to your connection with God and each other. If I don't hear timely, concrete feedback about how you are experiencing the worship services, I can't plan them in a way that contributes to your needs. The next time you are upset by changes in the church, would you please come and talk to me right away?"

To summarize, responding to criticism is an NVC multiple skill set; it involves the three basic skill sets of empathy, self-empathy, and honest expression. Whenever we receive a hard-to-hear message, we can go through the following steps at a later time as way of connecting with our needs and the other's needs:

1. Write down specifically what was said to you (the observation).
2. Write down all the specific evaluations of yourself or the other person in response to hearing this message. Notice the energy and intensity of these judgments.
3. Notice your body's response to these evaluations. Do you tense your muscles, clench your teeth, or have a churning stomach?
4. Identify and experience your feelings. Avoid moving into detached analysis of your emotions.
5. Connect your feelings to your underlying needs. What do you really want in this situation? Take time to remember how you feel emotionally and physically when this need is met. In other words, focus on the presence rather than the absence of this need.
6. Now turn your attention to the person who spoke this hard-to-hear message. What do you imagine that she or he was feeling and needing when she or he spoke to you? Write down these empathic guesses.
7. Focus your attention on the other person's possible needs. Imagine what it might be like for him or her to have these needs be unmet.
8. Notice how your own thoughts and feelings toward this person shift. Notice if you are now connecting with your needs for compassion, consideration, respect, and open communication with this person.

9. Having empathized with yourself and the other, consider what requests you might make of yourself. What connecting requests might you make of the other person?
10. Now consider how you might move toward honest expression with this person. What would you say using the basic OFNR pattern?

Compassionate Anger

"Be angry but do not sin," says the writer of the book of Ephesians. "Do not let the sun go down on your anger" (Eph. 4:26). While some of us struggle with the "do not sin" part of this exhortation, others of us struggle to "be angry." We fail to own our anger. Whether it is because we have been on the receiving end of someone's life-alienating anger, because our culture has socialized us to "be nice," or because our congregations have not modeled how to express anger in healthy and faithful ways (or some combination of these), many of us have attached negative evaluations to anger. These include:

Anger is dangerous
Anger is risky
Anger hurts people
Anger is irrational
Anger is contagious and addictive
I must control my anger
Nice girls don't get mad
We're not the kind of people who lose our tempers

When we hold these kinds of unconscious beliefs, we suppress our anger and miss out on the opportunity to mine it for the treasures buried within. Denying, avoiding, or minimizing our anger disconnects us from its life-giving capacity. And usually the suppression of our anger through one of these defense mechanisms leaves us feeling empty, without zest or vitality. Why? Because, as Rosenberg writes, "all anger has a life-serving core."[8] When we suppress our anger, we lose the pathway to its life-serving core.

At the core of anger lies an unmet need, frequently a chronically unmet need or cluster of needs. If I am angry because one of my colleagues has been talking for fifteen minutes of our fifty-minute faculty meeting, it is likely because I need and value consideration, respect, and inclusion of all voices. But I may not have access to those needs when

I am caught in anger because surrounding these core need(s) is a set of life-alienating beliefs: "He shouldn't be so domineering! How can he write a book about listening and then utterly fail to give room for anyone else to speak? What an idiot! Somebody should know how to facilitate meetings in a more inclusive way!" These kinds of evaluations are fueling the anger. The more we think these thoughts, the angrier we become. As neuroscientific studies demonstrate, "The longer we ruminate about what has made us angry, the more 'good reasons' and self-justifications we can invent. Brooding fuels anger's flames."[9]

Sometimes we engage in collective brooding in response to repeated, systemic dynamics. We share our angry evaluations with others and they join our choir of judgment and condemnation. If I leave a committee meeting, huddle together with fellow, disconcerted colleagues, and rant about our other colleague's "bad behavior," I reinforce my disconnection from my needs. I also reinforce our collective judgment about this person. And I contribute to an us versus them mentality in my workplace by blaming a particular person for our frustration. To draw on family systems theory again, we scapegoat this person and we triangulate. Instead of taking responsibility for our own feelings and needs, we turn outward and blame someone else. Instead of acting in self-differentiated ways, we fuse together and form an alliance against the person(s) whom we have identified as the source of our problems. Like the over-functioning/under-functioning reciprocity, these two relational patterns, scapegoating and triangulating, are reactive responses that ironically exacerbate the very anxiety that we long to alleviate.[10]

In contrast to these patterns, compassionate communication teaches us to connect with our needs whenever we feel angry and then to express ourselves honestly—fully and passionately—with an inner sense of connection to those needs. In order to connect with the precious needs embedded with our anger, we begin by consciously recognizing that anger is a sign that we are alienated from our needs. Rosenberg writes, "Anger can be valuable if we use it as an alarm clock to wake us up—to realize that we have a need that isn't being met and that we are thinking in a way that makes it unlikely to be met."[11] If we accept this basic premise, then we can differentiate the stimulus from the cause of our anger. In the example above, the stimulus for my anger is the observation that my colleague has talked for fifteen minutes; the cause of my anger is my unmet needs for consideration, respect, and inclusion coupled with my judging and blaming.

Whenever we feel angry, we can stop, slow down, and breathe. We can notice the thoughts that are fueling our anger. We listen to our judging and blaming fully. Perhaps we vent to a trusted friend with the intention to uncover the needs buried within our life-alienating thinking. The key here is our intention as well as clarity about what we are asking of this friend. That is, we are not triangulating or scapegoating; rather we are giving voice to our judgments for the sake of greater self-connection and thus greater compassion for ourselves and the other person. Our friend gives us space to be heard fully in support of self-connection. In this venting or voicing of our judgments, we place our gaze on ourselves, specifically on our own judgments, evaluations, accusations, and demands, not on the stimulus. Frequently these judgments will be expressed with the word "should." For example, note the "shoulds" embedded in my anger toward my colleague: "He shouldn't be so domineering! He shouldn't write a book about listening and then utterly fail to give room for anyone else to speak! Somebody should know how to facilitate meetings in a more inclusive way!"

Once we have identified our "should" thinking, then we translate it into needs. The evaluation, "He shouldn't be so domineering," points to my needs for respect and consideration. My exclamation, "How can he write a book about listening and then utterly fail to give room for anyone else to speak?" points to my need for integrity. "What an idiot," suggests that integrity matters deeply to me. The intensity of my evaluation is directly related to how much I value integrity. If I were only mildly triggered, I likely would not resort to name-calling. Finally, saying "somebody should know how to facilitate meetings in a more inclusive way" points to my needs for order, competence, and support.

After we have identified our needs, then we connect to their fullness. We dwell in them and ponder how much we value those needs. We consider what those needs mean to us, what feelings they evoke in us, and what we experience bodily when we are connected to their life-giving quality. If we connect to the beauty of our needs, our anger will shift. For anger is a secondary emotion that usually masks hurt or fear. Instead of anger, now we may feel sadness because we realize how frequently these needs are unmet. Or we may feel peace and contentment because we are grounded in our most cherished values. In any case, we are no longer blaming the other person for our feelings.

Once we experience this shift, we are ready to express our transformed anger in the form of passionate commitment to our needs and values. No longer "shoulding" on ourselves or others, we can speak assertively and compassionately. To do this, we follow the OFNR pattern. For instance, to my colleague who was facilitating the meeting, I might say the following: "Karen, I noticed that Tom spoke for fifteen minutes during our fifty-minute meeting. I'm feeling exasperated because I value inclusion and consideration of each committee member. Would you be willing to begin our next meeting with a request that we each share our perspectives concisely so that all our voices can be heard?" Or I might choose to make a request within the meeting itself if I've been able to practice some emergency self-empathy and thus connect to my needs in that moment. I may say to the whole group: "I'm noticing that we only have twenty minutes left in our meeting and so far only two people have shared their perspectives on this topic. I'm feeling concerned because I want all of our voices to be included in our decision-making process. I'm wondering if those of us who have not yet spoken would be willing to take two minutes each to share our thoughts on this matter." These two examples point to the variety of ways that we might express ourselves honestly once we have transformed our anger into passionate connection to the fullness of our needs.

Transforming anger enhances our own self-connection, and the resulting honest expression supports a communal life characterized by mutual encounters of care. In contrast to triangulating or scapegoating, we honor others as persons made in the image of God when we choose to express our feelings, needs, and requests to them. In contrast to avoiding or cutting off communication with those who trigger us, NVC honesty helps us to live out our interdependence as fellow members of the body of Christ.

Speaking the Truth in Love

Saying no, expressing ourselves honestly in response to criticism, and transforming our anger into passionate expressions of our needs are all forms of speaking the truth in love. As the writer of Ephesians tells us, this sort of speech "builds up" the body of Christ. It empowers others to become who they are. When we speak the truth in love, we participate in the Spirit's work of reminding us that we are children of God, loved by God, and created in God's image.

Speaking the truth in love also contributes to the mutual integration and adaptation of the members of the church toward one another. Truthful and loving honesty helps the church to become more interdependent, that is, to become who it is—an integrated organism comprised of the most diverse parts. As we encounter one another in love—in mutual seeing, hearing, speaking, and assisting—the Spirit knits our lives together in

Christ. As Karl Barth writes, "Without this integration and mutual adaptation, there can be no reciprocal dependence and support. And without this the community will inevitably fall apart and collapse."[12] For mutual support, encouragement, and adaptation are essential characteristics of the body of Christ. They are the foundation for the church's capacity to carry out its mission in the world.

Members of the church "need to be brought together, to be constituted, established, and maintained as a common being—one people capable of unanimous action," writes Barth.[13] By speaking the truth in love, we encourage and even empower each other to live out both our common and our unique callings in life. Each of us has a common calling to serve others, to live in solidarity with those who are suffering, and to witness to God's grace in word and deed. And each of us has been given gifts of the Spirit—mercy, service, administration, teaching, and so forth—in order to carry out this calling in our congregations, neighborhoods, families, and workplaces. Our communication with one another, according to the writer of Ephesians, ought to strengthen our communal and personal capacities to live out our callings to their fullest.

Finally, speaking the truth in love flows from an attitude of humility and results in mutual forbearance. "Lead a life worthy of the calling to which you have been called, with all humility and gentleness, with patience, bearing with one another in love" (Eph. 4:1–2). We are called by God to recognize our own finitude and thus our fallibility. We cannot know the heart of another person; indeed knowing our own heart is difficult enough. We cannot fully discern truth, "for now we see in a mirror, dimly, but then we will see face to face. Now I know only in part; then I will know fully, even as I have been fully known" (1 Cor. 13:12). We cannot, therefore, claim without doubt that our perspective or opinion is right and others' are wrong; that we know God's will and others do not, especially when those others are faithful Christians who also are attempting to discern the ways of God. So speaking the truth in love is couched in a commitment to mutual forbearance, a willingness to persist in relationship with one another in spite of our differences, disagreements, and outright conflict. As the Presbyterian Church (U.S.A.) *Book of Order* says, "There are truths and forms with respect to which men of good characters and principles may differ. And in all these we think it the duty both of private Christians and societies to exercise mutual forbearance toward each other."[14]

Part 3

Advanced Skill Sets
in Compassionate Communication

Chapter 8

Blessed Are Those Who Mourn

The Path of Healing

Blessed are those who mourn for they will be comforted.

Matthew 5:4

Scripture teems with stories of women, men, and children who discover God's presence in the midst of their pain and perplexity. Yahweh is with Joseph, the son of Jacob—whose brothers sold him into slavery—whenever Joseph finds himself in the pit or in prison (Gen. 38–39). Elijah unexpectedly receives God's provision and guidance in the midst of his terror, exhaustion, loneliness, and despair (1 Kgs. 19). In and through Ruth, God accompanies Naomi in her bitter bereavement—the loss of her husband, sons, home, and socioeconomic well-being (Ruth 1). The apostle Paul testifies that he has experienced the resurrection power of Christ precisely in the context of his suffering, in the midst of persecution and in spite of that persistent thorn in his flesh (2 Cor. 12:7).

Scripture gives voice to the lament of those who feel God's absence more than God's presence in moments of suffering, crisis, and bewilderment. Job receives no comfort and rails at God. An unnamed psalmist laments over God's absence, blames God for his unending sorrow, and fails to find hope. Psalm 88 ends as it begins, in darkness: "I suffer your terrors; I am desperate. Your wrath has swept over me; your dread assaults destroy me. They surround me like a flood all day long; from all sides they close in on me. You have caused friend and neighbor to shun me; my companions are in darkness" (vv. 15–18). Echoing another lament psalm, Jesus cries out on the cross, "My God, my God, why have you forsaken me?" (Matt. 27:46). Even the incarnate Son of God experi-

136

ences utter God-abandonment, the kind that plunges him into nonbeing, chaos, and dread. "He descended into hell."[1]

On the cross, Jesus says, "It is finished" (John 19:30). Ever since his resurrection and ascension, the church has repeated these words again and again, trusting that through his finished work, God's children have been reconciled to God and each other. In his life, death, and resurrection Jesus has put death to death and made sin impotent. He has liberated the oppressed, healed the wounded, saved the sinner. But we do not yet experience this fully. Violence, abuse, and grief remain with us. Sometimes comfort is not only unattainable but also unimaginable. In these moments, the body of Christ—Christ's presence on earth in the power of the Spirit—weeps with those who weep. This is the church's vocation: to bear the burdens of those who feel defeated, to be compassionately present with the brokenhearted, and to wait prayerfully for the fullness of reconciliation.

Pastoral ministry encounters the grief-stricken with tenderness, compassion, understanding, and healing words and deeds. It also seeks to empower the people of God for compassionate care of one another and the world. But sometimes, leaders and members are at a loss when it comes to participating in the healing ministry of Christ. Sometimes grief is unabated; guilt and shame persist. Consider, for example, Martha, a long-time member and lay leader at Christ Community Church. She recently divorced her second husband after he had an affair with a coworker. On some days she could barely function. She struggled to get her kids ready for school and herself off to work. On other days her anger seeped out at inappropriate times. She lashed out verbally at friends, family, and her pastor. Her pain was palpable and her shame so intense that she refused to receive the Lord's Supper because, as she put it, she couldn't forgive her ex-husband. She considered herself unworthy of God's love and acceptance. At the same time she was angry with God. How could God have let this happen?

As a way of offering pastoral care, church leaders referred Martha to a professional counselor and continued to meet with her on a monthly basis. Friends from the church visited her frequently. They listened to her, prayed with her, and read Scripture together—especially those passages that would remind her of God as Comforter and Healer. They pointed her to lament psalms when she felt abandoned by God. They tried to assure her of God's prevenient grace and healing power, all to no avail. She was paralyzed by grief, guilt, and shame, unable to connect authentically with God, others, or even herself.

Mourning and Healing in NVC

Marshall Rosenberg teaches a process of mourning as a way of dealing with our guilt, grief, and shame. As in self-empathy, in mourning we fully identify and experience our unmet needs when we have failed to act according to our core values. NVC mourning "is an experience of regret, but regret that helps us learn from what we have done without blaming or hating ourselves."[2] The key is to identify *both* the needs that we were trying to meet by taking the actions we now regret *and* at the same time, the needs that were unmet by taking those actions. As Rosenberg writes, we "empathically hold both parts of ourselves—the self that regrets a past action and the self that took the action in the first place."[3] Noticing and valuing both sets of needs moves us out of self-judgment and into self-compassion. In Martha's case, for example, she might identify her deep disappointment with herself when she recalls her exasperated tone when speaking with her pastor. She would connect with the needs that she was trying to meet when she spoke in this manner—a longing for understanding, expression, and healing. She would also identify the needs that were unmet—her values of consideration, care, and kindness. Honoring all those needs might elicit grief, but this would be the kind of grief that liberates rather than binds.

Beauty for Ashes

NVC trainers Robert Gonzales and Susan Skye expand on Rosenberg's understanding of mourning through their emphasis on the beauty of needs. As described in chapter 2, the "beauty of needs" refers to the life-giving quality of every human need. When we are fully connected to this quality, we can celebrate all our needs even when we cannot find ways to meet them. We shift out of frustration, anger, or grief into a profound sense of gratitude, even for the longing itself. Their process of "transforming the pain of unmet needs to the beauty of needs," (also called the transforming pain process), is an advanced form of self-empathy that requires the capacity to connect to the fullness (or beauty) of our needs.[4] This multiple skill set thaws frozen grief and breaks up the fallow ground of guilt and shame. It comprises six phases or steps, each of which involves basic compassionate communication skills described in previous chapters. While presented sequentially here, these phases rarely proceed in a strict, linear fashion. In real life, we move in and out of them, back and forth. Sometimes we enter the final phase, glimpsing the beauty of our needs, only to be thrust back into an earlier phase. See illustration 8.1 for a diagram of how this works.

Illustration 8.1. The Cycle of Transforming Pain

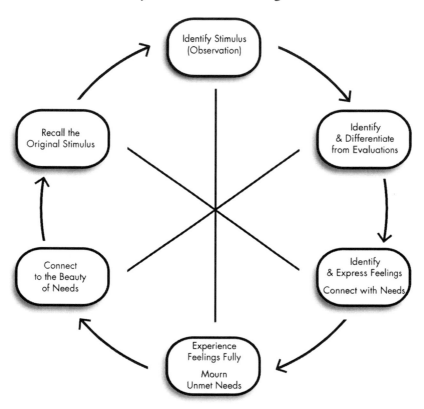

In the first step of the transforming pain process, we identify a stimulus that triggered a strong emotional reaction. In other words, we make an observation without an evaluation. In the second step, we bring to conscious awareness any life-alienating thinking related to this observation. We express all of our judgments and evaluations about ourselves, the other person(s), the situation, the world, or God. We express these emotion-laden thoughts not in a detached manner but in a fully embodied manner. Doing so enables us to connect with the potency of our judgments and evaluations. We speak them aloud and with energy. We give ourselves permission to vent or rant. Then we begin to differentiate ourselves from all these judgments. We consciously identify the judgments and evaluations as stories that we are telling ourselves. For each evaluation, we say aloud, "I'm telling myself that . . . ." When we have clearly differentiated these evaluations from the stimulus, we may notice a palpable shift in our bodies—for instance, the relaxation of tightened muscles or a decrease in our heart rate.

In the third step, we identify and express the feelings that are linked to our evaluations. Here we differentiate primary emotions (those surges of energy coursing through our bodies) into categorical emotions (distinct feeling words). Then we identify and name the needs embedded within each of the feelings. If new evaluations or judgments arise during this phase, we return to the previous phase: once again, we see each judgment as a story that we are telling ourselves.

In the fourth step, we experience our feelings fully. We enter into them. We surrender to them instead of suppressing them. We also relinquish our frantic attempts to find strategies to meet our needs and simply mourn the fact that they are unmet. To use the language of grief-work, we mourn our losses at this stage. In compassionate communication, our losses have to do with our unmet needs. We don't mourn what happened (the stimulus); instead we connect fully with the needs that were unmet in the situation and mourn their absence. In this way, we avoid re-traumatizing ourselves, which can occur when we immerse ourselves in the details of an event that has stimulated significant pain.[5] We stay in this phase until we experience a palpable sense of relief. This doesn't mean that we won't need to go through this process ever again. It does mean that we allow our thoughts and feelings to run their course, so to speak, in the moment.

In the fifth phase, we shift our attention from the pain of those unmet needs to the beauty of those needs. Rather than focusing on the need's absence (such as the absence of trust), we connect to its living energy, to use Gonzales's and Skye's language. We move from a deficiency mindset (my need for trust is not being met) to an abundance mindset (my need for trust is a precious quality that contributes to the flourishing of human life). (Or, "Trust in my intimate relationships is a quality that I cherish.") We avoid constructing strategies to meet our unmet needs at this point. Rather we bring into awareness just how much we value these needs. From a Christian perspective, we might notice how these needs point to those qualities of life that are fully ours in the kingdom of God. In God's kingdom, no one is lonely or without love. Each person finds a place of glad belonging in the community. If we still struggle to connect with the fullness of the needs that we have identified, we might recall a time in our life when they were met. As we remember how we felt when those needs were met, we seek to experience them bodily in the present. We bask in our relaxation, calm, happiness, contentment, or gratitude.

In the sixth and final phase, we bring the original stimulus back into our awareness while staying connected to the fullness of the need (its meaning, the feelings it evokes, and the accompanying bodily sense). We notice and speak any new thoughts about the stimulus. If judgments and evaluations reemerge, then we return to step two. Often, however, the evaluations and judgments have dissipated at least in part. We become aware of new feelings and needs. After identifying them, we can choose to construct a strategy to meet these needs. At this point we might make a request of ourselves or others. Now our requests emerge not from a place of judgment or suffering, but rather from centeredness in our identity. Having mourned our unmet need, we now are aware of how much this quality of life belongs to us. In some sense, it cannot ultimately be taken away. No longer desperate for the other to give us what we think we must have to live, we trust that we can get this need met elsewhere. From the standpoint of NVC, we connect with the fundamental goodness of life. From a Christian perspective, we rest in God's providential goodness and grace, which the Spirit showers on us in the here-and-now. Mourning leads to healing as we rest in the fullness and splendor of God's love.

Empathetic Coaching

We can mourn our unmet needs as an advanced form of self-empathy or with the empathetic coaching of another. Whenever grief overwhelms us, we are more likely to experience healing when a caring other journeys alongside us. To illustrate this coaching, we'll return to Martha's situation. How might a pastor or fellow church member guide Martha through the transforming pain process?

Identify the stimulus. First, the pastor would ask Martha to identify the stimulus. She would coach Martha to separate out her evaluations in order to make a clear observation. Because Martha's situation is complex, there may be many stimuli. She would choose one that seems most alive for her. Martha might say, "My husband told me that he was having a sexual relationship with one of his coworkers."

Identify and differentiate from evaluations. Here the pastor would encourage Martha to voice her judgments freely. (Obviously, a relationship of trust between Martha and the pastor would be one of the prerequisites for engaging this process.) Martha might express a whole series of evaluations of her husband and his coworker: "My husband's a lousy scumbag.

That woman is a slut. They deserve each other. How could he do this to me? How could he do this to our children? He's a despicable human being. What about our marriage vows? What an unfaithful, disloyal hypocrite! She's a home-wrecker. I hope they both die an early, painful death!" She might express judgments about herself: "What did I do wrong? If only I was more attractive. I should have seen this coming. I should have spent more time alone with him. How much more betrayal can I go through? I can't handle this." Or she might express judgments about God: "Why is God punishing me? How could God let this happen? Doesn't God care that my children won't grow up with their father and mother in the same house?" She might express evaluations about the situation or life in general: "Life isn't supposed to be this way. It's not supposed to be so hard. I guess some people get to be happy and others don't."

The pastor would encourage Martha to speak these evaluations with passion until her energy was spent. Since many of these statements are not direct judgments, the pastor would facilitate the process of differentiation by helping Martha translate her comments into stark evaluations. "What did I do wrong?" might be translated into "Somehow this is my fault." "If only I was more attractive" might be translated into "I should be more attractive." "What about our marriage vows?" might be translated into "He should have kept our marriage vows." Unlike the two previous evaluations, the pastor might actually agree with this last evaluation. But she wouldn't say so at this point. All evaluations and judgments need to be mined for the core values that are embedded within them, including those that are held precious by the community of faith. Thus "he should have kept our marriage vows" reveals Martha's core value of fidelity in marriage, or of following through on one's promises and commitments. The pastor wants to assist Martha to find her own core values. Expressing her agreement with Martha's evaluation would thwart the process because it would shift attention to the pastor and away from Martha's healing process.[6]

After this translation, the pastor would coach Martha to say, "I'm telling myself that my husband should have kept our marriage vows," and "I'm telling myself that somehow this is my fault. I'm telling myself that life isn't fair." In order to differentiate from these thoughts, Martha might repeat these statements multiple times. She would repeat the phrase, "I'm telling myself that my husband is a scumbag," until the energy embedded within this statement dissipates.

Identify and express feelings; connect with needs. As Martha differentiates herself from these thought patterns, she might feel anger, sorrow, confusion, or despair. The pastor would listen for, and help Martha to identify, the needs embedded within these feelings. Martha might feel sorrowful, because she needs trust, reliability, and companionship. She might feel confused because she needs wisdom about how best to support her children. She might feel despair because she needs hope for a meaningful and fulfilling future.

Experience feelings fully; mourn the unmet needs. As Martha identifies her unmet needs, she likely will move naturally into mourning. She might feel profound sadness when she realizes that her longings for trust and reliability are unfulfilled and when she sees that her need for intimacy with a life-partner is unmet. At this point, Martha would simply experience and express her feelings fully. The pastor would be completely present throughout this part of the transforming pain process, attentively listening in silence while holding the moment as sacred.

Connect to the beauty of the needs. Next, the pastor would coach Martha to focus her attention on the needs for trust, reliability, and intimacy. She might encourage Martha to think of a time in her life when these needs were met. Martha might think about a close friend with whom these needs are fulfilled. She would recall how she feels physically when these needs are met. Perhaps feelings of ease, peace, and happiness would surface. Martha would breathe deeply and stay connected to those memories and their present effects. The pastor would watch Martha, noting any changes in her posture, breathing, and facial expressions. A relaxed posture, slower breathing rate, or a smile would indicate that Martha is connecting with the beauty of trust, reliability, and intimacy.

Recall the original stimulus. In this phase, the pastor would encourage Martha to stay connected to the beauty of her needs and recall the original stimulus, asking: "What comes to mind now when you remember your husband telling you that he had an affair with a coworker?" Hopefully, by now Martha would have more empathy for herself. Perhaps she would feel proud of herself for placing such a high value on trust and loyalty. Maybe she would think, "With God's help, I can get through this." If she identified a need for support in the midst of mourning, she might now think of a specific request she can make of another person to give her the support she needs in the next few weeks. She might even feel empathy for her husband and wonder, "What unmet needs propelled him to choose to have an affair?" If this occurred, she would not be blaming herself but rather expressing genuine curiosity about his experience.

The process of transforming the pain of unmet needs to the beauty of needs is not a one-time fix. We might engage this practice many times, even returning to it years later whenever our grief rises to the surface. When empathetically coaching someone, we may not get through the entire process in one pastoral care session. For this reason, it is important to clearly communicate expectations whenever we coach someone else through it. There is no right timeframe for moving through this process. The phase of mourning could last an entire pastoral care session. Some people could decide that they simply do not want to continue the next steps. If so, then we can return to the process at a later time, starting with whatever is alive in the other person at that time. All the while we would be trusting the work of God's Spirit in this person's life. Likewise, transforming pain does not mean the elimination of pain once and for all. While we may long for closure—to be finished dealing with our suffering and sorrow—some losses remain open in this life. Chronically unmet needs might stimulate pain at unexpected moments. Thus we continue on this path of healing.

In summation, moving through the process of transforming the pain of unmet needs to the beauty of needs yields greater self-awareness and self-care. This kind of mourning frees us from our own undifferentiated pain by, paradoxically, allowing us to fully experience our feelings and needs. It opens us up to the comfort that has its source in God. Though we might need to walk this path of healing many times, our ashes of sorrow can be transformed, again and again, into joyous celebration: "You have turned my mourning into dancing; you have taken off my sackcloth and clothed me with joy" (Ps. 30:11).

Liberation from Shame

Like unresolved grief, shame blocks life-giving connection to God, self, and others. Shame is a deep-seated belief that one's self is fundamentally flawed, bad, inadequate, and unlovable. In contrast, guilt is the belief that one's behavior is wrong. Whereas guilt causes one to cry, "I have done wrong," shame causes one to cry, "I am wrong." Shame is "experienced as a deep abiding sense of being defective, never quite good enough as a person."[7] People who are prone to shame fall prey to self-loathing. Even the slightest of actions, words, gestures, or one's own thoughts can trigger a barrage of self-judgment.[8] The accompanying sense of worthlessness and humiliation of shame drives them into hiding from others and themselves.

The transforming pain process can be adapted in order to free us from the sticky cocoon of shame. In this adaptation, we seek to identify the core beliefs (what Skye and Gonzales call "core unconscious beliefs") that alienate us from God, self, and others. These deeply ingrained patterns of thought mediate our experience of the world and distort our own self-image. Because they emerge from early childhood experiences of deficiency and deprivation, they profoundly (though usually unconsciously) shape our identity. They include beliefs like, "I'm not good enough. I'm flawed. I'm inadequate. I'm unworthy. I'm unlovable. I'm undesirable."[9]

Because they function at the unconscious level, core beliefs are not easily accessed. However, they manifest themselves on the conscious level in clusters of related evaluations and judgments. If we unravel the cluster of related beliefs, we can discover the core belief. We know when we have identified a core belief by our bodily reaction. We might sigh, slump down into our chair, or exclaim, "Aha. That's it." This recognition is intuitive and embodied. It is not a product of detached analysis. As a means of checking if we actually have identified the *core* belief, we can ask ourselves, "Is there anything that seems deeper than this belief? Is there anything more devastating to me than this?"

To return to our case study, Martha would explore her myriad self-judgments in order to identify a core belief. It might go like this: "I'm telling myself that I'm unattractive. I'm telling myself that it's my fault that my husband had an affair. I'm telling myself that there's something wrong with me. I'm telling myself that I should have prevented this. I'm telling myself that I wasn't a good enough wife. That's it. That's exactly it. I'm not good enough. I've believed that my whole life. I've believed that I'm not good enough: not good enough to keep my parents from divorcing; not good enough to make my first marriage work; and now not good enough to keep my second husband."

Once we have identified a core belief, we notice its profound physical and emotional impact on our bodies and minds. We learn to identify the needs that are unmet when we live with this self-narrative. Martha might notice, "When I tell myself that I'm not good enough, I feel like I want to curl up in a ball and hide from the world. I can feel my shoulders and head pull inward. I feel so vulnerable. I feel embarrassed. I feel horribly ashamed. I want to like myself. I need acceptance, especially self-acceptance." This insight would lead to mourning. Martha might say, "I feel so sad when I think about how I have treated myself so harshly. When I think about how I blamed myself for my parents' divorce and for my two divorces, I feel heart-broken." As we recognize our unmet needs, we might feel sadness, sorrow, and grief. In this process, our self-flagellation turns to compassion toward ourselves as we acknowledge decades of pain.

Next we focus not on the absence but the presence of the need. We dwell in the beauty of the need. Thus Martha might remember a time when her needs for self-confidence and self-acceptance were fulfilled. As she thinks about her friendships over the years, she feels proud of her ability to be there for others and to give and receive love. In that moment of recollection, she reexperiences the centeredness, calmness, and empowerment related to these needs. She may take some time then to experience in a full emotional sense how wonderful it feels genuinely to like herself.

Finally, we bring the core belief into awareness while staying connected to the beauty of our needs. There may be a number of results: (1) the belief seems completely untrue; (2) the belief seems less potent, or its energy has diminished; or (3) self-judgments get triggered again. If the latter occurs, then we empathize with those evaluations until we reconnect with the beauty of the need. For example, Martha now brings her shame-based belief—"I'm not good enough"—into full awareness. Perhaps she sighs, "Oh, it's not true at all. I am acceptable. I am good enough. I am accepted and beloved in spite of my shortcomings or faults. I don't have to prove myself to anyone." When the core belief gets triggered in the future, she can access the beauty of her needs more readily by recalling this experience of finding a deep sense of self-acceptance.

To summarize, the process of transforming the pain of unmet needs into the beauty of needs provides one means of healing our grief and shame. Whether we are stuck in self-condemnation or seemingly impassable sorrow, it enables us to mourn the unmet needs that result from our choices or the choices of others. Through such mourning we connect with the intrinsic beauty of our needs. Present to the qualities of life that sustain all of humanity, our hearts open wide so that we can regard ourselves and others with compassion. We unravel tangled thoughts that plunge us into the pit of shame. We begin to develop new life-giving thought patterns that help us to thrive. While this practice is not a one-time fix for sorrow or shame, it is a practical pathway for living our most cherished values.

Transforming Pain, Building New Neural Pathways

Since its inception, modern psychology has posited mourning as central to healing. In his essay, "Mourning and Melancholia," Sigmund Freud argued for the necessity of grief-work in response to the death of loved ones or to the loss of cherished ideals.[10] Since Freud, theorists have specified stages, phases, and tasks of grief-work.[11] Some have emphasized the role of ritual. Others have focused on grief-work for those who experience childhood trauma and deprivation.[12] Most recently, developments in neuroscience have been applied to trauma and grief.[13] These latest insights and therapeutic practices resonate with the process of transforming the pain of unmet needs into the beauty of needs. In fact, interpersonal neurobiology illuminates how and why this advanced form of self-empathy actually heals the mind.

As described in chapter 3, emotions exist at various levels: primary emotions (a flow of energy and information through our brain); categorical emotions (naming those surges of energy as discrete feelings, such as sadness, anger, fear); and states of mind (patterns of brain activity that shape our "feelings, thoughts, memories, attitudes, beliefs, and desires").[14] States of mind profoundly influence our actions. They can last for a few moments or longer periods. They can become intractable and highly dysfunctional, as in the case of depression, anxiety, and shame.

States of mind can be altered, even when deeply ingrained, by regulating our emotions. Emotional regulation involves modulating the flow of both energy and information throughout the brain. Many forms of therapy focus primarily (if not exclusively) on the information aspect of emotion. They seek to change the interpretation and meaning of emotion through dialogue with a therapist. Interpersonal neurobiology demonstrates the need to alter the energy flow as well.

Altering energy flow is particularly important when we experience emotional flooding or hijacking. In emotional flooding, the brain is overwhelmed with intense arousal. Our ability to think and act becomes impaired. It may seem as though we are out of control.[15] Emotional flooding often occurs in response to repeated loss or trauma. Grief creates strong synaptic connections and easily accessed neural pathways. If a person experiences loss or trauma in early childhood when the brain is more plastic, then these neural pathways, which form a particular state of mind, are likely to be triggered by events later in life. In such instances, "we interpret the present situation, unconsciously, through the lens of the past."[16] Our case study exemplifies this. Martha's state of mind consists of intense anger directed at herself, a sense of being out of control, and an overall sense that her life has shattered. She is experiencing emotional flooding. Her state of mind "has pushed beyond [her] window of tolerance."[17] This state of mind has been triggered because her current situation is analogous to her interpretation of a painful childhood experience (she blamed herself for her parents' divorce) and the repetition of this loss (her previous divorce). She has experienced repeated activation of this state of mind throughout her life. An overwhelming volume of stress hormones surges through her brain in this state of mind, impairing her ability to think and act as she would normally. Modulating the flow of energy and information in Martha's brain would change her state of mind and thus restore her equilibrium. It also would construct new neural pathways to prevent flooding in the future.

Siegel's template for emotional regulation provides a map for restoring equilibrium to those who experience this kind of emotional hijacking. He stresses the importance of bringing both aspects of emotion—the energy and information—into conscious awareness. This awareness is the condition for making new choices in response to events that trigger ingrained grief, anxiety, shame, and so forth. In counseling, a trusted other sees and empathizes with our pain and vulnerability. We experience "feeling felt" when the counselor's state of mind aligns with ours. We experience affect attunement and emotional resonance, which strengthens our capacity to explore analogous painful or shame-inducing stimuli from our past.[18] As Siegel points out, the problematic state of mind—overwhelming anxiety, shame, dread, and so forth—will get triggered in therapy. In response, our counselor can utilize guided imagery, meditation, relaxation techniques, and internal override discussions to help build new neural pathways.[19]

The practice of transforming the pain of unmet needs into the beauty of needs incorporates these very elements of emotional regulation. At the most fundamental level, the transforming pain process brings our emotions into conscious awareness in the presence of a caring other. Second, when this other person empathizes with our feelings and needs, we "feel felt." This supports our capacity to mourn. Third, when we differentiate from our evaluations or shame-based beliefs, we are able to change our interpretation (or appraisal) of a debilitating experience. Fourth, this process alters the energy flow of our feeling state. When we connect to the beauty of our needs, we engage memory and imagery—the right hemisphere of the brain—in order to alter the energy flow of intractable grief, anxiety, or shame. Dwelling in the beauty of our needs is a kind of meditation that allows us to experience a flow of energy that opens our hearts and minds to new ways of being in relationship to others and ourselves. This energy surges with creativity and aliveness.

Most significantly, the culmination of the transforming pain process is the emergence of a new state of mind, such as peace, contentment, and trust. In this state of mind, we may be able to recall the previously debilitating stimulus ("My husband said he was having an affair with his coworker") or the shame-based belief ("I'm not good enough") without emotional flooding. New neural pathways have been created; pathways that we can access in the future. When we cultivate our capacity to connect with the beauty of our needs, we strengthen these neural pathways. Repeatedly tapping into this neural pathway by connecting to the beauty of needs reinforces the new state of mind so that it becomes more likely to persist for longer periods of time.

In summary, we have drawn on interpersonal neurobiology to further explain mourning and healing in compassionate communication. From our perspective, attunement and empathy are distinct though related processes that contribute to healing from unresolved grief and lingering shame. Attunement involves an alignment of the listener's and speaker's states of mind. This occurs naturally in all attachment relations and is evident, for instance, when the listener's posture and tone of voice mirror that of the speaker.[20] Rosenberg's definition of empathy does not quite account for this kind of attunement and lasting emotional resonance between speaker and listener. Empathy, according to Rosenberg, requires intense focus on the other person's experience; it requires us to bracket any of our own interpretations and feelings about the other. While this definition can help us to avoid projecting our feelings and interpretations onto another person, it does not capture all that occurs when we are fully present to another person. Our observation of experienced NVC trainers suggests that affect attunement and emotional resonance do occur when guiding someone through the transforming pain process. We suspect that the combination of attunement with primary emotions and empathy with categorical emotions in the context of one's deepest pain significantly enhance our capacity to connect to the beauty of needs and thus experience healing.

Mourning and Healing in the Midst of Church Conflict

Many dimensions of pastoral ministry call for the kind of mourning described above. Not only individuals like Martha but also entire congregations and denominations need to mourn their unmet needs. As mentioned in the introduction of this book, congregations today live in a maelstrom of conflict, crisis, and change. Conflict and grief live in close proximity to each other. Whenever conflict remains unresolved, grief follows. Grief is the natural response to loss, and entrenched conflict entails loss. When factions decide to leave a denomination after decades of being at odds with institutional structures, when demographic change leads to dwindling numbers and conflict about the congregation's identity and mission, when congregational leaders cannot see past their differences, when the church loses its cultural capital—its voice and influence—and is perceived as irrelevant: in all these situations, church leaders and members experience significant loss.

Responding to these conflicts and changes requires resilient, courageous, and compassionate leadership. It frequently involves the reconstruction of one's congregational identity and mission—radically new ways of being the people of God in particular locales. As Ronald Heifetz and Marty Linsky point out, leaders confront people with loss when they encourage change, particularly in response to adaptive challenges.[21] Adaptive challenges are those for which there are no known answers. Adaptive challenges require "experiments, new discoveries, and adjustments from numerous places in the organization or community" along with "changing attitudes, values, and behaviors."[22]

Just as change can trigger loss, so unresolved grief can complicate and escalate conflict. Experts in conflict resolution put it this way: "An inability to manage one's grief results in a greater inability to manage conflict."[23] Why? Because denial, anger, depression (and the many other dimensions of grief) will resurface with intensity if they have been ignored and suppressed. Living with chronically unmet needs for empathy and mourning inhibits our capacity to hear others, to enter into (let alone stay in) dialogue with them, and to lead congregations through conflict and change. As professors of peace studies and conflict resolution claim, "Without acknowledging grief, by denying its existence, the party [person or group in a conflicted relationship] attempts to cope with grief by deferring the pain and suffering associated with the process of grieving. Negotiation efforts, however, will be severely hampered by this deferment."[24]

For this reason, compassionate leaders ought to do their own griefwork.[25] Without attending to their own losses by mourning their unmet needs and connecting to the presence of these needs in Christ, leaders will falter in their pastoral and congregational care. As pastoral theologian Jaco Hamman puts it, "Facilitating conversation around the losses the congregation experienced is nearly impossible if you cannot converse about your own losses."[26] He goes on to say: "As an adaptive challenge, loss does not require authorities who have the drive to fix, but rather it seeks empowered people who can learn new ways of grieving and being together."[27] Compassionate, caring leaders support persons, families, and entire communities of faith in walking the path of mourning and healing. They trust, on the basis of God's work of healing in their own lives, that walking toward pain and perplexity—rather than seeking to escape from it or spiritualize it away with Christian platitudes—is the path to healing.

In other words, compassionate leaders are wounded healers. As Henri Nouwen has taught us, "In our woundedness, we can become a source of life for others."[28] The minister or leader as wounded healer examines his pain; invites God into the dark, shameful, and sorrowful places in his life; surrenders any images of the put-together minister; and walks the path from mourning to healing again and again. Wounded healers face their sorrow and shame not to glorify them but to make peace with them. There are times when this means that we seek peace in the midst of unmet needs. We live with longing and hope and without bitterness or despair.

Mourning and Healing . . . in God's Time

We witness to a God who has saved us from sin and healed our suffering. We trust that in Jesus Christ we have been reconciled to God and each other. Yet frequently we do not experience this in the here and now because our reconciliation to God and each other is as an event that exists in three modes or tenses.[29] Our reconciliation (our justification and sanctification) is something that has happened already (in the past), that will happen (in the future), and that continues to happen (in the present).

- *Our reconciliation to God and each other has already happened.* God has reconciled us not only to God but also to one another in the death and resurrection of Jesus Christ (Rom. 5:18; Col. 1:20). The kingdom of God has come to earth. As Jesus said, "It is finished!" (John 19:30). We have been incorporated into Christ's death on the cross. We are therefore at peace with God and each other.
- *Our reconciliation to God and each other will happen.* Reconciliation is not yet fully manifest in our lives. All of creation yearns for the full consummation of the kingdom of God, the day when "God will be all in all" (Rom. 8:22–25). In the time between Jesus' resurrection and the glorification of all God's children, the church prays for the coming of God's kingdom and participates in God's ongoing work of reconciliation in the world.
- *Our reconciliation with God and each other happens in the here and now.* This is not something that we orchestrate of our own will, but something that we participate in. What has happened in the past and will happen in the future breaks into the present. By the power

of the Holy Spirit, we are freed for lives of compassion, for lives of true encounter marked by mutual seeing, hearing, speaking, and assisting one another with gladness.

Trusting in the promise of God to bring about this universal reign of peace does not fully answer how to deal with our ongoing sin and suffering. We have been freed from sin, yet like the apostle Paul, we find ourselves not doing the good that we want but rather doing that which we despise (Rom. 7:15). We have been granted peace with God, yet anguish of heart and mind blinds our vision and squelches our hope. Like Martha, we sometimes get mired in grief and shame, unable to receive God's grace.

The New Testament teaches us to understand the irruption of sin and suffering in our lives as a participation in the cross of Jesus Christ. In the time between the times, after the resurrection and ascension of Christ yet before the full consummation when Christ will be all in all, we live the way of the cross. We interpret our sin as a contradiction of our identity in Christ. We remember that in our baptism we were united to Christ's death and resurrection (Rom. 6). Our old self, our sin, has been crucified and buried with Christ. We belong to God. Our true self is motivated by life together in the kingdom of God, by the gospel of peace, by the compassion of Christ. We trust that Christ suffers with us and for us. Rather than avoiding, denying, or minimizing our pain, we live with our woundedness. As Andrew Purves puts it, "In our suffering and dying we participate in [Christ's] Lordship over death and so his life and its power are at work within us. We do not suffer unto ourselves. Rather, the Christian's sufferings are now seen to have become Christ's sufferings. Understood now as suffering in Christ, our suffering announces the promise of life."[30]

If interpreted within the context of reconciliation set forth in the New Testament, the transforming pain process can assist us in living the way of the cross. It can become a concrete practice that helps us witness to the life and death of Jesus Christ. When incorporated into our faith, this multiple skill set in compassionate communication becomes a means through which we are reminded of our fullness of life in the kingdom of God and connected to our true identity as members of Christ's body. Again, look at Martha's experience. She could not forgive her husband and so she could not imagine that God could forgive her.[31] A barrage of self-incriminating thoughts reinforced her shame. These thoughts were louder and more persistent than any words of assurance from her pastor, friends, or the Bible itself. Her state of mind, the flood of emotion, and the tangled web of evaluations blocked her connection to her true identity in Christ. While these thoughts were hers, they did not come from her true self.

In the transforming pain process, she began to disentangle these thoughts from her true self. Identifying her evaluations and differentiating herself from them was a process of renewing her mind in which she sought to discern God's will for her life: "Do not be conformed to this world, but be transformed by the renewing of your minds so that you might be able to discern what is the will of God—what is good, acceptable and perfect" (Rom. 12:2). Having differentiated from this self-condemnation, Martha was able to feel the pain and disappointment associated with her unmet needs for care, consideration, and forgiveness in response to her loved ones. She mourned her myriad losses. At this point her consciousness shifted, actually freeing her to confess her dependence on God's grace.

Martha also experienced the absence of trust, intimacy, and companionship as significant loss. She surrendered to the accompanying sorrow and expressed her anguish authentically. She cried out to God in lament; she let her tears flow in the presence of a long-suffering God, even as the apostle Paul repeatedly cried out for healing and deliverance from his "thorn in the flesh" (2 Cor. 12:7b–10). Martha's connection to the beauty of these needs was one way she could meaningfully connect with the promises of Christ, and with an eschatological vision that yields faith, hope, and love. Through this renewal of her mind, the remembrance of her husband's confession no longer elicited crippling grief and shame.

When we practice transforming the pain of unmet needs into the beauty of needs, our hearts are broken wide open to the pain and joy in the world. Herein lies the paradox of both mourning and the way of the cross: we are fully alive when present to our deepest pain. Healing and wholeness come through mourning.[32] We experience koinonia—union and communion with God and each other—when we bear one another's burdens and accompany one another in our perplexity and pain. We become compassionate leaders, participating in God's ongoing ministry of healing and care in the world. As Andrew Purves writes, "it is precisely our woundedness, when it has been uncovered and accepted for what it is, which allows us to be ministers, and which in particular makes compassion possible for us."[33] When we incorporate these practices into the life of the church, it "becomes increasingly in practice the compassionate presence of its compassionate Lord."[34] Together we become truly human; we become the broken Body of Christ, daily dying and rising with Christ and thereby witnessing to the coming kingdom of God.

Chapter 9

Be of the Same Mind

Staying in Dialogue

If then there is any encouragement in Christ, any consolation from love, any sharing in the Spirit, any compassion and sympathy, make my joy complete: be of the same mind, having the same love, being in full accord and of one mind. Do nothing from selfish ambition or conceit, but in humility regard others as better than yourselves. Let each of you look not to your own interests, but to the interests of others.

Philippians 2:1–4

Michelle and Diane had been serving the same congregation for over fifteen years. As pastor and Christian education director, they had weathered the storms of clergy sexual misconduct (perpetrated by the previous pastor), a near-split of the church, and the comings and goings of other staff members. They were passionately committed to their congregants, young and old alike. Each worked more than sixty hours per week. If there was a special event, Michelle and Diane were there. If congregants were hospitalized, Michelle and Diane visited them. They led small groups, adult education series, weekly youth and children's services. Their practices of hospitality created a sense of welcome and belonging for church members.

On the surface, the two women seemed to work effectively together in leading the church and caring for its members. They co-coordinated special services and educational events during Advent and Lent, and they competently completed the tasks associated with their positions. Yet those who served with Michelle or Diane on committees or the church council quickly sensed the tension between them. Their rela-

154

tionship was strained by unresolved hurt. Fear and mistrust lurked underneath a thin veneer of collegiality and cooperation.

Michelle and Diane suppressed their feelings and needs by adopting a relational posture of détente. They stayed in their own "territory" as much as possible. Their differing positions in the church structure enabled them to do this without drawing attention to their strained relationship. Michelle did not interfere with educational programming and Diane did not participate in church council meetings. They didn't give each other feedback or share ideas about future events unless necessary. They carefully avoided inciting outright conflict with each other. Diane had long ago chosen silence instead of expressing her dissatisfaction to Michelle, yet her frustration leaked out in off-hand comments to others. Sometimes she unwittingly sided with those who were in conflict with Michelle. They griped to Diane about the pastor's so-called passive-aggressive communication, and she consoled them. She sympathized with them, for she, too, was angry with Michelle. Conversely, Michelle was convinced that Diane regularly undermined her pastoral authority. She expected respect and received none, or so she thought. She noticed that aggrieved staff, congregants, and elders often found their way to Diane's office. She tried to circumvent this triangulation by leading a staff retreat on conflict resolution. She preached on Matthew 18:15—"If another member of the church sins against you, go and point out the fault when the two of you are alone. If the member listens to you, you have regained that one"—and she warned staff about transgressing healthy boundaries in communicating with congregants. But she never directly addressed any of this with Diane.

Michelle and Diane felt considerable regret when they reflected on the impasse between them. Each longed for trust, harmony, and greater ease in their common work. Each wanted mutual understanding. However, neither believed that it was possible, for neither had the skill to communicate in a way that would move them toward a true encounter of mutual seeing, hearing and speaking, all with gladness.

For persons like Michelle and Diane—indeed for all of us—the NVC practice of staying in the dialogue (or authentic dialogue) provides a concrete means for connecting with others in the midst of disagreement and misunderstanding. It helps us to sustain empathy and honesty in an ongoing dialogue. It moves us out of patterns of distance into encounter, out of blame into understanding and acceptance. It encourages persistence in conversation when we are tempted to give up or give in.

Authentic Dialogue in Compassionate Communication

Authentic dialogue is a multiple skill set in compassionate communication that builds on and requires facility in honest expression, empathy, and self-empathy. Like all of NVC, the primary goal of authentic dialogue is connection. The goal is not to change the other person, the church, or ourselves. Authentic dialogue does not aim for a predetermined outcome. In fact, authentic dialogue depends on a willingness to relinquish attachment to outcomes. We are attached to an outcome whenever we cling to preconceived ideas of how a conflict ought to be resolved. Even if we believe that a particular strategy will meet our needs or the other's needs, doggedly holding onto it will block our capacity to be fully open to the other person. It likely will thwart the emergence of new, creative ways of thinking and relating. Thus if Michelle and Diane were to enter into authentic dialogue, they would set aside any agendas for their conversation. Michelle would surrender any demands for respect, and Diane would surrender any demands for inclusion in decision-making processes. Their sole intention would be connection. They would aim to be present to one another and to themselves.

Preparing for the Dialogue

Staying in dialogue requires a single-minded and open-hearted intention to connect to the feelings and needs of the other person while staying connected to our own. We shift our attention from strategies to needs. As Rosenberg writes, "To practice this process of conflict resolution, we must completely abandon the goal *of getting people to do what we want.* Instead, we focus on creating the conditions whereby *everyone's needs will be met.*"[1] In authentic dialogue, we value each person's needs. We acknowledge and honor those needs before we consider strategies to meet them. We connect with those needs as qualities that contribute to the flourishing of human life.

For this reason, cultivating and connecting to the beauty of one's own needs is a precursor to entering into authentic dialogue. It is important to identify the needs that have been stimulated in relation to the person(s) with whom we want to dialogue. If we are not connected to the full value of our own needs, we will speak out of the pain of our unmet needs. We may appear demanding, desperate, or urgent, all of which tend to foster defensiveness and resistance rather than trust and openness. If we practice the process of transforming the pain of our unmet needs into the beauty of needs prior to the dialogue, we will be more likely to speak calmly and clearly and to stay grounded in our intention to connect with the other. As described in the previous chapter, the transforming pain process creates new neural pathways that yield altered patterns of thinking and feeling. It fosters new states of mind that can be accessed whenever we get triggered emotionally. The more well-worn the newly created neural pathways are, the more quickly we can access new states of mind in tense situations. Rather than responding to criticism by blaming and shaming ourselves or the other person, we can shift into a more peaceful, nonreactive state in the midst of dialogue.

In situations of protracted conflict or high anxiety, such as with Michelle and Diane, transforming our core unconscious beliefs may be a necessary precursor to authentic dialogue as well. And in all cases, such inner work will contribute to our capacity to stay in the dialogue. While core unconscious beliefs take myriad forms, they all tend to view the self, others, the church, or the world in terms of deficiency. For example, they may say or think "I am inadequate"; "Life is all pain, no gain"; "My needs will never be met"; or "Authentic relationships are hurtful, even dangerous." If we are unconsciously operating out of these beliefs, then our capacity to stay in dialogue will be limited at best. If I believe that "my needs will never be met," then I may very well relinquish a part of myself in order to "keep the peace." I may decide that it's not worth the effort to persist in being heard and seen. If I have an unconscious belief that I am fundamentally flawed or inadequate in some way, then I may interpret hard-to-hear messages from another person as a personal attack precisely because it reinforces my own unconscious belief about myself. Instead of connecting with my own feelings and needs in self-empathy, I may devolve into a shame reaction. Rather than empathizing with the other, I may lash out verbally in blame, accusation, or judgment. If I believe that life is ceaseless struggle, I may give up on the dialogue when it becomes difficult. I may feel hopeless and despairing if I believe that I will never be understood. I may compromise, agreeing to a strategy that fails to meet my needs. Consequently, resentment may simmer under the guise of agreement.

Authentic dialogue does not seek a compromise between conflicted parties. As mentioned in chapter 2, compromise means that the parties are focusing their attention on strategies rather than needs. When attempting to reach a compromise, people usually are intent on crafting an action plan that will meet, at best, some needs but not all needs. Usually no one is completely satisfied with the compromise precisely because it fails to take *all* the needs into account. Conflicted parties may even adopt a strategy that appears to keep the peace but actually undermines stability and trust. In our case study, Michelle and Diane seem to have reached this kind of compromise. They agreed to interact only when church activities required them to do so. Though they coordinated their church responsibilities, they did not encounter each other authentically in their full humanity. They suppressed their needs for trust and interdependence and felt considerable pain and sometimes bitterness toward each other.

Compromise is rooted in a scarcity mentality: the belief that there are not enough resources to meet everyone's needs. Each person sacrifices something in order to reach an amicable resolution. This may breed disappointment if not discontent. It also may reinforce competition rather than open-hearted collaboration. Rather than promoting trust of the other, it may promote suspicion; instead of openness, it increases guardedness. In contrast, authentic dialogue is rooted in an abundance mentality, a belief that *everyone's needs matter*, a trust that resources exist to meet those needs, and openness to discovering strategies that utilize resources in meeting needs.

From a Christian theological perspective, an abundance mentality comes from trust in Jesus Christ, the one in whom and through whom the kingdom of God has come. "I came that they may have life, and have it abundantly," said Jesus (John 10:10). He is abundant life. We are united to him by the power of the Spirit, so that whatever is his, is ours (John 17). As discussed in the final section of this chapter, this abundance is an eschatological reality. It is not yet fully manifest in our midst. Nevertheless, we pray for it. We enter dialogue grounded in this knowledge: Christ has brought, brings, and will bring us abundant life.

When grounded in this kind of abundance mentality, we can value the autonomy of the other. We each accept responsibility for our own needs. We freely respond yes or no to any requests because we are tuned into our own freedom in Christ. And we refrain from seeking to meet our own needs at the expense of the other's needs. Doing so would undermine the mutuality, inclusivity, and interdependence characteristic of abundant life in community.

By entering the dialogue in this state of mind, we actually enhance the possibility that a creative strategy may emerge to meet everyone's needs. Surrendering our strategies and connecting to the beauty of our needs— and to the One in whom those needs are met—paradoxically creates the possibility for meeting needs in previously unimaginable ways. It may lead to a shift in one or both persons, such that we see how a former strategy actually does meet our needs. Or it may lead to a shift in which one or more needs rise to the surface as most pressing. Strategies then can be developed in response to those needs. Regardless, strategies are accepted freely and fully or not at all. They are not the telos of authentic dialogue but nevertheless may emerge organically when two or more people connect to the fullness of their common needs.

Staying in the Dialogue

Staying in the dialogue involves moving back and forth between empathy and honesty from a center of self-connection. The person who requested the dialogue typically begins with an honest expression of feelings and needs related to a concrete observation about an interaction with the other person. Sometimes it is beneficial for the one who is in the most pain (the most likely to be triggered by the other's sharing or the one who most needs empathy in the moment) to begin the dialogue. In any case, each person speaks until he or she has been heard fully, using connecting requests to sustain the dialogue. If the other person interrupts, then the one who was speaking shifts into empathy. An interruption reveals that the other has been triggered emotionally. Acknowledging this person's feelings and needs will support self-connection and aid mutual understanding. After this interlude for empathy, the one who was speaking prior to the interruption continues with honest expression.

Connecting requests are at the heart of staying in dialogue. As discussed in chapter 4, there are two kinds of connecting requests: (1) mirroring requests, which elicit feedback on what the other person heard us say; and (2) requests that elicit feedback on how our sharing has affected the other person. To discern if we have communicated our feelings and needs clearly we might ask, "Can you tell me what you heard me say?" To understand the other's response to our words, we might ask, "How do you feel now that you have heard me share this?" In the flow of authentic dialogue, we typically make the former request prior to the latter. We make an observation, followed by a full expression of our feelings and needs related to that event or interaction. Then we follow up with a mirroring request to discern whether or not we have communicated clearly and have been heard as we intend. If the other person's response indicates that they have not accurately and fully heard our feelings and needs, then we restate them with as much clarity as possible. To illustrate this process, let's examine the beginning of an authentic dialogue between Michelle and Diane.

Michelle: Diane, I had a disagreement with Karl and Marie two weeks ago about their small-group book study. I've seen them come to your office twice since then and I noticed that they look away from me when I glance at them. I'm worried because I'm imagining that they are complaining about me to you. I need some trust that you will support me in working out my disagreement with them. Could you share with me what you've heard me say?

Diane: Basically you're accusing me of talking to Karl and Marie about you behind your back.

Michelle: Thanks for that feedback. I can see that I have not been as clear as I would like to be. What I really want is open communication with Karl and Marie and with you. I want to trust that you will support my relationship with them. I'm wondering if you can share what you are hearing me say this time. I do not wish to attribute blame to anyone, but rather to ask for your support as I work out my disagreement with Karl and Marie.

Diane: It sounds like you want to have direct communication with all of us. You're hoping that I will encourage them to communicate with you directly. Is that right?

In her first statement, Michelle makes two observations: (1) she had a disagreement with Karl and Marie; and (2) she's seen them glance away from her when they've come to Diane's office since then. Michelle also shares her evaluation of these events, which she differentiates from her observation: she *imagines* that Karl and Marie are talking negatively about her to Diane. Then she expresses her feeling of worry and her needs for trust, support, and by implication, open communication. Even though Michelle differentiates her observation from her evaluation, Diane hears it as an accusation. Thus Michelle responds by focusing on her own feelings and needs again, followed by a connecting request. This time Diane hears the needs and reflects them back accurately. She also adds a connecting request—"Is that right?"—to determine if she has understood Michelle.

In authentic dialogue, we seek not only to understand intellectually what matters most to the other person and to ourselves, but also to enter into—to connect emotionally and bodily with—the fullness of our needs. We invite the other to understand cognitively and emotionally what matters to us about the issue at hand. We experience ourselves as being understood when the other is able to say in his or her own words the essence of what we are trying to communicate. We use the second kind of connecting request for two reasons: (1) to hear the other's authentic response to our sharing; and (2) to check if he or she has received the fullness of what we have shared. In regard to the latter, when other people connect with the beauty of our needs, their emotional response to us shifts in some way. Full connection to needs occurs on three levels: the meaning of the need (intellectual level); the feeling connected to the need (affective level); and how the need lives in our bodies (physical level). Whenever our listeners connect to all three dimensions of our need—to its beauty or intrinsic value—they experience a shift in their state of mind (and vice versa). Their thoughts, attitudes, and feelings change. In authentic dialogue, a shift in the others' thinking and feeling in response to our sharing or a shift in our thinking in response to their empathy suggests that we have authentically connected around the beauty of shared universal needs. Their response to our question, "How do you feel hearing me say this?" helps us understand if they have fully connected to what is at stake for us.

To demonstrate how to use a connecting request to check for connection to the beauty of needs, let's continue the dialogue between Michelle and Diane.

> **Diane:** It sounds like you want to have direct communication with all of us. You're hoping that I will encourage them to communicate with you directly. Is that right?
>
> **Michelle:** Yes. I also want support in this. I'm wondering how you feel when you hear me say this.
>
> **Diane:** I'm a bit annoyed. I'm not responsible for your relationship with Karl and Marie.
>
> **Michelle:** What I'm saying is that I need support in working out my conflict with Karl and Marie. When my need for support is met, I feel peaceful and at ease, and I have more confidence that I really can talk with Karl and Marie honestly. Can you tell me what you are hearing me say this time?
>
> **Diane:** I can try. [pause] It sounds like you are more peaceful when you trust that I will work side-by-side with you, that I will support your relationship with Karl and Marie.

Michelle: [sighing with relief] Yes. That's exactly it. I feel relieved because a sense of mutual understanding is important to me. How do you feel, hearing this?

Diane: I think I understand better now. I don't feel so annoyed or uptight. I feel relieved, too.

In this part of the dialogue, Michelle uses the second type of connecting request to facilitate mutual understanding and connection to the fullness of her needs. Diane's response—"I'm a bit annoyed"—indicates that she has not connected to the beauty of Michelle's need. Michelle has not communicated the embodied, energetic meaning of support and trust in her life. Thus she elaborates by referring to all three aspects of her need for support: (1) the *meaning* of support—it gives her confidence; (2) the *emotions* tied to respect—peaceful; and (3) how she experiences respect *bodily*—at ease, implying that she has let down her guard. Having heard the fullness of Michelle's need, Diane reflects it back to her with feeling. Michelle receives this mirroring with appreciation and asks again how her honesty has affected Diane. This time Diane shares that her own feelings have shifted from annoyance to relief. She has less tension in her body. She resonates with Diane. This signals that together Diane and Michelle have connected to the beauty of Michelle's needs for support and understanding. They have entered into authentic dialogue, an encounter of mutual seeing, hearing, and speaking.

Along with connecting requests, the capacity to express appreciation is a key element in staying in the dialogue. Expressing gratitude or appreciation is distinct from giving compliments or praise. The intention of expressing appreciation is to share how another person has contributed to our well-being. The intention in expressing compliments is not as clear. Sometimes praise aims to influence, change, or manipulate the other person. Even if the goal is authentic communication, compliments may come across as flattery. For example, if you say to your colleague, "You are the most supportive and understanding person I have ever worked with," she might suspect that you are trying to create an alliance over against others. Her trust might actually be undermined.

When we give compliments or praise, we are focused on the other person. Essentially compliments are judgments stated in positive language. As discussed in chapter 4, compliments may stimulate confusion and frustration. They may reinforce unconscious beliefs about needing to earn another's love and acceptance. For instance, if we say to a student, "You are brilliant," she might think, "I must have fooled her somehow." Or she might feel anxious, telling herself that she must continue to appear brilliant so as to earn our affirmation and love. In contrast, when we express appreciation, we are focused on ourselves. We speak openly from our hearts about how the other has influenced us in a life-giving way. We follow the basic pattern of OFNR. We might say to a colleague, "I so appreciate that you completed that project on time, as it really meets my needs for reliability and support." Or we might say to a student, "Wow! I so enjoyed reading your paper. I appreciated the creativity and clarity of thought (while adding the specific observations that we are evaluating as creative and clear)." Paradoxically, this focus on ourselves contributes to mutuality and greater understanding. It also gives the other person important information about herself (what she did to contribute to our well-being) and about us (what we value most).

When we express appreciation in authentic dialogue, we acknowledge the other person for empathizing with us and especially for connecting to the beauty of our needs. We communicate our gratitude for a willingness to persist in hearing us fully, especially when we are struggling to be heard with our own intention. When the other reflects back what matters most to us, we may feel a sense of relief, a relaxation in our bodies. Tension may dissipate. We may even be moved to tears. For empathic listening contributes to our most central and primal need, our need for love.

Expressing gratitude or appreciation often completes a full cycle of sharing in authentic dialogue. It signals that we have been heard fully regarding the particular concrete observation with which we began the dialogue. This does not mean that we won't have more feelings and needs to share. It simply means that, for the moment, our honest expression is complete. Therefore, after we express gratitude in authentic dialogue, we ask the other person to share anything that is alive in her, as in the conversation below.

> **Michelle:** Thanks for listening and for understanding how much I want and need support. I'm grateful that you heard me. I'm wondering if there are any aspects of our relationship that you'd like to talk about.
>
> **Diane:** You're welcome. Yes, there are some things I'd like to talk about.
>
> **Michelle:** Okay. I'm all ears.

This would begin the next cycle of the dialogue, now with Diane sharing her observations, feelings, and needs, using connecting requests to contribute to mutual understanding and connection to the fullness of her needs, and expressing gratitude and appreciation when Michelle empathizes with her.

While strategies are not the telos of authentic dialogue, they may emerge naturally after both persons have connected to the beauty of needs. One person may feel inspired to propose a strategy for meeting one or more needs that have been identified. Another person might request that they brainstorm together some strategies that might meet both their needs. In other words, we can propose action requests and strategizing requests as part of authentic dialogue. There would be no compulsion or desperation attached to these requests if both persons are connected to the beauty of their needs. If we could not agree freely and gladly, we would say no to the request. Whenever we say no to one request, it is because we are saying yes to needs that would not be met by fulfilling this request. In authentic dialogue, it is important to be able to hear the yes hidden inside a no response to our requests. In other words, we listen for the needs embedded within the no. We then seek to empathize with *those* needs, valuing them as we value our own. If a strategy to meet our needs does not naturally emerge in the course of the conversation we might feel disappointed. When that occurs it is helpful to practice NVC mourning, that is, to connect explicitly with all the needs that we have thus far identified but have not yet found a way to meet.

To illustrate, let's return to our conversation above. Michelle might propose an action request instead of a connecting request after she expresses appreciation for Diane's empathy. An effective action request is specific, stated in positive language, and doable. Michelle would empathize with Diane as needed and persist in proposing action strategies while staying connected to the beauty of her needs. Regardless of the outcome, she eventually would make a connecting request in order to hear Diane's feelings and needs, thus beginning the next cycle of the dialogue.

> **Michelle:** Thanks for listening and for understanding how much I want support. I'm grateful that you heard me. I think it would be helpful if you invited me into the conversation the next time that Karl and Marie come to your office. How does that sound?

Diane: [hesitating] I'm not comfortable with that. I don't want to be in the middle of your conflict with them. That might seem like we are ganging up on them.

Michelle: [taking her time] Okay. Is it that you want to sustain trust and openness with Karl and Marie and you want each of us to have our own relationship with them?

Diane: Yes. Exactly.

Michelle: I'm wondering, then, if you could encourage them to talk with me if they express any concerns about me. This would meet my needs for trust and support.

Diane: Yeah. I can do that.

Michelle: Thanks. I really appreciate your support. I'm also wondering if there are any aspects of our relationship that you'd like to talk about.

To summarize, authentic dialogue seeks to enhance connection and mutual understanding between two or more people. It is a multiple-skill set in compassionate communication, combining honesty, empathy, self-empathy, and mourning. It depends significantly on the capacity to make connecting requests and to express appreciation. While it always aims for mutual connection to the beauty of needs, it sometimes leads to meeting needs through action requests and strategizing requests. Though the process of authentic dialogue is particularly helpful in the context of high anxiety and conflict, it can be practiced in any relationship when we want to enhance mutual understanding.

Often people wonder if they can enter into authentic dialogue with someone who doesn't know NVC. Can we have authentic dialogue with individuals who are not conscious of their needs? With people who do not know the difference between connecting requests and action requests? Simply put, the answer is yes, though it does require more skill, particularly the capacity to speak colloquial NVC. Here are some basic guidelines for sustaining authentic dialogue with someone unfamiliar with NVC:

- Begin with a concrete observation, followed by feelings and needs stated in your own words (colloquial NVC).
- Use colloquial connecting requests to facilitate mutual understanding and connection to the beauty of needs.

- Listen for the needs underneath the other person's thoughts and feelings.
- Empathize after interruptions.
- Persist in being heard fully. Persist in hearing the other fully.
- Express appreciation for empathy.
- Hear the yes in the no.[2]
- If you are emotionally triggered, practice emergency self-empathy. If you are unable to stay self-connected, request to finish the conversation at another time. In the meantime, engage in a process of self-empathy as you reflect on the conversation, or reach out to a friend with empathetic skill, asking the friend to help you identify your feelings and needs.

Noticing our Anxiety

In order to stay in dialogue, it is essential to learn how to work with our own anxiety. Interpersonal neurobiology and family systems theory illuminate how anxiety shapes us intrapersonally, interpersonally, and communally.

As Siegel delineates in *The Developing Mind*, feelings are the glue that connect the mind and the body, persons, and entire systems.[3] Anxiety is a particularly strong connector in us, between us, and within groups. It is a flow of energy through the brain and body, which mobilizes us for action in response to a perceived or real threat. We may be conscious or unconscious of the anxiety that fuels our choices and behaviors, depending in large part on the shaping of neural pathways in our earliest years of life. How we experience and respond to anxiety is imprinted on our brains through interactions with our parents or primary caregivers. Brain research suggests that this is not simply a psychological phenomenon but also a neurobiological one. How the parents (or early caregivers) experience and express emotion shapes the patterns of brain activity in the child so that the child's brain imitates the parents' experience and expression of feelings. The parents' states of mind actually shape the formation of states of mind in the child. Therefore, how well our primary caregivers regulated their feelings of anxiety in our early years shapes our capacity to tolerate anxiety, how intensely we respond to it, and the basic posture we adopt in response.

While the level of tolerable anxiety varies from person to person, most of us typically adopt one of three patterns in response to overwhelming anxiety: fight, flight, or freeze. We attempt to subdue our anxiety either through aggressive speech and action, through withdrawal, or through indecision. Interestingly, recent research suggests that many women display a fourth kind of response to anxiety—"tend and befriend."[4] Though at first glance, it appears positive, this response can also be reactive or defensive. It is often an attempt to pacify, soothe, or calm another person, driven by the fear of losing the relationship and disconnected from an awareness of needs. The "tend and befriend" response will inhibit authentic connection when it is not accompanied by honesty as well as empathy. For example, a woman may try to pacify her angry supervisor as a strategy for harmony, but in so doing she might be disconnected from other essential needs, such as her own integrity, honesty, and autonomy. Returning to our case study, Michelle and Diane vacillate between a flight response and a tend-and-befriend response. Publicly they are collegial and considerate toward one another. Privately they retreat into their own work as much as possible, and they avoid talking about their differences and frustrations.

Family systems theory considers these four patterns to be forms of emotional reactivity, instinctual responses to real or perceived threats. In emotional reactivity, we focus on something or someone outside of ourselves in order to alleviate our anxiety. In families or larger groups, such as congregations, emotional reactivity manifests in more complex relational postures: chronic conflict, distancing, cut-offs, over-functioning and under-functioning, triangulation, repetitions, and secrets.[5] In all of these postures, persons focus on each other rather than on their own inner lives. They tend to blame each other or try to fix each other rather than take responsibility for their own feelings and needs. Smaller groups within the system may adopt an us versus them mentality or target another as "the identified patient" or "scapegoat." Though these relational postures seek to alleviate anxiety, they ironically perpetuate it further.

Emotional reactivity, regardless of the form it takes, inhibits authentic encounter among persons within a system. Emotionally reactive people fuse together. They are anxiously hooked into each other. They merge emotionally, giving up some aspect of themselves or taking on some aspect of someone else. They become less self-differentiated. Fusion and self-differentiation are distinct emotional processes in any system. As Ronald Richardson puts it, "They are about the degree of emotional merging and emotional separateness in our relationships with one another."[6] Authentic encounter, from a systems perspective, depends on self-differentiation. Self-differentiation involves the capacity to be separate, equal, and open in relationship to others.[7] The emotionally separate person maintains a sense of self in the midst of anxiety in the system. Equality means that one respects both the self and the other and enters into life-giving connection rather than life-alienating fusion. Openness implies mutuality and honesty in expression. It involves the willingness to share one's own thoughts, feelings, and needs while still valuing those of the other. Thus systems characterized by a high degree of self-differentiation not only tolerate but also welcome difference. Rather than suppressing or avoiding disagreement, self-differentiated persons can engage in authentic dialogue. In contrast, people who are fused together fear difference. Difference stimulates anxiety, which leads them to keep secrets from each other, remain aloof, or triangulate.

From the perspective of NVC, these relational postures, or forms of fusion, are complex, systemic strategies that are disconnected from needs. While they may be attempts to secure harmony or ease, they emerge from a scarcity mentality. These relational postures are motivated by fear rather than by trust that everyone's needs matter and that strategies can be found that value everyone's needs. Whenever we act out of such fear, we are disconnected from the fullness, or beauty, of our needs. Consequently our strategies—whether distancing, cut-offs, triangulation, secrets, or a complex combination of these relational postures—undermine a whole set of needs. We purchase a pseudo-harmony at the cost of our integrity, authenticity, and interdependence. Again, consider Michelle and Diane. They have adopted a pattern of emotional distancing,[8] marked by failure to address their differences and by periods of noncommunication. On the one hand, this creates a certain amount of ease in their relationship. On the other hand, their needs for honesty, trust, security, and integrity go unmet. Triangulation reinforces this pattern of distancing.[9] If Diane talks with Karl and Marie about Michelle, the three of them might feel connected and supported by each other. However, in doing so, they not only fail to engage Michelle honestly but also they fail to encounter one another fully. Their own relationship is indirect, mediated by outside concerns. When tension arises among them, most likely they will not trust each other enough to work it out.

In conclusion, these insights on the intrapersonal, interpersonal, and systemic manifestations of anxiety contribute to the kind of self-awareness that supports and encourages authentic dialogue. Anxiety expresses itself unconsciously; thus recognition of these relational patterns may be the first step in identifying what it is that keeps us from fully encountering others. At the personal level, we may reflect on our history of response to conflict and stress, noting our habitual response: fight, flight, freeze, or tend and befriend. When we find ourselves automatically reacting in any of these ways, we can make a conscious choice to slow down. Before speaking or acting, we may take the time to notice our bodily sensations, to connect them to our feelings of anxiety, and then to ask ourselves what we need. At the larger systemic level, we can pay attention to emotional reactivity. Are there patterns of triangulation, conflict, distance, or cut-off throughout a congregation's history? We can note whether or not the congregation's anxiety is chronic or acute. If chronic, some constellation of these patterns will be active. If acute, these patterns will manifest themselves typically during times of high stress.[10]

If we can recognize the common triggers of our anxiety as well as the relational postures we tend to adopt in response, then we can increase our capacity for tolerating anxiety in ourselves and others. This begs the question: How can we recognize and feel our anxiety without jumping into strategies that, in the long term, only perpetuate it? How can we move toward authentic dialogue rather than away from it when our anxiety rises? Family systems theory teaches strategies to increase self-differentiation and hence authentic connection when we find ourselves in emotionally reactive patterns. We can initiate connection, even in a small way, with persons who are cut off from our family or our congregation. We can sensitively reveal secrets with the intent to contribute to life.[11] We can avoid the temptation to scapegoat others by translating our moralistic evaluations into observations. We can encourage conversation between two parties with whom we are triangulated while simultaneously staying personally connected to each of them. In short, we can learn to maintain a nonanxious presence in the midst of situations in which the stimulation of particular needs and thought patterns give rise to anxiety. Paradoxically, becoming a nonanxious presence requires the capacity to identify, experience, and express our anxiety rather than attempting to escape our anxiety through reactive relational patterns. This is precisely what we learn to do as we practice authentic dialogue. We learn to observe the kind of situations that activate our anxiety. We learn to identify our anxiety and express it rather than act it out. We learn to connect the anxiety to the underlying need, whether for trust, respect, consideration, harmony, or community (or any other need). We learn to make connecting requests of ourselves and others and thereby short-circuit the anxiety that contagiously captures everyone in the system.

Authentic Dialogue in Theological Perspective

The telos of life, according to NVC, is connection to self and others, devoid of judgment and brimming with acceptance. As a multiple skill set of NVC, authentic dialogue fosters this kind of interpersonal relating in the context of anxiety and conflict. The telos of life, according to Christianity as we interpret it, is multi-dimensional koinonia, or union and communion with God, with fellow members of the church, and with the entire human family. While koinonia certainly is connection, it is also much more than that. It is a distinctively theological conceptual category that seeks to describe a complex reality that is more than simple connection. When understood within this larger theological framework of meaning, authentic dialogue can become a spiritual practice that contributes to koinonia.

The Beauty of Koinonia

At the end of his life, Jesus prayed to the Father for his disciples, "that they may be one, as we are one, I in them and you in me, that they may be completely one, so that the world may know that you have sent me and have loved them even as you have loved me" (John 17:23). In this prayer, Jesus revealed that koinonia constitutes the being of God, the church, and the world. Though often translated as "fellowship," koinonia is a much richer concept, which means something like mutual indwelling, coinherence, and coexistence.[12] As George Hunsinger explains,

> Koinonia . . . means that we are not related to God or to one another like ball bearings in a bucket, through a system of external relations. We are, rather, something like relational fields that interpenetrate, form, and participate in each other in countless real though often elusive ways. Koinonia, both as a term and as a reality, is remarkable for its range and flexibility and inexhaustible depth. . . . Koinonia stands for the final reconciliation and interconnection of all things through a living, luminous system of internal yet diverse relations.[13]

Koinonia means that we exist in the greatest possible intimacy with God and each other. It is an intimacy that has its origin in the very being of God and thus permeates God's work of creation, reconciliation, and redemption.[14]

Koinonia describes the mysterious union and communion of the Trinity. Father, Son, and Holy Spirit exist in a union and communion of free, self-giving love, knowledge, and creative action. From this koinonia flows new life. The abundant, overflowing love of God creates human beings for another kind of koinonia, a relationship of loving, communicating, and knowing between God and humanity. Yet humanity turns from this relationship again and again. We anxiously bend inward, retreating from God and each other. However, God does not retaliate against us or abandon us. As Karl Barth puts it, "The love of God always throws a bridge over a crevasse,"[15] reconciling us to God and each other in and through the life, death, and resurrection of Jesus Christ.

Jesus Christ reconciles us to God and to each other so that we can live in koinonia, in a mysterious and profound mutual participation in God and in one another's lives on account of Jesus. Jesus Christ lives in us and our lives are lived in and through him. This koinonia is already a reality for us in Christ. By the power of the Spirit, all humanity has participated in the death and resurrection of Jesus Christ. In one sense it is a perfect and completed work, as Jesus Christ accomplishes our reconciliation with God. However, koinonia is not yet fully experienced by us. All creation waits, whether consciously or not, for redemption. Only in eternity will the union and communion among persons, between persons and God, and within the entire cosmos be experienced in all its beauty, joy, peace, and love. Until then, our vocation is to witness to this koinonia in our words and deeds and to pray for its fullness in all creation.

We can identify a number of distinctions between koinonia with God and each other in Christ and connection in NVC. Whereas Rosenberg posits life-giving connection as an inherent quality of humankind, Christian theology posits koinonia as a gift that comes from outside of humanity. Our union and communion with God and each other come from and depend on divine action. Koinonia is not something that we accomplish on our own, by our will power, skills, or even training in NVC. We ultimately depend on and exist on account of God's love.[16] This brings us to a second distinction. Rosenberg tends to blur the lines between divinity and humanity. Referring to God as "Beloved Divine Energy," he writes, "I know Beloved Divine Energy by connecting with human beings in a certain way. I not only see Divine Energy, I taste Divine Energy, I feel Divine Energy, and I am Divine Energy."[17] In contrast, koinonia refers to an intimate indwelling between God and humanity in which there remains a qualitative distinction between Creator and creature. God remains God, and we remain human even in our deep communion with God. Third, koinonia will become completely manifest only in the eschaton, when God will be all in all, whereas Rosenberg seems to suggest that a life of unity and compassion can be achieved with proper socialization over time. He writes, "I believe . . . that a peaceful world is not only possible, it's inevitable. I think we're evolving in that direction."[18] Finally, our theology of koinonia affirms a distinction between the church and the world. While koinonia is a universal condition and definitive for all humanity, the church has been awakened to this reality. The church knows and proclaims and lives in light of the fact that all have been reconciled to God in Jesus Christ. Thus the church lives based on the promise of the full actualization of reconciliation in all creation. Its decisions and actions spring from and move toward koinonia. Even so, practices from outside the church can (and often do) reflect aspects of koinonia more faithfully than the church's ministry. In such instances, the church is called to recognize the truth of God wherever it is found, either within the church or outside its walls, and to reform its own life accordingly. We believe that this is exactly what the church does when it incorporates NVC into its own spiritual practices.

Authentic Dialogue as a Practice of Koinonia

After the apostle Paul encourages members of the church at Philippi to "be of the same mind, having the same love," he urges them to "work out your own salvation with fear and trembling; for it is God who is at work in you" (Phil. 2:2, 12, 13). In this short passage, Paul urges us to become who we are already—one people united in Christ, who together reflect the koinonia of the Trinity. "Let the same mind be in you that was in Christ" (Phil. 2:5).

This koinonia among the members of Christ's body takes visible shape in worship, prayer, and service. In these practices, our lives are knit together in love. By the power of the Spirit in our midst, we live in peace with each other, support one another, confess our sin to one another, practice hospitality toward one another, and bear each other's burdens. Yet when we persist in polarizing discourse and destructive conflict, we contradict our koinonia. Disunity in the church contradicts our very identity and scandalizes our witness. For how can the church be an ambassador of reconciliation when communities of faith are torn asunder by mutual recrimination, judgment, cut-offs and chronic conflict? How can we worship in spirit and truth and vilify those made in God's image, in whom God dwells?

It is precisely at this point, where the church persists in contradiction and thus jeopardizes its calling, that authentic dialogue can become an essential skill that supports our life in koinonia. Even though the church is *simul justus et peccator*, a communion of people who are simultaneously saints and sinners, and even though the church cannot attain koinonia on its own strength or skill, it can work out its unity, in part, through authentic dialogue. When tempted to fight or flee from one another in response to their anxiety, persons or groups in the church can speak the truth in love by using connecting requests and NVC appreciation. When tempted to splinter into more denominations, the church can enter a sustained process of honesty, empathy, self-empathy, and mourning. Authentic dialogue thus can become a practice that contributes to working out our reconciliation without reducing reconciliation or koinonia to connection.

To conclude, let's return to our case study and consider how Michelle and Diane might understand their authentic dialogue as a practice of koinonia. As a precursor to entering the dialogue, they could connect to the beauty of their needs as qualities of life that will become fully manifest only in the kingdom of God. Thus they would enter dialogue with a trust that they already are united with each other in Christ. They could rest in the fact that their union and communion is an objective reality. They could willingly surrender their strategies, trusting that "love does not insist on its own way" (1 Cor. 13:5). Connected to the beauty of koinonia, Michelle and Diane might learn the secret of being content in all situations (Phil. 4:11–12). Trusting in God's grace and mercy, which are abundant for them in Christ, they could pray for God's Spirit to unite them in the midst of their anxiety and conflict. Michelle and Diane could persist in an encounter of mutual seeing, hearing, and speaking not out of guilt or any tyrannical list of "shoulds" but rather out of the freedom to become who they are, a freedom given from above. They could confess any judgment, blame, or false witness borne against each other as manifestations of their sin and suffering. Rather than despair, they would hope for the day when their reconciliation to God and one another will be made manifest in all its fullness. In this way, the multiple skill set of authentic dialogue would help them live out their koinonia with each other. At the same time, their dialogue process would be undergirded by a broader set of koinonia practices, such as worship and prayer. By participating in God's ongoing ministry of reconciliation, their posture of détente might be transformed into peaceful fulfillment of their common vocation.

Chapter 10

Strive for God's Kingdom

Transforming Conflict in Church-Wide Crises

> Instead, strive for [God's] kingdom, and these things will be given
> to you as well.
>
> Luke 12:31

Leaders who are committed to the principles of compassionate communication, who are trained in its basic skills, and who are willing
to take the emotional risks involved in compassionate leadership, will
be able to navigate the terrain presented by a crisis or an impasse at a
church-wide level. Those, in other words, who dare to speak honestly,
listen with empathy, and practice self-empathy will have the necessary
tools to work effectively in crisis. This chapter offers a structure and out-
lines a process by which the skills elaborated in this book can be put to
work in navigating church-wide conflict.

Even under the best of circumstances, complex situations arise
that have the potential to spike the anxiety of the whole system. Conflicts that had once been relatively contained with a problem-solving
approach suddenly rage out of control.[1] Or a new pastor begins her
ministry in a promising church, only to uncover the well-kept secret
that the previous pastor left under a cloud of controversy. In the midst
of her shock and dismay, how can she grow to understand the ordeal
the congregation has suffered, as well as fathom its ongoing impact on
their life together?

Sometimes catastrophe strikes and the whole church is traumatized:
a beloved pastor and his wife are murdered by a teen in the youth group;
a pastor in a small town sets fire to the church building, writes a note
of confession, and then commits suicide; a federal building is bombed

in a downtown metropolis and clergy from the surrounding area are summoned to minister to the grief-stricken.[2] When the entire community is shocked by sudden calamity, feelings of anger, grief, perplexity, and disorientation typically arise. Only honestly acknowledging and working through these feelings will enable the community to forge a path forward. Under such circumstances, the church needs compassionate leaders who can truly *lead*, offering vision, encouragement, and finely honed practical skills as the congregation moves together toward healing.

Entrenched conflict can also bring about a state of disequilibrium. In some conflicted churches, secrets distort information, creating alienation for some and a false sense of companionship for others, thereby raising the level of anxiety system-wide. Cut-offs by key members intensify the anxiety of those left behind. Communication typically becomes more indirect as the congregational culture becomes more conflict-avoidant. Triangles form. The anxiety of the conflict between any two parties is siphoned off into a third party who listens to both of them but is powerless to resolve their differences.[3] Such conflicts can grow into true impasses, in which members can no longer recall what the real issues are. The conflict ceases to be about the issues and begins to be about persons instead. Labeling and diagnosing those with whom one disagrees become prevalent patterns. Power is no longer shared but is used by one group at the expense of another. Decision-making structures are altered to reinforce the power of the ruling faction.

Though such patterns are typically found in conflicted churches, each situation is unique and every context has specific cultural norms as well as particular challenges from the surrounding environment.[4] As such, it is impossible to provide guidelines that fit every situation. However, those leaders committed to practicing the NVC skills set forth in this book will notice the culture gradually beginning to change. David Brubaker, a highly respected congregational consultant, underscores the basic argument of this book when he asserts that "Congregations ultimately change when leaders change. . . . The key is that congregational leaders need to model the behaviors desired in the broader system. As leaders change their behaviors, the culture of the congregation will begin to shift."[5] Compassionate communication practiced by even a few key leaders might be seen as the smidgen of yeast that leavens the whole loaf. With the support and guidance of compassionate leaders, the church is able to tap into deeper wells of strength and resilience when conflict is not simply managed but rather is transformed.[6]

Practicing the skill set of honest expression, for example, would mean that "the elephant in the sanctuary" cannot remain there for long without some kind of explicit acknowledgment. Leaders who speak honestly will ask open-ended questions about those places where pain, anger, or discontent have arisen from pervasive unmet need. When those thoughts and feelings are heard with understanding, the anxiety of the system as a whole will decrease and bonds of trust will be forged. Because taboo subjects bring up visceral anxiety, it takes not only clarity of purpose but also the courage to persist in asking questions that will open up communication. This is the case in any authentic dialogue, of course, but now the scope of the conflict is wider and the task more complex. How might the whole church engage in a conversation that will allow for multiple points of view? In such a forum, multiple needs would doubtless be expressed. Finding creative strategies to meet those needs would be challenging. Trust and openness, as always, would provide the nutrients that enable the creativity of the group to flourish. Though the task is more complex than in a dyad or small group, the core principles are the same. Leaders committed to compassionate communication will move purposively but gently *toward* those issues that are generating anger, anxiety, or shame, refusing to let them be hushed up or buried unhealed.

In the case of widespread conflict, the leaders' chief aim is to restore a sense of belonging in the community by facilitating connection among all its members. The anxiety, isolation, and alienation that typically grow from relentless conflict are often its most destructive fruit. When persons shrink back in fear, they begin a negative spiral that only reinforces a sense of isolation. Anything that helps restore trust and connection, not only among individual members, but especially with the church as a whole, will contribute to the overall health of the community. Several suggestions follow:

- Share information about the crisis as accurately and transparently as possible on a regular basis.
- Remember that everyone's needs matter, including those of children, teens, and the homebound.
- Remember to attend to your own needs for self-care, making time for rest, renewal, support, inspiration, and prayer.
- Balance care for self with care for others.
- Take time to process feelings as they arise, remembering to connect your feelings with underlying needs and then to find strategies to address them.

- Find methods for collaboration and support from those outside the system; ask for help from other clergy, therapists, skilled chaplains or caregivers, church officials, and denominational organizations.[7]
- Plan any prayer services or gatherings for worship with a leadership team, remembering that worship provides pastoral care for the entire community.
- Consider inviting a denominational official or clergy colleague to preach for several weeks after a crisis to give the regular pastoral staff members time to work through their own shock and disorientation.
- Develop a highly respected planning team that will together envision a healing strategy for bringing all those affected by the crisis into constructive dialogue.[8]

Shifting the Congregational Culture

What processes help shift the congregational culture from one of fear and mistrust to one of greater trust and openness? All the strategies named above will help. What is most important is a clear commitment to practicing empathy, honesty, and self-empathy consistently, along with the more complex skill sets of mourning and authentic dialogue. In a highly anxious system, leaders themselves will need steady sources of empathy, where they can get support in connecting with their own core needs. Anxiety in a system is by definition highly contagious. Leaders will not be able to sustain compassionate openness toward their congregants unless they have developed strategies for regaining their calm center again and again, as often as it takes, by reaching out for support themselves. This means that knowing how to make requests for support is an essential leadership skill. Leaders committed to this practice not only will be highly effective in their leadership, but also will gain insight into the unmet needs of their congregants. *The whole is in the part*: because each of us internalizes the whole of which we are a part, we gain insight into the whole by becoming more aware of the particular dynamics within us. Naming those dynamics in a public forum helps lower anxiety because it gives people understanding of the overall context in which they are living.

Leaders who are centered and calm are able to provide a safe interpersonal context for members to express their myriad, often confused feelings; to connect with one another in a time of distress and instability; and to thereby stabilize valuable interpersonal relationships. By focusing on the underlying needs of the conflicted parties in a simple structure that enhances open communication, tensions can be eased, bringing renewed courage in its wake. The basic goal is to work constructively with *all* the members who have been affected by any specific event—a decision of a governing board, a painful incident in a church-sponsored event, an allegation of pastoral misconduct, or even a disaster that affects the wider community—and to hear and respond to their unmet needs. After the needs most pertinent to the present situation are identified, the collective wisdom of those affected can be called on to develop beneficial strategies for the entire body.

After each person's experience is heard with empathy, the participants will decide together what strategies might best serve the needs of the whole. Moving from needs to strategies, members may make requests of (or offers to) one another by describing specific (doable) actions that would meet the identified needs. In some cases, it can be challenging to think of something that will effectively meet the needs of the whole body. But when everyone is thinking *together* (rather than *over against* one another) it is striking, and often moving, to see the creativity of the group spur into action.

Compassionate Listening Circles

An established principle of compassionate communication is the conviction that it is singularly counterproductive to spend one's energy trying to decide who might be to blame for any conflict or crisis. Typically, many disparate conflicts arise over time with various people contributing to them. One person may see herself solely as the victim of another's hurtful action, while the other would identify *her* as the offender, focusing not on that action, but on the one immediately preceding it, to which he is simply responding. Levels of complexity in an interdependent body make it difficult to specify any *particular* action that might become the focus of a fruitful conversation. What, then, is the conflict about? How can church leaders identify a focus that will open up channels of communication about what is essentially at stake? Identifying a particular focus for a church-wide conversation requires the basic NVC skill of making a concrete observation, described in neutral terms without any evaluation attached to it. Stating a clear observation will assist the church in opening up the conversation without triggering initial reactivity.

If the aims of compassionate leadership are connection, belonging, and mutual understanding (and not blame, diagnosis, or finding a scapegoat), then in a certain sense it doesn't matter what the chosen focus is. Conflicts are like mushrooms in the forest, sprouting up in seemingly random fashion. Even though a mycologist would recognize these many mushrooms as a single plant, as distinct manifestations of a single rhizome (the horizontal root stem), to the ordinary observer it looks like a plethora of individual mushrooms. When persons are members of one another, there is often an underlying root conflict that is larger and more complex than any individual person can see. What might be the overall shape of the rhizome hidden from view? How does each member in the community conceive of it? The root system can be described adequately only through multiple perspectives. The purpose of an intentional process of compassionate listening, therefore, is to understand the meaning the root conflict has for each person, not to determine "what *really* happened."[9]

In order to set up a church-wide process of compassionate listening, it is only necessary to choose a single manifestation of the complex underlying conflict, a single mushroom that pops up in the forest. With careful listening, any particular focus will eventually lead to the hidden root, enabling those gathered to see the complexity of the conflict as well as its underlying unity. By intentionally choosing a single focus, the intricately woven interdependence of the community will be disclosed. Though the whole is hidden in any part (any particular mushroom will lead one to the hidden root system), it is helpful to choose a particular focus in the form of an observation that will prove significant to the community as a whole.

In any crisis, it is crucial to work collaboratively with a well-chosen planning team.[10] Such a team is best made up of lay leaders who are familiar with the issues the congregation is facing as well as with the long-standing hurts that need to be healed. Such leaders need to be members who are widely respected and who are sanctioned by the church governing body. If the congregation is polarized over a particular issue, it is important to have proponents of each of the "sides" on the team. It is generally unwise, however, to choose the most extreme representatives of one side or the other. It is most helpful to choose those who are more moderate in their opinions, especially those who are skilled in hearing those with whom they disagree. For this reason, it makes sense to provide these leaders with as much basic training in compassionate communication as possible. The success of any planning they undertake will depend in large part on their ability to work together as a team. The quality of their dialogue "tends to affect the quality of the overall dialogue within the congregation. . . . Their essential job is to advocate a fair process and not a particular outcome."[11]

The planning team's initial effort will be to design a compassionate listening forum in which the issues that need to be talked about can be brought forward safely. Such a forum is quite different—both in intent and in process—from a typical church meeting in which the pros and cons of a possible decision are discussed and voted on. Instead, a carefully constructed process is created, in which each person affected by the conflict or crisis can simply be heard. The extensive literature on what has come to be known as "restorative circles" can guide the planning team in developing a design for a compassionate listening forum in their particular church with its unique challenges and strengths.[12] The planning team has several key questions to consider:

- What will be the chosen focus of the first compassionate listening circle? (Ideally, the team will be able to state the explicit focus clearly in one sentence in the form of a concrete observation.)
- How will the purpose of such a listening circle best be communicated to the congregation?
- Is the planning team adequately trained to listen empathically even to those with whom they disagree (remembering that empathy does not equal agreement)?
- What kind of structure can be created so that everyone will be able to speak to the whole body? (Can one single circle be created or would it be better to offer a number of choices—both church-wide circles and smaller, more intimate circles—over a period of time if the church is facing a crisis of an ongoing nature?)

Setting Up a Compassionate Listening Circle

The basic structure of a compassionate listening circle entails a group of people who listen to one another about the meaning of any particular hot issue.[13] After introductions, they agree on a set of guidelines to facilitate communication.[14] A facilitator, or guardian of these guidelines, keeps track of the process and keeps the process on track. For larger, church-wide gatherings, it is advisable to have two co-facilitators. The facilitators' main tasks in a listening circle are

- to help the community come to an agreement about guidelines for the dialogue by explaining the overall aims of the compassionate listening circle;
- to make sure that each person who speaks is heard to his or her own satisfaction;
- to prepare each participant in a pre-circle process before the circle meets (pre-circles will be explained below);

- to schedule the date and time of the listening circle;
- to care for the space by choosing a quiet and symbolically meaning-ful place, and by having drinks, tissues, pens, and paper available;
- to set forth the process clearly for all participants; and
- to greet all persons as they enter the space, initiate a simple process for introductions to be made, and offer a clear opening sentence that reminds them of the intention that brought them all there.[15]

The listening circle's first task will be to adopt process guidelines. These typically include showing respect for each person by agreeing to keep what is said within the group (agreement regarding confidential-ity), and by having only one person speak at a time (agreement regarding fairness). The latter is often facilitated by the use of a "talking stick" or symbolic object that is held by the person who is speaking.[16]

Setting chairs in a circle communicates a commitment to valuing every person's voice. Kay Pranis, a national leader in using such listening cir-cles in a variety of contexts, writes of the core values that such circles tend to promote, asserting that "no person is more important than anyone else."[17] People who participate in structured listening circles are able to

- speak their truth
- drop masks and protections
- be present as whole persons
- reveal their deepest hopes and longings
- acknowledge mistakes and fears
- work together as a team of equals
- act in accord with their core values[18]

The particular focus of any circle should be intentionally described in neutral terms in the form of an observation in order to avoid blaming any particular person(s). Whatever happened is an event that cries out for mutual understanding. If this event involves an actual crime, legal processes might occur concomitantly to the circle process. It is crucial to distinguish between necessary legal procedures and the congregation's urgent needs for ongoing care and healing. In many churches, fears about legal ramifications effectively muzzle the congregation's leaders and members alike at the very time that they most need to hear from one another.

If discord has arisen in the body, it is of fundamental importance to have a safe process to address it without rancor. Imagine a scenario, for instance, where differing factions are polarized over whether to have a capital campaign to buy land adjacent to the church so that a parking lot can be built. Anxiety is rising, rumors are spreading, and the pastor hopes to quell them before they get out of hand. He can request a compassionate listening circle. Together, the planning team would choose a single action as the specific focus of the circle. The focus might be described thus: "Two weeks ago, the church council (or governing board) voted 7–5 to begin a capital campaign to buy the land where Kmart used to be. How do you think this decision affects our congregation? How does it affect you, personally?"

In this hypothetical example, three basic components are clearly in evidence: the act, the author of the act, and the recipient of the act.

- The act: the decision of the church council to begin a capital campaign to purchase a certain tract of land (set forth as an observation without evaluation).
- The author of the act: the church council is authorized to make such a decision.
- The direct recipient of the act: in this case, the entire congregation is affected.

By using these descriptive—author, act, and recipient—rather than evaluative terms, leaders indicate the restorative intent of the circle. They underscore their commitment to hear from all persons who have a stake in the outcome without blaming any particular individual or group. The same principles would hold true if a community is responding to tragedy or trauma. The purpose would still be to deepen or restore interpersonal relationships, disclosing step-by-step the core values that this community lives by, without looking for scapegoats.

The focus questions for a compassionate listening circle are best when they are not elaborate or complicated.

- What do you want others to know about how you are now in relation to the church council's vote? What impact has this decision had on you personally? On the congregation as a whole? *(Focus on the present.)*
- What do you want others to know about what you were looking for when you responded to the vote as you did (or, for the church council members, when you voted as you did)? *(Focus on the past.)*

- What would you like to see happen next? Is there a specific request (or offer) that you could make that would address the needs of the community, as you understand them?[19] *(Focus on the future.)*

Those trained in compassionate communication will notice how these questions enable people to speak about their feelings, needs, and requests in the context of a specific situation. In order for each person to experience being fully heard, it is crucial to hear needs and values in the context of expressed opinions. Such empathic listening deepens the conversation so that the participants begin to sense their shared humanity. Leaders who are able to differentiate between needs and strategies (as requests of self or other) will be able to help people identify their core needs—which serves to deepen each individual's sense of belonging to the whole—before moving ahead to seeking strategies to meet those needs.

Mutual understanding grows when dialogue helps people to connect around their most fundamental needs. The suggested questions in our example would give all members of the church council an opportunity to explain the thinking that led to their particular vote either for or against purchasing the land. It would also provide a forum for members of the congregation who have strong feelings about the decision to express them fully as they focus on the impact that the decision has had on them and others. Any strong feelings (either for or against) can be stated passionately, *because they are matters for compassionate listening, not matters for debate.* The circle is not designed to be a forum for winning proponents, persuading others to one's point of view, or making the opposing party look bad. Such tactics only increase ill feelings and lend themselves to greater polarization. A circle is successful if all participants bring all of their passion and enthusiasm (or worry and concern) forward to be heard by the whole body. If harm has been done, these questions (modified for the particular occasion) would give each person an opportunity to take responsibility for her choices, in some cases by expressing regret and seeking ways to make amends. The second question: "What do you want others to know about what you were looking for when you made the choice(s) that you did?" helps each person to take responsibility for himself and his choices (including choices not to participate, for example, because of a fear of conflict). Such questions invite a deeper level of reflection than is usually afforded in meetings marked by persuasion, debate, and argument.

Dominic Barter[20] identifies three central aims for these listening circles: mutual understanding, self-responsibility, and an action plan.

Mutual understanding is secured when each person has an opportunity to be heard about the *significance* of the act, the meaning that it holds for him or her now. After each person speaks, the facilitator asks the one specifically addressed, "What did you hear is important to her?" The person replies with a summary of the essence of what he heard. Then the facilitator turns to the person who spoke first and asks her "Is that what you wanted understood?" By taking these steps, the person who shares her hurt openly gets feedback right away as to whether she is being heard as she wants to be heard. The facilitator keeps going back and forth between the persons until the speaker is satisfied that she has been heard as she wishes. Little facilitates mutual understanding more readily than the experience of being heard as one hopes to be heard. The intention of the process is to focus on the people present and how they see each other, to reestablish a sense of connection. The facilitation helps the participants to gain trust in the process as well as insight into those with whom they disagree. The process will not move forward significantly until everything that has been said has also been heard to the satisfaction of the person who spoke. It can be tempting to skip over this step of empathic listening in the interest of saving time. However, the whole purpose of the compassionate listening circle is defeated if the participants do not experience being fully heard as they wish to be heard.

Secondly, self-responsibility takes place when each person in the community owns the choices he or she has made in reference to the act. The second set of questions helps all persons to see the impact of their choices in response to the act. The author and the direct recipients of the act are not the only ones who need to take responsibility, but also every member of the community. For every member of the community contributed to the context or cultural ethos in which the act took place. As members of the congregation become more able to identify their needs, they will gain skill in articulating the core motivations of their actions (or inaction). Naming them aloud before the community helps each person to take responsibility for his or her own needs, which decreases blame and increases a sense of empowerment. The more we take responsibility for our needs, the more empowered we are to act on the basis of them. This step helps each person to see his or her power to affect others. It also helps each one see others as human in making the choices they did.

The whole atmosphere of the conversation usually shifts palpably once there is a shared sense of mutual understanding and self-responsibility. Only then do the facilitators move to step three, toward the mutual creation of an action plan: "What would you like to see happen next?" or "What would you like to offer?" Once the heavy emotions have been successfully negotiated (steps one and two), this third step in the process can bring a flowering of creativity to the group, as ideas for repairing the harm begin to flow. An often-exciting sense of collaboration grows. Recalling the principles regarding requests, any proposed action needs to be concrete, specific, and doable within a particular time frame. The action plan aims to take into consideration *all* the needs that have been expressed. Often a creative, symbolic action is suggested that meets the expressed needs of both the author and direct recipients. For example, teenagers who destroyed a small prayer garden could offer to spend four hours every Saturday for the next ten weeks restoring it to beauty. Such an offer would show their sense of responsibility for the harm done and their commitment to make amends. Those most hurt by the destruction of the garden might even volunteer to help with the garden's restoration, thereby using the harm as an opportunity to build relationships with the youth of the community. Such a plan would be agreed on by all members of the circle and would be carried out within a specific period of time. A post-circle would be called at the end of the entire process to ascertain whether the actions have been carried out to the satisfaction of all or whether a new action plan needs to be constructed on the basis of newly emerging needs.

It is not the responsibility of the facilitators to resolve the conflict, for this is the work of the entire community. Because all these processes are voluntary, the persons who commit themselves to gather are those willing to take responsibility for any decision about next steps. All listening circles are completely voluntary. This means that those who do not wish to take part in the circle are free to decline. However, the circle will proceed without them. When a compassionate listening circle is in place, no one has the power to sabotage the healing of the community by his or her choice not to participate.

Pre-circles

There are three distinct phases to the overall process: pre-circles; the compassionate listening circle itself; and the post-circle. The facilitator meets with each group (or each individual, depending on the scope and the particulars of the event to be discussed) represented in a pre-circle meeting. That is to say, the facilitator meets with those who are the authors of the act, those who are the direct recipients, and those who are part of the larger community (those indirectly affected) in three different pre-circles. The facilitator's goals in these pre-circles are:

- to connect empathically with each person involved
- to gain clarity about the precise nature of the act (the particular incident that will be the chosen focus of the circle) by distinguishing observations from evaluations
- to support each person's choice to participate (or not) by describing the purpose of the circle, the underlying principles at stake, and the process involved
- to ask who else needs to be included in the circle in order to resolve the conflict

The facilitator ends each pre-circle by asking each person whether he or she would like to participate. At all times, the facilitator aims to adapt the form to the local context and culture as much as possible so that it will truly serve the people involved. In other words, the facilitator seeks to discover what needs the persons imagine will not be met by participating. By entering into dialogue about the purpose, principles, and process, the facilitator provides a fuller picture for potential participants, such that they become willing to take the risk of participating.

The facilitator's attitude of collaboration is crucial. He or she seeks at the outset to take the participants' needs to heart. Knowing the church and its culture is crucial to connect with what matters most to this *particular* church community. What will give the members the safety, awareness, and empowerment that will serve the whole body? The more flexible the facilitator is in adapting the precise form to the local conditions, the more restorative the results will be. The facilitator is flexible as to the exact formulation of the questions, for example, but needs to stay faithful to the core principles of the work. As the facilitators connect empathetically with the needs of the participants in the pre-circle process, they will gain their trust, which will more likely increase the number of those who want to participate. The greater the degree of voluntary participation, the more restorative the result.[21]

Post-circles

A post-circle is called by the facilitator at an agreed-on time set by the action plan. In the listening circle, all the participants will have agreed to take certain actions that they believe will bring about greater harmony or ease, make amends, or provide occasions for mutual support. Now, in the post-circle, members of the community gather once again to check on the well-being of the community and to celebrate together the actions that took place. If the actions that they thought would meet their needs did not fully do so, the post-circle gives everyone an opportunity to explore possible new actions.

As before, the facilitator is sure to ask each person who expresses herself whether she is heard as she wishes to be heard. This step, when pursued until the person is satisfied with how she is heard, effectively closes the communication loop and increases trust in the process. How satisfied are the members with the actions that they and others have taken? Does anything further need to be done to meet the current needs of the community?

If the agreed-on actions did not succeed in meeting participants' needs as anticipated, those needs can be expressed again. Now each person has the opportunity to dig deeper into the meaning that these actions carry for him personally as he is now newly aware of them. Is there an action that could be taken that would capture the full scope of what is at stake? What new circumstances might have arisen between the time the action plan was constructed and the time it was intended to be carried out that now need to be taken into consideration?

If the agreed-upon actions were not carried out as the group intended, the post-circle offers an opportunity to explore why by investigating what needs were met by not following through on those actions. That is to say, what are the reasons for anyone's choice not to follow through on the action plan? These reasons will likely be connected to still other (previously unidentified) needs that would not be met by the agreed-on action. The post-circle, then, is seen as an opportunity to fine-tune the action plan, not to blame or shame those who did not follow through on the earlier agreement. Now they have an opportunity to investigate what needs they were trying to meet by not undertaking the action. In terms of compassionate communication, what are they saying yes to by saying no to the previous agreement? These newly articulated needs may then lead to a new action plan within a new time frame.[22]

Systemic Structure for Compassionate Listening Circles

Compassionate listening circles will be most effective in transforming conflict if they are nested within larger systemic structures that support them. While it is relatively easy to see how such processes are undergirded by the gospel of peace, few churches have explicit structures in place that enable members to work through their conflicts before they grow into actual impasses. Imagine a church that had known processes in place by which any member, from the senior pastor down to the youngest Sunday school child, from the head deacon to the most isolated homebound member, could initiate a compassionate listening circle to resolve an important conflict. Years ago, in her book, *Toward a New Psychology of Women*, Jean Baker Miller wrote:

> Productive conflict can include a feeling of change, expansion, joy. It may at times have to involve anguish and pain too; but even these are different from the feelings involved in destructive or blocked conflict. Destructive conflict calls forth the conviction that one cannot possibly "win" or, more accurately, that nothing can really change or enlarge. It often involves a feeling that one must move away from one's deeply felt motives, that one is losing the connection with one's most importantly held desires and needs. . . . Adults have been well schooled in suppressing conflict but not in conducting constructive conflict. Adults don't seem to know how to enter into it with integrity and respect and with some degree of confidence and hope.[23]

If a church lacks structures to undertake constructive conflict, it is little wonder that its members have minimal confidence that initiating conflict might lead to a satisfying outcome. Many dread conflict because they have never been part of a family or community that has taught them how to enter it. The only kind of conflict that they knew about was suppressed, blocked, or destructive conflict. Putting a system in place that is sanctioned by the whole body would empower members to take responsibility for their conflicts.

- A restorative system requires a community or institutional agreement that gives legitimacy to the compassionate listening circles described here.
- It requires an actual physical space in which such circles can take place. The more inviting and comfortable the space, and the more symbolically meaningful, the more it communicates the value of the listening circle.
- Adequate human resources need to be available to facilitate listening circles—in particular, members of the community that have the interest, the time, and the gifts to facilitate such circles. Ideally, many members of the congregation would share in this work.

- The steps for the overall compassionate listening process, along with its underlying principles, need to be made known to everyone in the community by whatever technological means are available, from bulletin boards to newsletters, from Web sites to community e-mails.
- The process needs to be made accessible to every member. How any person in the community can request a listening circle must be clear. No one needs to ask permission of anyone else. Every member is equally empowered.[24]

Introducing a Compassionate Listening Circle in a Church-wide Process

Because it can be challenging to imagine how to initiate such compassionate listening circles in a congregation, we are providing a possible script that attempts to capture the essential elements involved, followed by some basic guidelines for moving into the rest of the circle process.

1st facilitator: Today, our primary purpose is to have a church-wide conversation about _____ by setting up a compassionate listening circle. Our intention is to develop a process where it is safe to express yourself with honesty and forthrightness. It is our presupposition that everyone's needs matter and that everyone has something important to contribute. Our planning committee (*introduce each member of the committee*) has given a great deal of thought to how to set up a process that is in alignment with our church's core beliefs and values.

- We have placed our chairs in a circle because we believe it visibly shows our unity in Jesus Christ even when we are in distress because of discord in our community. Jesus Christ is at the center of our compassionate listening circle. Because we belong to Jesus Christ, we belong to each other as well. Because Jesus listens to each of us with compassion, so we want to listen to one another with compassion.
- We want to honor the presence and dignity of every participant. Every voice in this circle is equally valued.

- We cherish the contribution of all who are willing to speak as well as the contribution of each person who listens with respect.
- We want to support emotional and spiritual connection by asking each of you to speak honestly and openly about your concerns.

The process we have created is as follows: My colleague (*give name*) and I, as cofacilitators, will sit in the inner circle with four (to eight) empty chairs. Anyone in the surrounding concentric circles who wishes to join the conversation can come forward at any time and sit in one of the empty chairs. We ask each speaker to leave your chair after you have been heard as you wish to be heard in order to make room for others who would like to speak. We hope that many of you will participate. Some of you may wish to come forward more than once as the conversation unfolds. Again, we want to hear from as many of you as time allows. To maximize this possibility, we are requesting that if you wish to participate more than once that you wait until all others who wish to speak have done so before rejoining the inner circle."[25]

2nd facilitator: For this format to work as intended, we are suggesting three basic guidelines.

1. Speak only when you are in the inner circle.
2. "Speak the truth in love" (Eph. 4:15). By that we mean, speak as honestly as you can and also with care and kindness toward your listeners.
3. Listen with respect. In practice, this means that we are requesting that no one offers cheers of support or boos of disapproval, or any clapping.

All are welcome to participate, but all communication must occur only in the inner circle. We are asking you to be silent unless you are sitting in one of these chairs. We are requesting that you do not speak to your neighbor in a side conversation if someone says something you especially like or dislike. Agreeing to these guidelines will enable us to proceed with trust that all voices will be heard with respect and consideration. Is there anyone here who cannot support these basic guidelines?"

1st facilitator: (*speaking directly to the second*) Would you be willing to remind us of this agreement if at any point we forget?

(*Now turning to address the group*) Our plan is to listen to one another until 10:30 AM, at which time we plan to take a fifteen-minute break. Then we will meet again for more listening until 11:30 AM. We then will have a time of closure, aiming to finish by noon.

There is a depth of past history in the church that we do not wish to rehash. Instead, we want to know what matters to you *now* about what happened *then*. The goal is not to negotiate the past or figure out what happened when, or who said what to whom; rather the goal is for each person to hear and connect with the community. We ask that you speak about how you experience things as a member of this community now and what you most want at this juncture. We want to support you in taking responsibility for your own feelings and values, rather than blaming others.

I would like to begin by requesting a minute of silence so that each of us can focus on what we most want from today's compassionate listening circle. Take a minute to reflect on your own heart's desire. What do you want known, and by whom, about how you are now in relation to the church council's vote?"

(*After a full minute of silence, the facilitator proceeds.*) "I'd like to invite six members of the congregation who want to begin the conversation to come forward and sit in the inner circle.

After beginning in this way, the conversation unfolds as the facilitators ask the open-ended questions that have been constructed.

Throughout the circle process, be sure to include time for hearing each person with care. Depending on the time constraints and the complexity of the impasse or crisis, the listening circle would close when there are clear agreements about next steps in an action plan. Sometimes several circles may be needed over time depending on the severity of the polarization. As people experience increasing connection over previously experienced impasses, there will be greater and greater willingness (even eagerness) to participate in such circles. With each new circle that is called, the same three questions are asked:

1. What is it you want known (and by whom) about where you are right now in relation to what happened?
2. What were you looking for at the time you chose to act?
3. How do we move forward from here? (What would you like to offer or to request?)

As each person answers the question for himself, he will experience the satisfaction of having another say what matters to him most about the conflict, as she has heard it. Being heard in this way builds connection and trust.

Restorative Practices and Christian Theology

If universal needs represent qualities of life in the kingdom of God, then compassionate listening circles provide a concrete means for congregations to strive for God's kingdom of peace. As members recognize the needs most alive in their own hearts, they might gain the insight that these are also needs of those with whom they (perhaps vehemently) disagree. In this way, they might recognize anew their profoundly mutual involvement in the kingdom. No difference or disagreement can ultimately separate them from one another because together they participate in Christ, in whom and through whom the kingdom has come, is coming, and will come. In other words, by acknowledging and honoring needs, compassionate listening circles reveal the hidden presence of God's kingdom in the midst of even the most distraught Christian community. Whether in the form of lament or praise, those who focus on God's kingdom of peace, compassion, and mutual respect will be given what they need when their church is in turmoil. Even in the darkest of hours, when the body seems torn asunder, trust in God's promise of the coming kingdom can sustain church members in faith, hope, and love.

Compassionate listening circles provide opportunities for the whole church to learn more honest and empathic ways to communicate. They give visible shape to the church's fundamental commitment to speaking the truth in love, not as an abstract ideal to strive for but rather as a growing skill that empowers the community to take responsibility for its own conflicts. Working through interpersonal pain is one way of trusting in God's grace. In honoring the interdependent needs of every member, in facilitating mutual understanding, and in offering opportunities for real accountability, the gospel of Jesus Christ can be lived out. These practices have the potential to develop each member's capacity to see the human beings with whom they are in conflict as precious members of the body of Christ—brothers and sisters made in the image of God—not as opponents to be controlled or conquered. The circle process enables members to connect with what matters most to them in their vision of God's kingdom. They enable each person to participate as a fully equal and valued member of the community. All members are given an opportunity to cocreate constructive solutions. In the process, every member who participates will learn crucial skills in how to undertake dialogue in a respectful way. Through all of this, the circle offers significant opportunities for Christian education and formation.

Christian communities are shaped in fundamental ways by biblical, theological, and ecclesial norms, as well as norms from the particular culture in which they are situated. In any church conflict, it is important to lift up those core affirmations to which the whole assembly can assent. These might include such things as a belief that every person is worthy of respect because each is created in the image of God. Core beliefs about our unity in Christ, the importance of mutual forgiveness, biblical teachings about reconciliation and loving our enemies, together set a positive context for this work. Every voice is valued as the whole body together seeks God's kingdom. "Again, truly I tell you, if two of you agree on earth about anything you ask, it will be done for you by my Father in heaven. For where two or three are gathered in my name, I am there among them" (Matt. 18:19–20). The fundamental interdependence of the members of the body is essential to this understanding. Emphasis is squarely placed on the unity of the body of Christ, even though each member plays a unique, indispensable role. We are members of one another and "if one member suffers, all suffer together with it" (1 Cor. 12:26). Jesus reminds his disciples over and again that even "the least of these" matter in the kingdom of God. Compassionate listening circles offer a structure in which the members of the church can experience the truth that everyone does in fact matter.

The apostle Paul reminds the church that we are to "bear one another's burdens" (Gal. 6:2) as a way of fulfilling the law of Christ. At the same time, we are admonished to take responsibility for our own actions: "For all must carry their own loads" (Gal. 6:5). The compassionate circle process highlights the fact that all our choices are made in the context of mutual accountability. As we listen to one another, we gain a wider vision of how our words and actions have affected others in the community. If we regret our choices, we are given an opportunity to make amends. Since all members are treated with basic respect, it is not a matter of humiliation to acknowledge regret. On the contrary, to do so is a sign of the Holy Spirit's work in our midst.

As Christian leaders offer a secure holding environment to strengthen frayed bonds of trust, and as they call on God to minister to the community in its pain, they offer space to each person to express what has wounded her most. In some cases, nearly everyone in the community has been hurt, but in strangely diverse ways. It is essential for leaders to refrain from moralizing or blaming, and instead to position themselves in such a way that all persons can be heard. The church that gathers to share their common pain will find new, and often surprising, ways to move forward as a community.[26]

When marriage partners have ceased to listen to one another because their pain is so intense, they might seek a counselor who offers a safe space where the two partners can hear each other. Compassionate listening circles offer a similar opportunity on a larger scale. They offer a safe structure, a clear process, and a healing intention for members of the body to hear one another's stories in a public forum. Now the hurting parties can be heard respectfully. It takes time to heal. Even more importantly, it takes willingness. No one can make another willing to begin such a healing journey, but without clear processes in place, no healing journey can ever be begun. Such listening circles offer the church a way to strive for God's kingdom of genuine peace, for working through church-wide impasses where mutual understanding, genuine accountability, and basic trust are the core needs of the community. Out of such honestly faced conflict, new life and hope will, by the grace of God, transpire.

Conclusion

As we reflect on our myriad efforts to bring about peace and harmony in our communities of faith, we will do well to recognize our human limits. We can take to heart the words of Oscar Romero, who risked (and lost) his life for the sake of peace. Human beings do not usher in God's kingdom, no matter what level of skill they have achieved. God alone has the power to bring it about. But we can work together in active fellowship and constant prayer, trusting in Christ's prayer that the church will be made one, even as the Father and the Son are one (John 17). As Romero wrote:

> It helps now and then to step back and take the long view. The kingdom is not only beyond our efforts, it is even beyond our vision. We accomplish in our lifetime only a tiny fraction of the magnificent enterprise that is God's work. Nothing we do is complete, which is another way of saying that the kingdom always lies beyond us. No statement says all that could be said, no prayer fully expresses our faith. No confession brings perfection. No pastoral visit brings wholeness. No program accomplishes the Church's mission. No set of goals and objectives includes everything. This is what we are about.
>
> We plant the seeds that one day will grow. We water seeds already planted, knowing that they hold further development. We provide yeast that produces effects far beyond our capabilities. We cannot do everything. And there is a sense of liberation in realising that.
>
> This enables us to do something, and to do it well. It may be incomplete, but it is a beginning, a step along the way, an opportunity for the Lord's grace to enter and do the rest. We may never see the end results, but that is the difference between the master builder and the worker. We are workers, not master builders, ministers, not messiahs. We are prophets of a future not our own.[27]

Conclusion

Learning the Secret of Contentment

I know what it is to be in need, and I know what it is to have plenty. I have learned the secret of being content in any and every situation, whether well fed or hungry, whether living in plenty or in want. I can do all this through him who gives me strength.

Philippians 4:12–13 NIV

Times of cultural and ecclesial change, conflict, and crisis present significant challenges for church leaders: how to lead communities of faith in which members are pitted against one another; how to relate to crumbling denominational structures; how to practice our faith with imagination when old ways of doing things no longer work; how to foster hope and healing in the face of widespread grief, anxiety, or despair; how to reach out to those who are ethnically, socioeconomically, and culturally different from us; and, not least, how to steward our particular call in the midst of it all. These are but a few of the challenges facing Christian leaders today.

If this list seems daunting, then it is good to be reminded that times of ferment and change are also times of opportunity. Compassionate communication is a cultural form that gives the church concrete practical skills as it seeks to embody God's mighty work of reconciliation in small but significant ways. Those who are rooted and grounded in Christ's love are able to move confidently *toward* conflict, trusting in God's will to create a just peace. Such conflict, when embraced rather than avoided, bears within it seeds of transformation, the possibility for new life, and the opportunity to live truly as interdependent members of Christ's body. When we approach conflict in an attitude of prayer, when we use our

196

basic NVC skills to shift our attention toward God's compassion, we discover a deep well of vitality and an ongoing source of hope. This life-giving discovery—embodied in our own experience and witnessed in the lives of our colleagues in ministry—has undergirded every page of this book.

We have sought to describe and to illustrate how the practical skills of compassionate communication can foster a leader's connection to God, self, and others in the midst of difference, disagreement, distress, interpersonal impasse, and entrenched systemic conflict. When integrated into our Christian faith, these skills enable us to hear criticism as constructive feedback rather than as blame or shame. When we are disappointed in ourselves or regret the choices that we have made, self-empathy enables us to identify our exact unmet needs, which we can then take to God in prayers of petition, lament, or confession. At the same time, we believe that compassionate communication gives the church concrete practical guidance in speaking the truth in love. Believing that only honesty will build up the body of Christ, we long for more church members to find the courage—and the skill—to speak about what is truly in their hearts and minds. As more and more of us take the risk of speaking up, we believe that trust will grow as we find that our core human needs are shared by everyone in the community that we love.

By learning to say no in order to say yes to those things that we care about passionately, we avoid the stress and burnout that ensues when we do our duty joylessly or succumb to others' expectations. When we attend to the movement of God's Spirit within, we learn to trust ourselves and respect our own human limits. By transforming anger or outrage into ardent commitment to what really matters, we find new courage both to speak and act in situations that cry out for justice. At the same time, we have found that empathic connection with those we serve supports our capacity to participate in Christ's ongoing ministry of compassion and healing. When we hear and understand the ache and longing in the hearts of our brothers and sisters in Christ, we find our own hearts opened anew even toward those we had previously regarded as irritating or demanding.

We are made for God and for each other. As Karl Barth put it so beautifully, we are meant to exist in mutual encounters of love, which are marked by seeing and being seen, speaking and hearing, and assisting one another with gladness.[1] From the standpoint of Christian faith, the freedom to give of ourselves is possible only on the basis of God's ongoing outpouring of grace. We are dependent on God's Spirit to lift us up when we fall, again and again, into old habits of evaluating, judging, and labeling others. Whenever we gather for worship we are reminded not only of God's continued goodness and love toward all that God has created, but also of our solidarity in sin with our fellow human beings. Our prayers of confession support us in translating our judgments of others into an acknowledgment of our limits, our values, and our deep-seated wounds. By acknowledging our common need for redemption, we are motivated to persist in translating our life-denying judgments into life-affirming needs. In this way, we are able, by the grace of God, to keep our hearts open toward those with whom we perennially, and perhaps antagonistically, disagree.

When our debates in church and culture get mired down in accusation, blame, and reified enemy images, we can pray for the courage, skill, and perseverance to transform conflict from the inside out. By God's grace we can be reminded that underneath the pain of the cacophony of unmet needs is the exquisite beauty of the needs themselves, including our own. When we connect with that beauty, anger and discouragement melt away as they are transformed into longing and hope. As we learn to how to bring our core unconscious beliefs into awareness, they no longer have the capacity to mire us in shame and anxiety. Then we are freed to enter into dialogue with new energy. As the Spirit of God moves in and among our dialogue with others, we are enabled to discover new, faithful, and creative ways of being the church together for the sake of the world.

The transformation of conflict into compassionate connection entails, even necessitates, a transformation of church leaders as well as our patterns of leading. Because we internalize the conflicts in our churches, we need continually to find ways of including ourselves in the transformation that we long for. This is the key to compassionate leadership in action. For at its heart, compassionate leadership emerges from compassionate leaders. Our very personhood is deeply implicated in leadership, which is why that leadership calls for the ongoing formation and transformation of our entire being—head, heart, and hands. Our knowledge of God, ourselves, and others—including our opinions, beliefs, and evaluations—must be transformed again and again by the Spirit of God. When we commit ourselves to translating our judgments and interpretations into feelings and needs, our hearts are opened anew to the world that God so dearly loves. Compassionate communication, as we have described it in light of our Christian faith, supports, strengthens, and builds our capacity to lead communities of faith with humility, generosity, courage, and love.

At the same time, it gives us concrete tools to deal constructively with ongoing disappointment, perplexity, or fear.

Compassionate communication itself cannot create faith, hope, or love. Our trust in God—nurtured by worship, fellowship, and prayer—is what keeps us from losing heart. Whenever we are overwhelmed by the suffering and injustice around us, we rely on God again and again to anchor us in a transcendent hope. Compassionate communication helps us keep our ears and eyes open to the cries of the human heart so that our pastoral care, teaching, and preaching might speak powerfully to a world in need.

At the end of his life, the apostle Paul penned these words in his closing exhortation to the church at Philippi: "I have learned the secret of being content in any and every situation, whether well fed or hungry, whether living in plenty or in want" (Phil. 4:12b NIV). It is a curious statement given that not all is well in Paul's life. He has been imprisoned unjustly. Even worse, other Christian leaders seem to be rejoicing in his imprisonment as they seize the moment to promote themselves in the very communities that Paul has nurtured and loved (Phil. 1:17). Still others threaten the well-being of the Philippians' faith by suggesting that Gentile converts must be circumcised. The very issue that Paul confronted earlier in his ministry at Galatia now faces him in Philippi. Certain teachers promote a deadening form of works righteousness (Phil. 3:2–4). Chronic unmet needs for honesty, integrity, generosity, and love have eroded this community's life together, manifesting in a perduring conflict between two church leaders (Phil. 4:2), a conflict that seems to threaten the unity of the congregation.

Paul believes that the core gospel message is at stake. His life's work seems utterly threatened. His crown of boasting (1 Thess. 2:19–20) appears to be toppling. Given all this, it is astounding that Paul claims to be *content*. What has happened to the fire-brand apostle who was so infuriated by the circumcision group that he hoped that they would just go all the way and castrate themselves (Gal. 5:12)? Here at the end of his life, facing entrenched conflict, dishonesty, and perhaps even malice, Paul speaks of a secret he calls contentment. This secret is not some form of spiritual enlightenment. It is not born of intellectual analysis, research, nor even by virtue of any personal quality of being. Instead, it has been formed in the depths of his soul out of a crucible of pain and perplexity.

This contentment is clearly a gift of God that enables Paul to hold fast through the storms of life. In this letter alone, we witness Paul's arduous effort to remind the Philippians of their unity in Christ. Abhorring the factions of the church, he admonishes them to:

- "Be of the same mind, having the same love, being in full accord and of one mind" (2:2).
- "Do nothing from selfish ambition or conceit, but in humility regard others as better than yourselves" (2:3).
- "Let each of you look not to your own interests, but to the interests of others" (2:4).
- "Let the same mind be in you that was in Christ Jesus" (2:5).
- "Do all things without murmuring and arguing" (2:14).
- "Do not worry about anything, but in everything by prayer and supplication with thanksgiving let your requests be made known to God" (4:6).
- "Keep on doing the things that you have learned and received and heard and seen in me" (4:9).

Finally, he reminds them to keep their focus on God's goodness in Jesus Christ by meditating on truth, honor, justice, purity, loveliness, grace, excellence, and anything worthy of praise: "Finally, beloved, whatever is true, whatever is honorable, whatever is just, whatever is pure, whatever is pleasing, whatever is commendable, if there is any excellence and if there is anything worthy of praise, think about these things" (4:8). This focus on goodness, loveliness, and excellence resonates with those who learn to keep their focus on the precious life-giving human needs that motivate human speech and action. We believe that the skills of compassionate communication give us concrete practical tools for keeping our minds focused on the goodness of God. By seeing human needs as positive, life-affirming qualities of being, compassionate communication reminds Christians to live in anticipation of the fullness of life promised to us in the kingdom of God.

After Paul has done all that he can to contribute to the peace, harmony, and unity of the Philippian church, he rests in God. He is content, not simply happy or satisfied but rather at peace with himself, with others, and with God. Acceptance of all that he has suffered and hoped for shapes his fundamental disposition in life. He can simultaneously fulfill his vocation and accept the situation at hand—contention in the church, his imprisonment, and even his impending death—because he trusts that God will fulfill the promised redemption in Jesus Christ. Living in the tension between the inbreaking of the kingdom in Christ's resurrection and its ultimate destiny in the redemption of both heaven and earth, Paul is sustained by hope. Paul's serenity does not depend on the outcome of his ministry but rather on the steadfast faithfulness of God in Jesus Christ.

Contentment is a disposition desperately needed for today's Christian leaders. How else can our work for healing, justice, peace, and unity be sustained? How else can we keep from burning out, from frantically trying to "fix" our communities of faith, or from disconnecting and cutting off from our sisters and brothers in Christ? How else can we rest in God when moral deliberation degenerates into polarization and even our best skills in compassionate communication fail to renew relationships as we would like?

As a consequence of faith, contentment is not something that we can manufacture on our own. It is a gift of God. We can learn contentment, even as we accept that its presence in our lives is a mystery. Contentment blossoms over a lifetime of abiding in God through worship, prayer, and life in the Spirit. Praying the Psalms, singing praises, meditating on Scripture as our daily bread until it is digested fully into our bodies and souls, taking Sabbath rest, and contemplating the fulfillment of human need as a partial description of what it means to live in the kingdom of God: all these practices, by the power of the Spirit, create a kind of peace even in the midst of pain and longing. This is the peace that emerges from the unseen work of the Spirit which nourishes whole communities in trust when they find themselves in the midst of painful conflict.

What is contentment? It is neither apathy nor resignation, neither frantic fretting nor desperate striving. It does not deny sin and offer cheap grace, nor does it turn a blind eye to suffering and injustice. It is a radical acceptance that comes as an unexpected gift when we trust God in plenty and in want, in joy and in sorrow, even in traumatic loss. Paradoxically, contentment and mourning go together because we live in a fallen world. Mourning and lament keep our hearts open to God's promises of new life in the midst of tragedy and trauma. We do not need to harden our hearts against suffering when we believe in a God who can—and does—bring light out of darkness, transform evil into good, and raise up new life out of death. The full weight of sin and death has been borne by another on our behalf and for our sakes. We are therefore free to rejoice in the word and work of God, keeping our hearts open in longing as we await the consummation of God's kingdom to be brought to earth. By the grace of God in Jesus Christ we can participate in this hope using the skills of compassionate communication to keep our focus on God's work of transformation.

Feelings Inventory

The following are words we use when we want to express a combination of emotional states and physical sensations. This list is neither exhaustive nor definitive. It is meant as a starting place to support anyone who wishes to engage in a process of deepening self-discovery and to facilitate greater understanding and connection between people.

There are two parts to this list*: feelings we may have when our needs are being met and feelings we may have when our needs are not being met.

Feelings When Your Needs Are Satisfied

Affectionate

compassionate
friendly
loving
open hearted
sympathetic
tender
warm

Confident

empowered
open
proud
safe
secure

Engaged

absorbed
alert
curious
engrossed
enchanted
entranced
fascinated
interested
intrigued
involved
spellbound
stimulated

Inspired

amazed
awed
wonder

Excited

amazed
animated
ardent
aroused
astonished
dazzled
eager
energetic
enthusiastic
giddy
invigorated
lively
passionate
surprised
vibrant

Exhilarated

blissful
ecstatic
elated
enthralled
exuberant
radiant
rapturous
thrilled

Grateful

appreciative
moved
thankful
touched

Hopeful

expectant
encouraged
optimistic

Joyful

amused
delighted
glad
happy
jubilant
pleased
tickled

Peaceful

calm
clear headed
comfortable
centered
content
equanimous
fulfilled
mellow
quiet
relaxed
relieved
satisfied
serene
still
tranquil
trusting

Refreshed

enlivened
rejuvenated
renewed
rested
restored
revived

Feelings When Your Needs Are Not Satisfied

Afraid	Confused	Embarrassed	Tense
apprehensive	ambivalent	ashamed	anxious
dread	baffled	chagrined	cranky
foreboding	bewildered	flustered	distressed
frightened	dazed	guilty	distraught
mistrustful	hesitant	mortified	edgy
panicked	lost	self-conscious	fidgety
petrified	mystified		frazzled
scared	perplexed	*Fatigue*	irritable
suspicious	puzzled		jittery
terrified	torn	beat	nervous
wary		burnt out	overwhelmed
worried	*Disconnected*	depleted	restless
	alienated	exhausted	stressed out
Annoyed	aloof	lethargic	
aggravated	apathetic	listless	*Vulnerable*
dismayed	bored	sleepy	fragile
disgruntled	cold	tired	guarded
displeased	detached	weary	helpless
exasperated	distant	worn out	insecure
frustrated	distracted		leery
impatient	indifferent	*Pain*	reserved
irritated	numb		sensitive
irked	removed	agony	shaky
	uninterested	anguished	
Angry	withdrawn	bereaved	*Yearning*
enraged		devastated	envious
furious	*Disquiet*	grief	jealous
incensed		heartbroken	longing
indignant	agitated	hurt	nostalgic
irate	alarmed	lonely	pining
livid	discombobulated	miserable	wistful
outraged	disconcerted	regretful	
resentful	disturbed	remorseful	
	perturbed		
Aversion	rattled	*Sad*	
animosity	restless	depressed	
appalled	shocked	dejected	
contempt	startled	despair	
disgusted	surprised	despondent	
dislike	troubled	disappointed	
hate	turbulent	discouraged	
horrified	turmoil	disheartened	
hostile	uncomfortable	forlorn	
repulsed	uneasy	gloomy	
	unnerved	heavy hearted	
	unsettled	hopeless	
	upset	melancholy	
		unhappy	
		wretched	

Needs Inventory

The following list of needs* is neither exhaustive nor definitive. It is meant as a starting place to support anyone who wishes to engage in a process of deepening self-discovery and to facilitate greater understanding and connection between people.

---

* Copyright © 2005 by Center for Nonviolent Communication. Reproduced with permission. To contact the Center for Nonviolent Communication, visit www.cnvc.org or e-mail cnvc@cnvc.org or call 505-244-4041.

Needs Inventory

Connection

acceptance
affection
appreciation
belonging
cooperation
communication
closeness
community
companionship
compassion
consideration
consistency
empathy
inclusion
intimacy
love
mutuality
nurturing
respect/self-respect
safety
security
stability
support
to know and be known
to see and be seen
to understand and be understood
trust
warmth

Physical Well-Being

air
food
movement/exercise
rest/sleep
sexual expression
safety
shelter
touch
water

Honesty

authenticity
integrity
presence

Play

joy
humor

Peace

beauty
communion
ease
equality
harmony
inspiration
order

Autonomy

choice
freedom
independence
space
spontaneity

Meaning

awareness
celebration of life
challenge
clarity
competence
consciousness
contribution
creativity
discovery
efficacy
effectiveness
growth
hope
learning
mourning
participation
purpose
self-expression
stimulation
to matter
understanding

Conflict Intensity Chart

A Resource for Ministry Committees
Presbyterian Church (U.S.A.)

Introduction

The Conflict Intensity Chart[*] is intended to provide members of Ministry Committees and others with a diagnostic instrument to assist in determining the intensity of a given conflict, to outline an ongoing training process and to provide relevant resources. Please note the following features of this chart:

A. Purpose is to De-escalate a Conflict:
The purpose of the chart is to provide the skills needed to de-escalate a conflict, and to lower each level above the first to a more manageable level if possible.

B. Levels are not Discrete:
There usually are not clear distinctions between conflict levels, and there is often overlap of characteristics. Intensity levels will vary from individual to individual and from group to group, requiring a consultant to examine a broad database before deciding the conflict level.

---

[*] This Conflict Intensity Chart is a resource of Presbyterian Church (U.S.A.). The original resource was produced by a 1986 General Assembly Task Force on Conflict consisting of the following persons: Ms. Margaret Bruehl, Mr. Roy W. Pneuman, Rev. Jill Hudson, Rev. Allan Swan, Ms. Mary V Atkinson, Rev. Alan G. Gripe. The writer/editor of this piece was Rev. Allan Swan. Permission to use the general categories and the descriptions of the Levels of Conflict has been granted by the Rev. Speed Leas of the Alban Institute, Bethesda, Maryland.

C. Characteristics are Inclusive:

As a corollary to the above note, the diagnosis of a particular conflict level of intensity ought to be derived from looking at all characteristics, rather than one or two that seem to dominate.

D. Team Approach should be Considered:

The suggested leadership skills acknowledge that no one person may have all the skills needed to manage a higher-level conflict. Other team members are needed to share insight and, especially at higher levels of intensity, to share the emotional stress of conflict intervention.

E. Training Required for all Intensity Levels:

It is recommended that all members of a Ministry Committee be trained to handle level one conflict. For those persons identified to act at levels two and three, additional training is required. Level four and five usually require professional outside consultants in conflict management.

LEVEL ONE: PROBLEM TO SOLVE

Characteristics:	
1. Issue	1. Real disagreement; conflicting goals, values and needs, etc.
2. Emotions	2. Short-lived anger quickly controlled; parties begin to be uncomfortable in presence of other.
3. Orientation	3. Tends to be problem oriented rather than person-oriented.
4. Information	4. Open sharing of information.
5. Language	5. Clear and specific.
6. Objective	6. Solving the problem. Move toward unanimous agreement. Utilize collaborative style.
7. Outcome	7. Collaborative agreement if possible. Win/win final resolution with acceptable, mutually agreed solution.
Skills Needed:	1. Trust/rapport building skills. 2. Ability to think theologically. 3. Good listening skills. 4. Working knowledge of the *Book of Order* and of the church. 5. Problem-solving and decision-making skills. 6. Consulting skills. 7. Knowledge of available resources.
Training Strategies:	1. Skills to be taught all members of Committee on Ministry on a continuing basis. 2. Develop resources using audio, visual and printed materials. 3. Use of case studies and role playing for skills training.

LEVEL TWO: DISAGREEMENT

Characteristics:	
1. Issue	1. Real disagreement; mixing of personalities and issues; problem cannot be clearly defined.
2. Emotions	2. Distrust beginning. Caution in association; less mixing with the "other side."
3. Orientation	3. Begin personifying problem; shrewdness and calculation begin.
4. Information	4. Selective holdback of information occurs on both sides.
5. Language	5. More vague and general; "some people . . ." "they . . . ," hostile humor, barbed comments and put-downs.
6. Objective	6. Face-saving; come out looking good. Tend to move toward consensus. Not yet win/lose conflict.
7. Outcome	7. Attempt collaborative solution; or negotiate acceptable agreement; win/win with real effort.
Skills Needed:	1. All skills under level one; in addition: 2. Analytical skills. 3. Understanding of power dynamics and issues. 4. Mediation skills. 5. Self-awareness skills.
Training Strategies:	1. Selected persons from Ministry Committee with additional specialized training/leadership. 2. Regionally-based year-long training in 5-6 segments or, 3. Attendance at weeklong workshop. 4. Use of simulation for training.

LEVEL THREE: CONTEST

Characteristics:	
1. Issue	1. Begin the dynamics of win/lose. Resistance to peace overtures. Focus on persons representing the enemy.
2. Emotions	2. Not able to operate in presence of "enemy"; however, admire worthy opponent. Not willing/able to share emotions/feelings constructively.
3. Orientation	3. Personal attacks. Formation of factions/sides Threat of members leaving. Need third party consultant from Ministry Committee or outside.
4. Information	4. Distortion is major problem. Information shared only within factions.
5. Language	5. Overgeneralizations: "You always . . ." "We never . . ." Attribute diabolical motives to others.
6. Objective	6. Shifts from self-protection to winning. Objectives are more complex and diffuse; clustering of issues.
7. Outcome	7. Decision-making = mediation, compromising, voting. Possible that some will leave the church.
Skills Needed:	1. All skills under level one and two; in addition: 2. Designing and negotiating contracts. 3. Clear recognition of one's own limits. 4. Understand interaction of personality types. 5. Facilitator in-group process. 6. Skilled in developing clear process of decision-making.
Training Strategies:	1. Presbytery-based crisis intervention team screened by Ministry Committee and trained by experiential methods. 2. Facilitator's limits have tested in advanced experiential training. 3. Long-term, continuing training through national and regional training events. 4. Have access to individual trained to administer and interpret instrument for self/other awareness, e.g., Myers/Briggs Type Indicator.

LEVEL FOUR: FIGHT/FLIGHT

Characteristics:	
1. Issue	1. Shifts from winning to getting rid of person(s). No longer believe other can change, or want to change.
2. Emotions	2. Cold self-righteousness. Will not speak to other side.
3. Orientation	3. Factions are solidified. Clear lines of demarcation. Last place for constructive intervention by third party consultant.
4. Information	4. Limited only to the cause being advocated; will not accept/listen to contrary information.
5. Language	5. Talk now of "principles," not "issues." Language solidifies into ideology.
6. Objective	6. No longer winning; now eliminate other(s) from the environment. Hurt the other person/group.
7. Outcome	7. High probability of split within the church with significant number of persons leaving church.
Skills Needed:	1. All skills under level one, two and three; in addition: 2. Ability to assess need for additional skill building. 3. Proven experience (track record). 4. Knowledge of broader, more specialized resources. 5. More formal networking; knowledge of those qualified to work in related areas. 6. Careful adherence to the *Book of Order*.
Training Strategies:	1. Ability to determine if a commission is needed. 2. Member of an identified cadre. 3. Practical training based on skills/needs assessment. 4. Acknowledgment at this level, intervention is helpful to "pickup the pieces" and negotiate a settlement, not to resolve the issue. 5. Use of specialists in networking. "(See skills needed #5—above")".

LEVEL FIVE: INTRACTABLE

Characteristics:	
1. Issue	1. No longer clear understanding of issue; personalities have become issue. Conflict now unmanageable.
2. Emotions	2. Relentless obsession in accomplishing the objective(s) at all costs. Vindictive. No objective control of emotion.
3. Orientation	3. Sees person as harmful to society, not just to the offended group or person.
4. Information	4. Information skewed to accomplish the objective at any cost.
5. Language	5. Focuses on words that imply the destruction and/or elimination of the other.
6. Objective	6. To destroy the offending party/persons; i.e., to see that the fired pastor does not get a job elsewhere.
7. Outcome	7. Highly destructive. Use of compulsion to maintain peace. May be necessary to remove members from church. Possible formation of administrative/judicial commission.
Skills Needed:	1. All skills under level one through four; in addition: 2. Adequate personal support system and strong inner resources. Able to practice personal stress management techniques. 3. Careful adherence to the *Book of Order*, especially the "Rules of Discipline." It is acknowledged that at this level no reconciliation is possible. Consultant's purpose is to minimize damage of conflict and enable person/institution/group to be able to function again.
Training Strategies:	1. Develop plan for the rebuilding of relationships. 2. Support for all members of the church.

Notes

Introduction

1. See Marshall Rosenberg, *Nonviolent Communication: A Language of Life* (Encinitas, CA: Puddle Dancer Press, 2003), 1–4.
2. See The Center for Nonviolent Communication, www.cnvc.org.
3. See especially http://nvctraining.com for a description of the wide variety of trainers, retreats, and teleclasses.
4. Both authors of this book teach courses on compassionate communication at our respective seminaries: Princeton Theological Seminary in Princeton, New Jersey and Luther Seminary in St. Paul, Minnesota. Many creative projects exist around the globe—too numerous to mention. NVC has been used in settling national disputes, businesses, coaching, psychotherapy, mediation, programs of prisoner rehabilitation, training hospital staff, working with the homeless and dispossessed, and working with Native American tribes. See www.cnvc.org; www.baynvc.org; or www.nvcti.com for a description of some of these projects.
5. Peter Steinke, *Congregational Leadership in Anxious Times: Being Calm and Courageous No Matter What* (Herndon, VA: The Alban Institute, 2006), vii.
6. Jean Baker Miller, *Toward a New Psychology of Women* (Boston: Beacon Press, 1986), 13.
7. Though this is our wording, the substance of this vision can be found on the Princeton Seminary Web site, http://www.ptsem.edu/NEWS/StrategicPlan/strategicplancollaborations.php.
8. We are indebted to NVC trainer Robert Gonzales for conceptualizing Nonviolent Communication in terms of basic skills, skill sets, and advanced skill sets. For more information on his approach to NVC, see www.living-compassion.org and www.nvcti.com.

Chapter 1: By the Renewal of Your Mind

1. This quotation appears in approximately 65 Web sites, attributed to Richard Rohr, but nowhere footnoted. See http://www.journey-through-grief.com/trauma-awareness-and-healing.html.
2. Nils Christie, "Conflicts as Property," *The British Journal of Criminology* 17, no. 3 (Jan. 1977): 8.

3. Jean Paul Lederach makes some important conceptual distinctions between conflict resolution and conflict transformation. Though we present a different conceptual framework from Lederach's, we agree with the distinctions he sets forth: (1) Conflict transformation not only seeks to end something destructive but also to build something desired. (2) It is relationship centered (rather than content centered). (3) It looks not merely at immediate symptoms, but at the larger system from which those symptoms arise. (4) It seeks to be responsive to crisis over the long term, rather than set goals that address only immediate pain or anxiety. (5) It acknowledges the ebb and flow of conflict with the need to de-escalate or escalate conflict depending on what will best serve constructive change. See John Paul Lederach, *The Little Book of Conflict Transformation* (Intercourse, PA: Good Books, 2003), 33.

4. Hermann Hesse, *Siddhartha* (Boston: Shambhala, 2000), 82. We are indebted to Dian Killian for this reference.

5. An earlier version of portions of this chapter can be found in Deborah van Deusen Hunsinger, "Practicing Koinonia," *Theology Today* 66, no. 3 (October 2009): 346–69.

6. See Miki Kashtan, "Truth, Care, and Words," The Fearless Heart, http://baynvc .blogspot.com/2011/07/truth-care-and-words.html: "What I am fundamentally aiming for is to live the values that speak to me about the NVC consciousness. The words used in practice are in support of this consciousness, not a substitute for it. I want my words to arise from the truth that lives in me. I aim for more and more fluidity in my holding of NVC consciousness, to stay grounded in principles of NVC and adapt the language to the circumstances."

7. Daniel Goleman, *Emotional Intelligence: Why It Can Matter More Than IQ* (New York: Bantam, 2006), 23.

8. Marshall Rosenberg, *Nonviolent Communication: A Language of Life* (Encinitas, CA: Puddle Dancer Press, 2003), 54–55.

9. For information on NVC Dance Floors, see www.nvcdancefloors.com; for GROK Card Games, go to www.nvcproducts.com; for information on the empathy labyrinth, see www.theempathylabyrinth.com; for interactive activities, see www.nvctoolkit.org.

10. Rosenberg frequently uses variations of this phrase in his workshops. See Jane Marantz Connor and Dian Killian, *Connecting across Differences: Finding Common Ground with Anyone, Anywhere, Anytime*, 2nd ed. (Encinitas, CA: Puddle Dancer Press, 2012), 156.

11. Marshall Rosenberg, "The Spiritual Basis of Nonviolent Communication: A Question and Answer Session," http://www.cnvc.org/learn-online/spiritual-basis/ spiritual-basis-nonviolent-communication.

12. Ibid.

13. For an earlier version of this argument, see Theresa F. Latini, "Nonviolent Communication as a Humanizing Educational and Ecclesial Practice," *Journal of Education and Christian Belief* 13, no. 1 (2009): 19–31.

14. Karl Barth, *Church Dogmatics*, Vol. III, Part 2 (Edinburgh: T. & T. Clark, 1960), 203ff.

15. Ray S. Anderson, *Self-Care: A Theology of Personal Empowerment and Spiritual Healing* (Pasadena, CA: Fuller Seminary Press, 2000), 238.

16. Barth, *Church Dogmatics*, 274.

17. Ibid., 251, 257.

18. Ibid., 259.

19. Ibid., 263, 264.

20. Ibid., 271–72.

21. Ibid., 272.

22. Rosenberg, "The Spiritual Basis of Nonviolent Communication."

Chapter 2: Rooted and Grounded in Love

1. We learned this emphasis on "the beauty of needs" or "the living energy of needs" from NVC trainers Robert Gonzales and Susan Skye. For more information on their work, see www.nvcti.com and www.living-compassion.org. For a short video describing the beauty of needs, see http://nvcprinciples.com/interviews/robert-gonzales-dwelling-in-the-beauty-of-needs.

2. By "enemy images," we mean static assessments of persons or groups whereby we pathologize them. Such sweeping evaluations allow us to dismiss others rather than encounter them as fellow creatures made in the image of God. In fact, when we hold enemy images of others, we dismiss them with lightning speed. Even before they speak, we have written them off. For instance, the labels "liberal" and "conservative" frequently function as enemy images in the church. Once we apply one of these labels (the label that we dis-identify with) to another person or group, we disconnect, or worse yet, ignore, demean, and dehumanize them. See Raj Gill, Lucy Leu, and Judy Morin, *NVC Toolkit for Facilitators* (Charleston, SC: BookSurge Publishing, 2009), 487–91.

3. Abraham Maslow, *Toward a Psychology of Being* (Radford, VA: Wilder Publications, 2011).

4. Adapted from "Needs Inventory," www.cnvc.org. For the complete "Needs Inventory," see Appendix 2.

5. Gershen Kaufman, *Shame: The Power of Caring*, 3rd ed. (Rochester, VT: Schenkman Books, 1992).

6. See Deborah van Deusen Hunsinger, *Theology and Pastoral Counseling: A New Interdisciplinary Approach* (Grand Rapids: Eerdmans, 1995), 177. Chapter 5 describes an extended case study of a woman afflicted with chronic shame, arising from multiple unmet needs from her earliest days.

7. Kaufman, *Shame*, 51.

8. Ibid., 53.

9. Ibid., 58.

10. Ibid., 61.

11. Ibid.

12. Ibid., 67.

13. Ibid., 68.

14. Jane Marantz Connor and Dian Killian, *Connecting Across Differences: A Guide to Compassionate, Nonviolent Communication* (New York: Hungry Duck Press, 2005), 65–78.

15. This abbreviated list is adapted from the card game, GROK, designed by Jean Morrison and Christine King, both CNVC certified trainers. See www.nvcproducts.com for more NVC games and materials.

16. Here we are defining *power* as the capacity to mobilize resources in order to meet needs. These resources include things like role, age, gender, race, physical size and stamina, wealth, job skills, information and access to knowledge, self-awareness, life experience, community, and so forth. Thus power is highly contextual; we are empowered in relation to others. Marie Fortune writes, "Power is a measure of

one person's (or group's) resources as compared to another person's (or group's) resources. Those who command greater resources than others *have power relative* to them; those who command *fewer* resources *are vulnerable relative* to them. As ministers, we possess a certain degree of power in relation to our congregants, clients, students, employees, staff members, etc.; and they are vulnerable in relation to us" (Marie Fortune, *Clergy Misconduct: Sexual Abuse in the Ministerial Relationship* [Seattle: Faith Trust Institute, 1997], 39, 40). We are in a *power-over* position when we have more internal and external resources to meet needs. We are in a *power-under* position when we have fewer. We exercise *power over* others whenever we mobilize resources to meet our needs to the neglect of others' needs and whenever we attempt to control or coerce others and thereby fail to respect their needs for choice, autonomy, and freedom.

17. Rosenberg, *Nonviolent Communication*, 54–55.

Chapter 3: Search Me and Know My Heart

1. Rosenberg, *Nonviolent Communication*, 41.
2. Ibid., 42–43.
3. Daniel Siegel, *The Developing Mind: How Relationships and the Brain Interact to Shape Who We Are* (New York: Guilford Press, 1999), 10.
4. T. Green, S. F. Neinemann, J. F. Gusella, "Molecular Neurobiology and Genetics: Investigation of Neural Function and Dysfunction," *Neuron* 20, 427, quoted in Siegel, *The Developing Mind*, 13.
5. Again Siegel writes, "Creating ratification or didactic boundaries between thought and emotion obscures the experiential and neurobiological reality of their inseparable nature" (ibid., 159).
6. Ibid., 142, 123.
7. Ibid., 126.
8. Ibid., 125.
9. Ibid., 127.
10. Ibid., 130.
11. Siegel explains that this axiom (Hebb's Axiom) is basic to understanding the brain as a whole as well as to understanding the way that primary and categorical emotions are experienced. See ibid., 26.
12. Sometimes, states of mind become so pervasive that together they form what Siegel calls a "self-state" (ibid., 231). We might think of a self-state as a cluster of basic states of mind. Self-states may be functional or dysfunctional, enabling a person to grow and adapt in an ever-changing world or inhibiting a person's ability to view life from a variety of perspectives.
13. We have created this image on the basis of Goleman's description of families of emotions. See Goleman, *Emotional Intelligence*, 291–92.
14. Goleman, *Emotional Intelligence*, 24. Elsewhere Goleman's model has been summarized as addressing four clusters of emotional competence. These include self-awareness, self-management (management of one's own emotional responses), social awareness, and relationship management. See "Emotional Intelligence," Wikipedia, http://en.wikipedia.org/wiki/Emotional_intelligence.
15. Goleman, *Emotional Intelligence*, 43.
16. Siegel, *The Developing Mind*, 136.

17. Ibid., 136.
18. Based on insights from neurobiology, we can explain the short-circuiting of emotional processing in the following manner: The brain responds to a stimulus with increased attentiveness (phase one). The brain discerns the most basic meaning of the stimulus, whether it is harmful, helpful or neutral (phase two). In accordance with the appraisal, the brain becomes more aroused; it transmits energy and information throughout its neural network (phase three). The body responds. The person experiences a primary emotion. All of this occurs in less than one second. Then instead of differentiating the primary emotion into a categorical emotion, the individual disconnects or suppresses that primary emotion. At best, he or she is aware of the primary emotion. At worst, the person is unaware of any level of feeling.
19. Siegel defines emotional resonance as an experience of "feeling felt." It occurs as a result of the alignment of states of mind between the caregiver and young child, and then continues throughout life as an important emotional and relational capacity. Failure to experience emotional resonance leads to isolation.
20. Eugene Gendlin, *Focusing* (New York: Bantam Books, 1981), 140.
21. See P. Ekman's research summarized in Siegel, *The Developing Mind*, 128.
22. Here we are implicitly drawing on Rational Emotive Behavioral Therapy (REBT), formulated by Albert Ellis (1913–2007) as one of the earliest forms of cognitive-behavioral therapy. According to Ellis, Activating events (A), combined with Beliefs about those events (B), yield emotional Consequences (C). These beliefs may be considered rational or irrational, accurate or inaccurate interpretations of events, contexts, and persons, including the self. These beliefs may either hinder or foster personal growth and interpersonal connection. Unlike Ellis's theory and therapeutic practice, compassionate communication would consider such judgments and evaluations of people and their actions to be life-alienating. In using compassionate communication, therefore, we would avoid terms like "rational" and "irrational." Unlike Ellis's practice, compassionate communication advocates a form of counseling grounded in empathy rather than in logical disputation. Further, in compassionate communication, we seek to connect to needs underneath or embedded within our beliefs and feelings. See Albert Ellis, "Rational Emotive Behavior Therapy," in *Current Psychotherapies*, ed. Raymond J. Corsini and Danny Wedding, 6th ed. (Itasca, IL: F. C. Peacock, 2000).
23. Anderson, *Self-Care*, 59.
24. Ibid., 87.
25. Ibid., 86.
26. Abraham J. Heschel, *The Prophets*, vol. 2 (New York: Harper and Row, 1962), 4; quoted in Anderson, *Self-Care*, 57.
27. For a depiction of the Spirit's work in the life of Jesus, see Luke 10:21–22; John 5:15–24; 14:1–31.
28. Wolfhart Pannenberg, *Anthropology in Theological Perspective*, trans. Matthew J. O'Connell (London: T & T Clark, 2004), 259; quoted in Anderson, *Self-Care*, 56.
29. Deborah van Deusen Hunsinger, *Pray without Ceasing: Revitalizing Pastoral Care* (Grand Rapids: Eerdmans, 2006), 123.

Chapter 4: Do Not Judge

1. We are not suggesting that psychological diagnoses should be eliminated from therapeutic practice. *The Diagnostic & Statistical Manual of Mental Disorders* (*DSM*) enables

psychiatrists and psychotherapists to understand and contribute to the healing of persons who are suffering. We are suggesting, though, that clinical diagnoses not become the primary or only filter through which persons understand themselves or others. A clinical diagnosis does not define the totality of a person's identity. We hope that psychological diagnoses can be utilized in such a way as to open us up to the humanity of the person before us rather than blinding us to it.

2. We could also refer to value judgments as "ethical judgments" or "moral judgments" with the following understanding: All persons make ethical judgments as they seek to discern how to live with integrity according to their values in a complex world. Christians make ethical judgments on the basis of their faith. We seek to discern how best to live in a way that is faithful to Jesus Christ. We seek to discern how to participate in the work of God's kingdom. Compassionate communication teaches us how to make and communicate these ethical judgments in a way that both respects the dignity of all people and acknowledges our own fallibility. Translating our moralistic judgments into value judgments keeps us from identifying ourselves as "right" and others as "wrong." It also anchors our attention on the values that we are seeking to uphold and honor in our decisions and actions.

3. Martin Luther, "The Babylonian Captivity of the Church," http://www.lutherdansk.dk/Web-Babylonian%20Captivitate/Martin%20Luther.htm.

4. For examples of this violence, see "Antisemitism," Encyclopedia Britannica Online, http://www.britannica.com/EBchecked/topic/27646/anti-Semitism.

5. Ulrich Mauser, *The Gospel of Peace: A Scriptural Message for Today's World* (Louisville, KY: Westminster John Knox Press, 1992), 46.

6. Ibid., 77.

7. Ibid., 78.

8. At this point, we diverge significantly from Marshall Rosenberg's spirituality. Rosenberg believes that human beings have an innate compassionate nature that has been corrupted, not by a break in relationship with God, but rather by socialization into violent forms of interaction. Thus, for Rosenberg, the remedy is socialization rather than salvation. See *Practical Spirituality: Reflections on the Spiritual Basis of Nonviolent Communication, a Q&A Session with Marshall Rosenberg* (Encinitas, CA: Puddle Dancer Press, 2004).

9. Craig Keener points out that this was tantamount to calling the Pharisees "the epitome of morally vile persons." Craig Keener, "Brood of Vipers (Matthew 3:7; 12:34; 12:33)," *Journal for the Study of the New Testament* 28.1 (2005): 8.

10. Mauser, *The Gospel of Peace*, 42.

11. For detailed exegesis and contextual analysis, see ibid., 65–82.

12. Our intent here is not to reinforce or accept gender stereotypes but to acknowledge the power and gendered nature of these myths. For example, we recognize that men can take on the role of self-sacrificing parent. Culturally, however, myths about gender, which function at the subconscious level, do tend to imagine women in this category. Consequently, cultural norms, practices, and structures arise that seek to keep this myth (and hence women) in this role. (We could say the same about the hero myth as well.) For a vivid description of the power of this myth, see Bernice Martin, "Whose Soul Is It Anyway? Domestic Tyranny and the Suffocated Soul" in *On Losing the Soul: Essays in the Social Psychology of Religion*, edited by Donald Capps and Richard Fenn (Albany: SUNY, 1995), 69–96.

13. For a more thorough discussion of the cross of the Christian, see Theresa F. Latini, "Grief-work and the Cross: Illustrating Transformational Interdisciplinarity," *Journal of Psychology and Theology* 37.2 (2009): 87–95.

14. For an extended interpretation of the interdependence of the "true church," see Karl Barth, *Church Dogmatics*, Vol. IV, Part 2 (Edinburgh: T & T Clark, 1958), 614–41. According to Barth, members of Christ's body are "brought together, constituted, established and maintained as a common being—one people capable of unanimous action. . . . Without this integration and mutual adaptation, there can be no reciprocal dependence and support. And without this, the community will inevitably fall apart and collapse. It cannot then be the provisional representation of the humanity sanctified in Jesus Christ" (635, 636).

Chapter 5: God's Compassion Is over All

1. Andrew Purves, *The Search for Compassion: Spirituality and Ministry* (Louisville, KY: Westminster John Knox Press, 1989), 16.

2. Ibid., 12.

3. Ibid., 16.

4. Karl Barth, *Church Dogmatics*, Vol. II, Part 1 (Edinburgh: T & T Clark, 1957), 369–70.

5. Purves, *The Search for Compassion*, 12.

6. Dietrich Bonhoeffer, *Life Together: Prayerbook of the Bible* (Minneapolis: Fortress Press, 1996), 98. See also Deborah van Deusen Hunsinger, *Pray without Ceasing*, 51–78.

7. "Compassion," in *Baker's Dictionary of Theology*, ed. Everett F. Harrison (Grand Rapids: Baker Book House, 1960), 132.

8. Desmond Tutu, *No Future without Forgiveness* (New York: Image Book Edition, 2000; Doubleday, 2000).

9. Judith V. Jordan, "The Meaning of Mutuality," in *Women's Growth in Connection: Writings from the Stone Center*, by Judith V. Jordan et al. (New York: Guilford Press, 1991), 87–88.

10. Siegel, *The Developing Mind*, 138.

11. Ibid., 117.

12. "Death is the great leveler, so our writers have always told us. Of course, they are right. But they have neglected to mention the uniqueness of each death—and the solitude of suffering which accompanies that uniqueness. We say, 'I know how you are feeling.' But we don't." Nicholas Wolterstorff, *Lament for a Son* (Grand Rapids: Eerdmans, 1987), 25.

13. Deborah van Deusen Hunsinger, *Pray without Ceasing*, 55–56.

14. Heinz Kohut, *The Restoration of the Self* (New York: International Universities Press, Inc., 1977), 253.

15. Carl Rogers, "The Necessary and Sufficient Conditions of Therapeutic Personality Change," in Howard Kirschenbaum and Valerie Land Henderson, eds., *The Carl Rogers Reader* (London: Constable, 1990), 226.

16. Siegel, *The Developing Mind*, 290.

17. Ibid., 272.

18. Ibid., 290.

19. Alexandra G. Kaplan, "Women and Empathy: Implications for Psychological Development and Psychotherapy," in Jordan et al., *Women's Growth in Connection*, 46.

20. Siegel, *The Developing Mind*, 143.

21. Kaplan, "Women and Empathy," in Jordan et al., *Women's Growth in Connection*, 46.
22. Deborah van Deusen Hunsinger, *Pray without Ceasing*, 67.
23. Kaplan, "Women and Empathy," in Jordan et al., *Women's Growth in Communication*, 47.
24. Ibid.
25. Jean Baker Miller and Irene Pierce Stiver, *The Healing Connection: How Women Form Relationships in Therapy and in Life* (Boston: Beacon Press, 1997), 30. See also Deborah van Deusen Hunsinger, *Pray without Ceasing*, 57.
26. William Faulkner is reputed to have said, "The past is not dead; it is not even past." See William Faulkner, *Requiem for a Nun* (New York: Random House, 1951).
27. Jane Marantz Connor and Dian Killian, *Connecting Across Differences*, 126.
28. Variations on these twelve can be found in a number of NVC sources. The original "typical twelve" came from Thomas Gordon's *Parent Effectiveness Training* (New York: New American Library, 1970), 41–44. His list is focused particularly on how parents respond to children in less than empathic ways: ordering, admonishing, moralizing, advising, lecturing, criticizing, praising, ridiculing, analyzing, reassuring, interrogating, and diverting.
29. Skill building in empathy can be especially lively and fun for groups. Jean Morrison and Christine King have developed a variety of interactive games called GROK, based on two packs of cards, one containing FEELINGS and the other containing NEEDS. GROK: Nonviolent Communication (NVC) Card Games for Discovery, Connection, and Fun. Galloping Giraffe Enterprises: www.nvcproducts.com. See examples of three of the fifteen possible games below.
    - *Feelings Charades:* A player draws a feeling card, holds it up for the group to see but does not look at it himself. The group members demonstrate the feeling with their faces and bodies, while the player tries to guess what feeling word is on the card.
    - *I might feel that way if . . . :* A player draws a feeling card, and without looking at it, shows it to the group. Members each describe a situation where they might feel that feeling. The player guesses what feeling is on the card.
    - *Group GROK:* A player describes a situation that is currently unresolved in his life in five to six sentences. He then chooses five FEELING cards that describe his feelings about the situation. The other players each have seven to eight NEEDS cards in their hands. They proceed to guess which NEEDS are connected to the FEELING cards that have been laid on the table. At the end the player scans the NEEDS cards and selects those that most accurately describe what he or she is needing in this situation.
30. Siegel, *The Developing Mind*, 337.

Chapter 6: Loving Your Neighbor as Yourself

1. This partial list of biblical passages is found in Anderson's *Self-Care*, 105.
2. John Calvin, *Institutes of the Christian Religion* Vol. 2, ed. John T. McNeill (Philadelphia: Westminster Press, 1960) 3.2, 691.
3. Ibid., 3. 4, 694.
4. Ibid., 3. 6, 696.
5. Anderson, *Self-Care*, 106.
6. We recognize that this passage of Scripture has been interpreted throughout church history in ways antithetical to the vision for mutual love that we are setting forth in this

chapter. Specifically, it has been used to subjugate women and deny their full humanity. We are suggesting that contrary to these interpretations, Ephesians 5, when interpreted in light of the whole New Testament as well as the context in which it was written, encourages respectful, mutual, and compassionate care in marriage.

7. See Karen Horney, *Neurosis and Human Growth*, especially chapter 3, "The Tyranny of the Should" (New York: W. W. Norton and Company, 1991).

8. Margaret Kornfeld, *Cultivating Wholeness: A Guide to Care and Counseling in Faith Communities* (New York: Continuum, 2000), 52–58.

9. Gendlin, *Focusing*, 34.

10. These questions are paraphrases of several questions Gendlin asks in the "short form" summary in the book's appendix. See ibid., 174.

11. I first learned of this practice in 2005 when Jane Connor and I were both participants in a year-long training program for those wishing to teach NVC, through the Bay Area Leadership Program. See www.baynvc.org.

12. Rosenberg, *Nonviolent Communication*, 132.

13. This example shows how NVC can be used over a period of time to promote emotional maturity in a person who is committed to a process of growth.

14. Several NVC trainers follow a format similar to this one in learning to transform self-judgments to underlying feelings, needs, and requests. For example, see "Freeing Ourselves of Self-Violence" in Gill, Leu, and Morin, *NVC Toolkit for Facilitators*. This version represents our own synthesis of the steps involved in transforming self-judgments through self-empathy and connecting them to our life of faith.

15. *Episcopal Clergy Wellness: A Report to the Church on the State of Clergy Wellness, June 2006* (Memphis: Credo Institute, 2006), 8.

16. Michael Jinkins, *Survey of Recent Graduates Working in Pastoral Ministry* (Austin, TX: Austin Presbyterian Theological Seminary, 2002), 4.

17. Gwen W. Halaas, *The Right Road: Life Choice for Clergy* (Minneapolis: Augsburg, 2004), 3.

Chapter 7: Speaking the Truth in Love

1. For a robust definition of authenticity, see Charles Taylor, *The Ethics of Authenticity* (Cambridge, MA: Harvard University Press, 1991).

2. Here we are using the term "reactive" as it is used in family systems theory. In systems theory, reactivity refers to an automatic, instinctual response to anxiety by which we focus on something outside of ourselves instead of dealing with our own internal responses to our environment. Some standard types of emotional reactivity are compliance, rebellion/resistance, power struggles, and distancing. See Ronald Richardson, *Becoming a Healthier Pastor* (Minneapolis: Augsburg Fortress Press, 2004), 15.

3. Susan Syke and Robert Gonzales, "The Living Energy of Needs," (NVC training, May 2007, Winter Harbor, ME).

4. Rosenberg, *Nonviolent Communication*, 120–21.

5. Other reactive relational patterns include triangulation, chronic conflict, distancing, repetitions, and cut-offs. See Roberta M. Gilbert, *Extraordinary Relationships: A New Way of Thinking about Human Interactions* (New York: John Wiley & Sons, 1992).

6. Ibid., 65–72.

7. Ibid., 98–103.

8. Rosenberg, *Nonviolent Communication*, 144.

9. Goleman, *Emotional Intelligence*, 60.
10. Entire systems—families, small groups, congregations, and other organizations—will sometimes identify a particular person as the problem instead of recognizing how their own responses contribute to the pattern. Edwin Friedman and others refer to this person as the "identified patient" in a system. This person may be blamed for the problems in the system, or this person may exhibit symptoms that emerge because of a lack of health in the overall system. See Edwin Friedman, *Generation to Generation* (New York: Guilford Press, 1985).
11. Rosenberg, *Nonviolent Communication*, 144.
12. Karl Barth, *Church Dogmatics*, Vol. IV, Part 2 (Edinburgh: T & T Clark, 1958), 636.
13. Ibid., 635.
14. *The Constitution of the Presbyterian Church (U.S.A.)*, Part II, *Book of Order* (Louisville, KY: Office of the General Assembly, Presbyterian Church (U.S.A.), 2007), G-1.0305.

Chapter 8: Blessed Are Those Who Mourn

1. "The Apostles' Creed," in *The Constitution of the Presbyterian Church (U.S.A.)*, Part I, *Book of Confessions* (Louisville, KY: Office of the General Assembly, Presbyterian Church (U.S.A.), 2004), 7.
2. Rosenberg, *Nonviolent Communication*, 133.
3. Ibid., 134.
4. We first learned this process from Robert Gonzales and Susan Skye at an NVC training event, "The Living Energy of Needs," in May 2007, Winter Harbor, ME. For a written description of this process, see Gregg Kendrick, "Transforming the Pain of Unmet Needs to the Beauty of Needs," www.basileia.org/PDFs/TransformingthePainofUnmetNeeds.pdf.
5. We are not suggesting that sharing the details of trauma or loss is problematic; in fact, this can contribute significantly to healing. For example, recounting one's experience of childhood abuse in the presence of an accepting other seems to be necessary for healing from shame. Resonance with another as we tell our story contributes to emotional regulation and restoration to healthy functioning. At the same time, some popularized notions of grief-work suggest that we must recount traumatic events over and over again as a kind of catharsis until our anxiety or shame subsides. This approach is potentially re-traumatizing. In this regard, compassionate communication offers an alternative, because it focuses not on the stimulus—one's experience of abuse—but rather on the unmet needs in that situation. Focusing on the unmet needs enables one to mourn fully without re-inflicting trauma because it is the *meaning* of the abuse or neglect that finally enables one to transform the pain. Simply repeating the story can inscribe the sense of trauma more deeply.
6. For a discussion of moral outrage and its place in healing, see chapter 7 in Ray S. Anderson, *Spiritual Caregiving as Secular Sacrament: A Practical Theology for Professional Caregivers* (Philadelphia: Jessica Kingsley Publishers, 2003). Anderson describes the experience of abuse as a moral injury to the self, resulting in moral outrage that demands justice. He writes, "In the case of a victim of domestic violence or child abuse, there is a deep-seated moral offense which has been committed against the person abused. The victim will need to be supported and affirmed in making a judgment against the offense as well as against the offender." Failure

to make a moral verdict keeps moral outrage suppressed and potentially turned against the self, leading to shame, depression, or self-injurious acts. "The moral issue can often lie hidden in the pain caused by the abuse. Once this judgment has been rendered as rightfully directed against the offender, the victim no longer is caught in self-blame. The feelings of outrage have now been dealt with. The feelings of anger can be allowed to be processed as emotion" (163). NVC deals with moral outrage by identifying the core values or needs embedded in our moral judgments. This focus on needs enables us to feel our anger and rage without dehumanizing the person who has committed the abuse. Nevertheless the capacity to name abuse as abuse is liberating and may be a precursor to going through the transforming pain process.

7. Kaufman, *Shame*, 73.

8. See chapters 1 and 6 for further discussions of shame. See also Deborah van Deusen Hunsinger, *Theology and Pastoral Counseling*, chapter 5.

9. It is important to note that these beliefs about ourselves are usually laced together with similar beliefs about life in general—e.g., life is always a struggle; life is unfair; there's not enough time, money, love, resources for all of us; no pain, no gain; the world is not safe; some people are good, some are bad; etc. While we are focusing here on shame-based beliefs, Gonzales and Skye use this process for transforming these other core beliefs as well.

10. For a helpful summary of Freud's essay, see Nicholas Ray, "Trauer und Melancholie [Mourning and Melancholia]," *The Literary Encyclopedia* (March 2008), http://www .litencyc.com/php/sworks.php?rec=true&UID=16917.

11. See Elisabeth Kübler-Ross, *On Death and Dying* (London: Tavistock, 1969); John Bowlby, *Loss: Sadness and Depression* (New York: Basic Books, 1980).

12. See Alice Miller, *The Drama of the Gifted Child* (New York: Basic Books, 1997).

13. In recent years, for example, psychological and neurobiological insights have been utilized to develop EMDR, Eye Movement Desensitization and Reprocessing, a highly effective treatment of Post Traumatic Stress Disorder. For an extensive bibliography of articles on EMDR, see EMDR Institute, Inc., http://www.emdr.com.

14. Siegel, *The Developing Mind*, 211.

15. Siegel explains: "When the intensity of an aroused state moves beyond the window of tolerance, a flood of emotion may bombard the mind and take over a number of processes, ranging from rational thinking to social behavior. At this point, emotions may flood conscious awareness. Some have called this an emotional 'hijacking,' 'break-down,' or 'flooding.' In such a situation, one's behavior may no longer feel volitional, and thoughts may feel out of control. Images may fill the mind's eye with visual representations symbolic of the emotional sensation" (ibid., 258).

16. Ibid., 257.

17. Ibid., 258.

18. Ibid., 268.

19. Siegel explains internal override discussions as a means of altering the brain's appraisal of stimuli. As he illustrates, early childhood trauma may create neural pathways that get re-triggered in the future, creating a flood of anxiety throughout the brain. This anxiety can create physical and mental disturbances when triggered by a similar situation in the present. Even though one knows that one is safe, the state of mind nevertheless gets triggered. If a person can become conscious of this

process, he or she can engage in a kind of internal dialogue that acknowledges the fear triggered in the present, appraises that fear differently (as unnecessary), and then imagines his or her amygdala relaxing. Over time, this can reduce the effects of the anxiety, making it manageable (ibid., 248–50).

20. Siegel illustrates this with an abbreviated case study of a therapist who notices that his bodily reaction to his client mirrors her posture, eye gaze, facial expression, and anxiously tapping foot. Noting his resonance with her, the therapist "guesses" at what she might be feeling, which elicits a flood of emotion from his client. In this instance and others like it, the therapist's state of mind has been influenced by his client's state of mind. She experiences "feeling felt" and interprets it as being understood. This kind of resonance is intrinsic to the human capacity to connect with others. It is necessary for the development of our brains; it is necessary for relationships to be established and to grow. Siegel goes on to say that the trained therapist knows when to allow such attunement to occur and when to take a more autonomous posture in the counseling process. While the trained therapist recognizes the alteration in his state of mind as a response to his client's state of mind, he does not therefore assume that he knows what that person is thinking, feeling, and needing. He simply is able to guess intuitively on the basis of resonance (ibid., 69–70).

21. Ronald A. Heifetz and Marty Linsky, *Leadership on the Line: Staying Alive through the Dangers of Leading* (Cambridge, MA: Harvard Business Press, 2002).

22. Ibid., 13.

23. Arnoud Stimec, Jean Poitras, and Jason J. Campbell, "Ripeness, Readiness, and Grief in Conflict Analysis" in *Critical Issues in Peace and Conflict Studies: Theory, Practice, and Pedagogy*, eds. Thomas Matyok, Jessica Senehi, Sean Byrne (Lanham, MD: Lexington Books, 2011), 148.

24. Ibid., 149.

25. Heifetz and Linsky, *Leadership on the Line*, 95–96.

26. Jaco Hamman, *When Steeples Cry: Leading Congregations through Loss and Change* (Cleveland: The Pilgrim Press, 2005), 98.

27. Ibid., 36.

28. Henri Nouwen, *The Wounded Healer: Ministry in Contemporary Society* (New York: Image Books, 1979), front cover.

29. See Karl Barth, *Church Dogmatics*, Vol. II, Part 1 (Edinburgh: T & T Clark, 1957), 262; Theresa F. Latini, *The Church and the Crisis of Community: A Practical Theology of Small-Group Ministry* (Grand Rapids: Eerdmans, 2011), 80–81.

30. Purves, *The Search for Compassion*, 103.

31. Martha understood forgiveness as a demand from God rather than as a capacity granted to her by the power of the Holy Spirit. The grace of God was twisted into law. When she connected with the beauty of her needs, her consciousness shifted so that forgiveness became a work of God in her heart and mind to be completed, if not in the here and now, then in the future tense of reconciliation. For further discussion of the psychological and theological dynamics involved in forgiveness, see David W. Augsburger, *Helping People Forgive* (Louisville, KY: Westminster John Knox Press, 1996).

32. For a fuller explanation of the paradoxical nature of grief-work and participation in the cross of Jesus Christ, see Theresa F. Latini, "Grief-work in Light of the Cross," 87–95.

33. Purves, *The Search for Compassion*, 119.
34. Purves, *The Search for Compassion*, 126.

Chapter 9: Be of the Same Mind

1. Marshall Rosenberg, *We Can Work It Out* (Encinitas, CA: Puddle Dancer Press, 2005), 2; italics in original.
2. When others say no to a request, it is because they are saying yes to (usually unstated) needs that they do not believe would be met by this request. Instead of reacting to the no, we listen empathically for what they might be saying yes to. What are the needs they want to meet, that they cannot meet by saying yes to our request? Thus we enter more deeply into dialogue, as together we seek to find a strategy that will meet both our own needs and theirs. For more information, see chapter 7, pp. 122–25, "Saying 'No.'"
3. Siegel, *The Developing Mind*, 18.
4. Shelley E. Taylor, *The Tending Instinct: How Nurturing Is Essential to Who We Are and How We Live* (New York: Times Books, 2002), 120–22, quoted in Peter L. Steinke, *Congregational Leadership in Anxious Times: Being Calm and Courageous No Matter What* (Herndon, VA: The Alban Institute, 2006), 52. While current research shows that the "tend and befriend" response is more common among women, this does not rule out the fact that some men may also exhibit this response.
5. For detailed descriptions of each of these relational postures, see Gilbert, *Extraordinary Relationships*.
6. Ronald W. Richardson, *Creating a Healthier Church: Family Systems Theory, Leadership, and Congregational Life* (Minneapolis: Augsburg Fortress Press, 1996), 80.
7. Gilbert, *Extraordinary Relationships*, 98.
8. "Signs of distancing include: excessive periods of noncommunication when one is emotionally reactive, workaholism, overuse of substances such as alcohol, excessive time spent on hobbies, a tendency to be quiet when anxiety rises, talk that includes nothing of personal importance, an inability to relate to some of the people in one's immediate or original family" (ibid., 5).
9. "The basic law of emotional triangles is that when any two parts of a system become uncomfortable with one another, they will 'triangle in' or focus upon a third person, or issue, as a way of stabilizing their own relationship with one another" (Friedman, *Generation to Generation*, 35).
10. Steinke lists thirteen common triggers of anxiety in congregations: money; debates about sexuality; pastoral leadership style; lay leadership style; questions about growth and survival; maintaining boundaries; trauma, such as damage to church building; staff conflict or resignation; harm done to a child or death of a child in the congregation; decisions to develop new programs and practices; debate about worship style; gap between vision for the church and reality of the church's situation; and building, constructing, or buying new space (*Congregational Leadership in Anxious Times*, 15–17).
11. "Keeping secrets" and "upholding pastoral confidentiality" are not the same. Ministers and therapists are rightly expected to keep confidence—not to reveal in any way the details of another's personal sharing. The one exception to this would be when a person discloses that a minor, an older adult, or someone with disabilities is being abused or neglected, or when someone's life is in danger. In these instances, we are obligated (legally and ethically) to intervene by reporting this harm (or suspected harm) to civil authorities, such as child protective agencies. See Marie

Fortune, "Confidentiality and Mandatory Reporting: a Clergy Dilemma?" http://www
.faithtrustinstitute.org/resources/articles/child-abuse. Ministers and therapists are not,
however, expected to keep secrets—to collude with another person or group in hiding
important, valuable, or liberating information from others. If a person reveals a secret
to us, we wouldn't simply tell others this secret. Rather we would encourage this person
toward more openness for the sake of healing. We may, in some instances, share that we
are unwilling to keep certain secrets, giving the person(s) a choice to continue the same
pastoral care relationship with us. For example, if in the course of providing pastoral
care to a couple, one partner reveals that he or she is having an affair, we might communicate, preferably using OFNR honesty, that we believe that reconciliation in marriage
can occur only if the person having the affair shares this information with their marital
therapist and his or her spouse. (If the couple doesn't have a marriage and family therapist, we should refer them to one.) We might identify our own needs for integrity, care,
and contribution to their lives and thus our inability to participate in keeping this secret.
The same principles would hold true if a group in the congregation is keeping secrets
from others—e.g., three families in the congregation have petitioned a few members
of church council to fire two youth pastors in a row. Telling the secret would not necessarily mean that every congregant needs to be informed about all the details of the
situation (depending on the circumstances), but it would mean that the whole church
council should open up conversation about the needs of youth, the responsibilities of
youth ministers, and transparent decision making before succumbing to any pressure to
fire or hire church staff members.

12. George Hunsinger, *How to Read Karl Barth: The Shape of His Theology* (Oxford, New
    York: Oxford University Press, 1990), 238–42; George Hunsinger, *Disruptive Grace:
    Studies in the Theology of Karl Barth* (Grand Rapids: Eerdmans, 2000), 257 and follow-
    ing. See also Deborah van Deusen Hunsinger, *Pray without Ceasing*, chapter 1.

13. George Hunsinger, *Disruptive Grace*, 257.

14. For a more extensive presentation of this argument, see Theresa F. Latini, *The Church
    and the Crisis of Community*.

15. Karl Barth, *Church Dogmatics* Vol. II, Part 1 (Edinburgh: T & T Clark, 1957), 278.

16. Barth expounds, "It does not belong to us to have being, and when we have it, it does
    not belong to us in this being of ours to be the objects of the love of God. We might not
    be at all, and we might be without being the objects of His love. God does not owe us
    either our being, or in our being His love. If we are, and if we are objects of the love of
    God, that means that we on our side are debtors to God, without God owing anything
    to us. If He loves us, if He has preferred our being to our not-being, our lovableness to
    our unlovableness, that is for us the ever-wonderful dynamic of His love. It is grace and
    not nature. For it takes place in the whole intervention of the divine action and being"
    (ibid., 281).

17. Marshall Rosenberg, "The Spiritual Basis of Nonviolent Communication," http://
    www.cnvc.org/learn-online/spiritual-basis/spiritual-basis-nonviolent-communication.

18. Marshall Rosenberg, *Speak Peace in a World of Conflict* (Encinitas, CA: Puddle Dancer
    Press, 2005), 173.

Chapter 10: Strive for God's Kingdom

1. See Appendix 3: Conflict Intensity Chart, in order to make an assessment of any specific
   conflict situation in your church.

2. These are three actual case studies, which are discussed at length in a helpful book titled *Congregational Trauma: Caring, Coping and Learning* by Jill M. Hudson (New York: Alban Institute, 1998).

3. See Friedman's *Generation to Generation* for a thorough discussion of each of these points. He describes his "law" regarding triangles as follows: "When any two parts of a system become uncomfortable with one another, they will 'triangle in' or focus upon a third person, or issue, as a way of stabilizing their own relationship with one another." Later he points out that though "the most triangled person in any set of relationships is always the most vulnerable; when the laws of emotional triangles are understood . . . it tends to become the most powerful" (35, 39).

4. David R. Brubaker identifies four factors that need to be examined in any particular congregational conflict: issues of congregational culture, organizational structure, adaptation to environmental changes, and leader effectiveness. See his *Promise and Peril: Understanding and Managing Change and Conflict in Congregations* (Herndon, VA: Alban Institute, 2009).

5. Ibid., 97.

6. Carolyn Shrock-Shenk differentiates among the goals of conflict practitioners in recent years as they have moved from conflict *resolution* (a term which implies the need to eliminate or be done with conflict); to conflict *management* (which implies "keeping the lid on" it or putting conflict into "acceptable parameters"); to conflict *transformation* (which seeks to transform the interpersonal relationships of those in conflict). The first approach is more problem-focused, the second more process-focused, and the third more people-focused, though all three approaches include all three dimensions: problem, process, and people. See *Making Peace with Conflict: Practical Skills for Conflict Transformation*, eds. Carolyn Shrock-Shenk and Lawrence Ressler (Scottsdale, PA: Herald Press), 35.

7. For example, the Presbyterian Disaster Assistance (PDA) trains volunteers to enter conflicted or traumatized churches to offer concrete help in an emergency, focusing "on the long term recovery of disaster impacted communities." See http://presbyterianmission.org/ministries/pda/who-we-are/.

8. Many of these ideas are adapted from Hudson's *Congregational Trauma*.

9. The single rhizome of the mushroom plant as an extended metaphor to describe conflict in community was developed by Dominic Barter in his workshop on "Building Compassionate Justice for the 21st Century," October, 2008, St. Paul, MN.

10. See "Forming a Reference Committee in Congregational Change or Conflict," in Brubaker, *Promise and Peril*, 147–50.

11. Brubaker, *Promise and Peril*, 149.

12. The following Web page describes the key components of restorative circles as developed by Dominic Barter: "An Overview of Restorative Circles," Psychologists for Social Responsibility, http://www.psysr.org/issues/restorative/.

> A Restorative Circle is a community process for supporting those in conflict. It brings together the three parties to a conflict—those who have acted, those directly impacted and the wider community—within a chosen systemic context, to dialogue as equals. Participants invite each other and attend voluntarily. The dialogue process used is shared openly with all participants. The process ends when actions have been found that bring mutual benefit that nurtures the inherent integrity of all those involved in the conflict.

Restorative Circles are facilitated in three stages that arise in an approximate sequence and identify the key factors in the conflict, reach agreements on next steps, and evaluate the results. As circles form, they invite shared power, mutual understanding and self-responsibility within community.

Restorative Circles are facilitated by community members who identify themselves as impacted by the conflict at hand. They commit to serving the emergent wisdom of the participants through their willingness to offer agreed upon questions and to track the co-creation of meaning and action by those present.

13. For practical ideas and useful suggestions for setting up such circles in a community setting, see Ron Kraybill, *The Little Book of Cool Tools for Hot Topics: Group Tools to Facilitate Meetings When Things Are Hot* (Intercourse, PA: Good Books, 2007).

14. When facilitating such a circle it is crucial to the process to hear each person with respect, give each person an opportunity to be heard without interruption, and keep confidentiality. These guidelines function as promises made to one another and as gentle reminders of the shared commitment to create a safe space for everyone. See Kay Pranis, *The Little Book of Circle Processes*, 12–13.

15. We are drawing here on our understanding of the key elements required of facilitators as presented by Dominic Barter in his workshop, "Building Compassionate Justice."

16. "The use of a talking piece allows for full expression of emotions, deeper listening, thoughtful reflection, and an unhurried pace." See Kay Pranis, *The Little Book of Circle Processes*, 12.

17. Ibid., 8.

18. Ibid., 3–10.

19. The basic questions that each member addresses have been posed in a number of ways. In a criminal justice context, Terry O'Connell of *Real Justice* asks these questions of each participant: (1) What did you think when you realized what had happened? (2) What impact has this incident had on you and others? (3) What has been the hardest thing for you? (4) What needs to happen to make things right? See www .realjustice.org and www.iirp.org. Note that O'Connell's order moves from the past, through the present and toward the future. Both victims and perpetrators of crime return to their initial thoughts and feelings about the crime and share them openly with the group. Only after hearing the initial impact does the circle move forward in time to the present. By contrast, the questions as we have posed them follow an order suggested by Dominic Barter. It begins in the present as a way to ground the participants in the here and now. This step helps people to connect with what matters to them most now as they face one another in the circle. After grounding in what matters most in the present, the focus shifts to the past as each person takes responsibility for the choices he or she made at the time.

20. We are indebted to Dominic Barter's teaching of the processes, principles, and structures of restorative circles. Barter is certified as a trainer by the Center for Nonviolent Communication and is an internationally recognized proponent of restorative practices. See his Web site for more information on his work in Brazil and his teaching throughout the world. Here we have recounted our understanding of his teachings and we have contextualized them specifically for the church. See http:// www.restorativecircles.org/.

21. Barter suggests three criteria by which to evaluate the process: (1) the more flexible I am in the way I adapt the form to local conditions, the more restorative the result; (2) the more faithful I am to the core principles of the work, the more restorative the result; (3) the greater the degree of voluntary participation, the more restorative the result.

22. The aims and procedures of both pre- and post-circles represent our understanding of Dominic Barter's teachings as presented in his workshop on "Building Compassionate Justice for the 21st Century," October, 2008, St. Paul, MN.

23. Jean Baker Miller, *Toward a New Psychology of Women* (Boston: Beacon Press, 1976), 129.

24. The basic requirements for setting up a restorative system represent our understanding of Dominic Barter's teachings as presented in his workshop on "Building Compassionate Justice for the 21st Century," October, 2008, St. Paul, MN.

25. This format was adapted from the description of a Samoan Circle in Ron Kraybill's *The Little Book of Cool Tools for Hot Topics*, 51–53.

26. See Deborah van Deusen Hunsinger, "Bearing the Unbearable: Trauma, Gospel and Pastoral Care," *Theology Today* 68:1 (2011), 8–25.

27. Oscar Romero, quoted in "Prophets in a Future Not Our Own," trans. Kenneth E. Unterner, http://www.worldwideopen.org/en/resources/detail/833.

Conclusion: Learning the Secret of Contentment

1. See Karl Barth, *Church Dogmatics*, Vol. III, Part 2 (T & T Clark, 1960), 222–84.

Bibliography

Anderson, Ray S. *Self-Care: A Theology of Personal Empowerment and Spiritual Healing.* Pasadena, CA: Fuller Seminary Press, 2000.

———. *Spiritual Caregiving as Secular Sacrament: A Practical Theology for Professional Caregivers.* Philadelphia: Jessica Kingsley, 2003.

Augsburger, David W. *Helping People Forgive.* Louisville, KY: Westminster John Knox Press, 1996.

Barter, Dominic. "An Overview of Restorative Circles." Psychologists for Social Responsibility. http://www.psysr.org/issues/restorative/.

———. Workshop. "Building Compassionate Justice for the 21st Century." October, 2008, St. Paul, MN.

Barth, Karl. *Church Dogmatics,* Vol. II, Part 1. Edinburgh: T & T Clark, 1957.

———. *Church Dogmatics,* Vol. IV, Part 2. Edinburgh: T & T Clark, 1958.

———. *Church Dogmatics,* Vol. III, Part 2. Edinburgh: T & T Clark, 1960.

Bonhoeffer, Dietrich. *Life Together: Prayerbook of the Bible.* Minneapolis: Fortress Press, 1996.

Bowlby, John. *Loss: Sadness and Depression.* New York: Basic Books, 1980.

Brubaker, David R. *Promise and Peril: Understanding and Managing Change and Conflict in Congregations.* Herndon, VA: Alban Institute, 2009.

Calvin, John. *Institutes of the Christian Religion.* Edited by John T. McNeill. Philadelphia: Westminster Press, 1960.

Christie, Nils. "Conflicts as Property." *The British Journal of Criminology* 17, no. 3 (Jan. 1977): 1–15.

Connor, Jane Marantz and Dian Killian. *Connecting Across Differences: A Guide to Compassionate, Nonviolent Communication.* New York: Hungry Duck Press, 2005.

The Constitution of the Presbyterian Church (USA), Part I, *Book of Confessions.* Louisville, KY: Office of the General Assembly, Presbyterian Church (U.S.A.), 2004.

The Constitution of the Presbyterian Church (USA), Part II, *Book of Order.* Louisville, KY: Office of the General Assembly, Presbyterian Church (U.S.A.), 2007.

Ellis, Albert. "Rational Emotive Behavior Therapy." In *Current Psychotherapies*, 6th ed. Edited by Raymond J. Corsini and Danny Wedding. Itasca, IL: F. C. Peacock, 2000.

Episcopal Clergy Wellness: A Report to the Church on the State of Clergy Wellness. Memphis: Credo Institute, 2006.

Faulkner, William. *Requiem for a Nun.* New York: Random House, 1951.

"Feelings Inventory." Center for Nonviolent Communication, 2005. http://www.cnvc.org/Training/feelings-inventory.

Fortune, Marie. *Clergy Misconduct: Sexual Abuse in the Ministerial Relationship.* Seattle: Faith Trust Institute, 1997.

———. "Confidentiality and Mandatory Reporting: A Clergy Dilemma?" http://www.faithtrustinstitute.org/resources/articles/child-abuse.

Frankl, Victor. *Man's Search for Meaning.* New York: Beacon, 2006.

Friedman, Edwin H. *Generation to Generation: Family Process in Church and Synagogue.* New York: The Guilford Press, 1985.

Gendlin, Eugene. *Focusing.* New York: Bantam Books, 1981.

Gilbert, Roberta. *Extraordinary Relationships: A New Way of Thinking about Human Interactions.* New York: John Wiley & Sons, 1992.

Gill, Raj, Lucy Leu, and Judi Morin. *NVC Toolkit for Facilitators: Interactive Activities and Awareness Exercises Based on 18 Key Concepts for the Development of NVC Skills and Consciousness.* Charlotte, NC: BookSurge Publishing, 2009.

Goleman, Daniel. *Emotional Intelligence: Why It Can Matter More Than IQ.* New York: Bantam Books, 2006.

Gordon, Thomas. *Parent Effectiveness Training.* New York: New American Library, 1970.

Halaas, Gwen W. *The Right Road: Life Choice for Clergy.* Minneapolis: Augsburg, 2004.

Hamman, Jaco. *When Steeples Cry: Leading Congregations through Loss and Change.* Cleveland: The Pilgrim Press, 2005.

Harrison, Everett F., ed. *Baker's Dictionary of Theology.* Grand Rapids: Baker Books, 1960.

Heifetz, Ronald A. and Marty Linsky. *Leadership on the Line: Staying Alive through the Dangers of Leading.* Cambridge, MA: Harvard Business Press, 2002.

Heschel, Abraham J. *The Prophets*, vol. 2. New York: Harper and Row, 1962.

Hesse, Hermann. *Siddhartha.* Boston: Shambhala, 2000.

Horney, Karen. *Neurosis and Human Growth.* New York: W. W. Norton and Company, 1991.

Hudson, Jill M. *Congregational Trauma: Caring, Coping and Learning.* New York: Alban Institute, 1998.

Hunsinger, Deborah van Deusen. "Bearing the Unbearable: Trauma, Gospel and Pastoral Care," *Theology Today* 68, no. 1 (2011): 8–25.

———. *Pray without Ceasing: Revitalizing Pastoral Care.* Grand Rapids: Eerdmans, 2006.

———. "Practicing Koinonia." *Theology Today* 66, no. 3 (2009): 346–67.

———. *Theology and Pastoral Counseling: A New Interdisciplinary Approach.* Grand Rapids: Eerdmans, 1995.

Hunsinger, George. *Disruptive Grace: Studies in the Theology of Karl Barth.* Grand Rapids: Eerdmans, 2000.

———. *How to Read Karl Barth: The Shape of His Theology.* Oxford, New York: Oxford University Press, 1990.

Jinkins, Michael. *Survey of Recent Graduates Working in Pastoral Ministry*. Austin, TX: Austin Presbyterian Theological Seminary, 2002.

Jordan, Judith V. et al. *Women's Growth in Connection: Writings from the Stone Center*. New York: Guilford Press, 1991.

Kashtan, Miki. "Truth, Care, and Words." The Fearless Heart. http://baynvc.blogspot .com/2011/07/truth-care-and-words.html.

Kaufman, Gershen. *Shame: The Power of Caring*. 3rd ed. Rochester, VT: Schenkman Books, 1992.

Keener, Craig. "Brood of Vipers (Matthew 3:7; 12:34; 12:33)." *Journal for the Study of the New Testament* 28, no.1 (2005): 3–11.

Kohut, Heinz. *The Restoration of the Self*. New York: International University Press, 1977.

Kornfeld, Margaret. *Cultivating Wholeness: A Guide to Care and Counseling in Faith Communities*. New York: Continuum, 2000.

Kraybill, Ron. *The Little Book of Cool Tools for Hot Topics: Group Tools to Facilitate Meetings When Things Are Hot*. Intercourse, PA: Good Books, 2007.

Kübler-Ross, Elisabeth. *On Death and Dying*. London: Tavistock, 1969.

LaCugna, Catherine. *God for Us: The Trinity and Christian Life*. San Francisco: Harper, 1993.

Latini, Theresa F. "Grief-work in Light of the Cross: Illustrating Transformational Interdisciplinarity." *Journal of Psychology and Theology* 36, no. 2 (Summer 2009): 87–95.

———. "Nonviolent Communication as a Humanizing Educational and Ecclesial Practice." *Journal of Education and Christian Belief* 13, no. 1 (2009): 19–31.

———. *The Church and the Crisis of Community: A Practical Theology of Small-Group Ministry*. Grand Rapids: Eerdmans, 2011.

Lederach, John Paul. *The Little Book of Conflict Transformation*. Intercourse, PA: Good Books, 2003.

Loder, James E. *Logic of the Spirit: Human Development in Theological Perspective*. San Francisco: Jossey-Bass, 1998.

Luther, Martin. "The Babylonian Captivity of the Church." Available at http://www .lutherdansk.dk/Web-Babylonian%20Captivitate/Martin%20Luther.htm.

Martin, Bernice. "Whose Soul Is It Anyway? Domestic Tyranny and the Suffocated Soul." In *On Losing the Soul: Essays in the Social Psychology of Religion*. Edited by Donald Capps and Richard Fenn, 69–96. Albany: SUNY, 1995.

Maslow, Abraham. *Toward a Psychology of Being*. Radford, VA: Wilder Publications, 2011.

Mauser, Ulrich. *The Gospel of Peace: A Scriptural Message for Today's World*. Louisville, KY: Westminster John Knox Press, 1992.

Miller, Alice. *The Drama of the Gifted Child*. New York: Basic Books, 1997.

Miller, Jean Baker. *Toward a New Psychology of Women*. Boston: Beacon Press, 1986.

Miller, Jean Baker and Irene Pierce Stiver. *The Healing Connection: How Women Form Relationships in Therapy and in Life*. Boston: Beacon Press, 1997.

"Needs Inventory." Center for Nonviolent Communication. http://www.cnvc.org/Training/ needs-inventory.

Nouwen, Henri. *The Wounded Healer: Ministry in Contemporary Society*. New York: Image Books, 1979.

Pannenberg, Wolfhart. *Anthropology in Theological Perspective*. Translated by Matthew J. O'Connell. London: T & T Clark, 2004.

Pranis, Kay. *The Little Book of Circle Processes: A New/Old Approach to Peacemaking*. The Little Books of Justice and Peacebuilding Series. Intercourse, PA: Good Books, 2005.

Purves, Andrew. *The Search for Compassion: Spirituality and Ministry*. Louisville, KY: Westminster John Knox, 1989.

Ray, Nicholas. "Trauer und Melancholie [Mourning and Melancholia]." *The Literary Encyclopedia*. March 2008. http://www.litencyc.com/php/sworks.php?rec=true&UID=16917.

Richardson, Ronald W. *Becoming a Healthier Pastor*. Minneapolis: Augsburg Fortress Press, 2004.

———. *Creating a Healthier Church: Family Systems Theory, Leadership, and Congregational Life*. Minneapolis: Augsburg Fortress Press, 1996.

Rogers, Carl. "The Necessary and Sufficient Conditions in Therapeutic Personality Change." In *The Carl Rogers Reader*. Edited by Kirschenbaum, Howard and Valerie Land Henderson, 219–36. London: Constable, 1990.

Rohr, Richard. "Trauma Awareness and Healing Class Reflections." Journey through Grief. http://www.journey-through-grief.com/trauma-awareness-and-healing.html.

Rosenberg, Marshall. *Nonviolent Communication: A Language of Life*. Encinitas, CA: Puddle Dancer Press, 2003.

———. *Practical Spirituality: Reflections on the Spiritual Basis of Nonviolent Communication, a Q&A Session with Marshall Rosenberg*. Encinitas, CA: Puddle Dancer Press, 2004.

———. *Speak Peace in a World of Conflict*. Encinitas, CA: Puddle Dancer Press, 2005.

———. "The Spiritual Basis of Nonviolent Communication: A Question and Answer Session." http://www.cnvc.org/learn-online/spiritual-basis/spiritual-basis-nonviolent-communication.

———. *We Can Work It Out*. Encinitas, CA: Puddle Dancer Press, 2005.

Schenk, Bruce and Terry O'Connell. "Actively Living Reconciliation and Restoration: The Restorative Framework and Faith Communities." Paper presented at the International Institute of Restorative Practices. Bethlehem, PA, October, 2008.

Shrock-Shenk, Carolyn and Lawrence Ressler, eds. *Making Peace with Conflict: Practical Skills for Conflict Transformation*. Scottsdale, PA: Herald Press, 1999.

Siegel, Daniel J. *The Developing Mind: How Relationships and the Brain Interact to Shape Who We Are*. New York: Guilford Press, 1999.

Steinke, Peter. *Congregational Leadership in Anxious Times: Being Calm and Courageous No Matter What Happens*. Herndon, VA: Alban Institute, 2006.

Stimec, Arnoud, Jean Poitras, and Jason J. Campbell, "Ripeness, Readiness, and Grief in Conflict Analysis." In *Critical Issues in Peace and Conflict Studies: Theory, Practice, and Pedagogy*. Edited by Thomas Matyok, Jessica Senehi, and Sean Byrne. Lanham, MD: Lexington Books, 2011, 143–58.

Taylor, Charles. *The Ethics of Authenticity*. Cambridge, MA: Harvard University Press, 1991.

Taylor, Shelley E. *The Tending Instinct: How Nurturing Is Essential to Who We Are and How We Live*. New York: Times Books, 2002.

Tutu, Desmond. *No Future without Forgiveness*. New York: New Image Books, 2000.

Wolterstorff, Nicholas. *Lament for a Son*. Grand Rapids: Eerdmans, 1987.

Index of Scripture

Index of Subjects

Italic page locators indicate tables.

CPSIA information can be obtained at www.ICGtesting.com
Printed in the USA
BVOW04s1416250714

360466BV00008B/76/P